THE EDUCATION OF BORSTAL BOYS

INTERNATIONAL LIBRARY OF SOCIOLOGY
AND SOCIAL RECONSTRUCTION

Founded by Karl Mannheim
Editor: W. J. H. Sprott

A catalogue of books available in the INTERNATIONAL LIBRARY OF SOCIOLOGY AND SOCIAL RECONSTRUCTION and new books in preparation for the Library will be found at the end of this volume.

THE EDUCATION OF
BORSTAL BOYS

A Study of their Educational Experiences
prior to, and during, Borstal Training

ERICA STRATTA

LONDON
ROUTLEDGE & KEGAN PAUL
NEW YORK: HUMANITIES PRESS

First published 1970
by Routledge and Kegan Paul Ltd
Broadway House, 68–74 Carter Lane
London EC4
Made and printed in Great Britain
by C. Tinling and Co. Ltd
London and Prescot
© Erica Stratta 1970

SBN 7100 6605 8

Contents

Contents

Foreword

by

T. P. MORRIS

The idea that education, or rather the lack of it, is a contributory factor in the crime of the young is far from new. Throughout the 19th century it was a recurring theme in the writings of almost anyone concerned with the 'moral reclamation' of juvenile delinquents. The elementary skills of the three 'Rs', and especially reading, were regarded by many advanced reformers as of crucial importance; on occasion the enthusiasm could be excessive, and for a time the emphasis in the regime of the Berkshire County Gaol led to its being known among its habitués as the 'Read-Read-Reading Gaol'.

To a modern observer it seems scarcely surprising that at a time when the mass of the common people had but minimal access to primary education, the average young offender would be unable to read and write. The moral aspect of education was seen by reformers in terms of increasing the exposure of the lower orders to the benefits of moral education through the printed word.

Joseph Fletcher wrote in 1848:
Without a proportionate advancement in the morality of society each new change in material civilisation will lead to frequent incentives to disorder among the people at large . . . amidst those classes whose moral ties to the existing framework of society are feeblest, and least felt or understood, and to many of whom Socialism, or any other destructive theory would appear as consistent with their well-being as the most cherished axioms of Political Science, or even the words of Christian Truth Itself.

Literacy then, was to be a bulwark against moral decay and the Bible of King James a principal instrument of moral education.

The sociologist who is given to excursions within the thickets of such pompous Victorian prose must be forgiven if, when

vii

reading some of the letters addressed nowadays to the Editor of *The Times*, he experiences a sense of *déja vu*. But whereas the intensity, quality and duration of popular education in the last century was recognized as limited, the same cannot be said for developments within the lifetime of those now living. There is little doubt that the improvements have been massive since the turn of the century. It has been said that we now spend more on education and delinquency is of a more complex nature. The pioneer work of Sir Cyril Burt in the 1920's demonstrated that among delinquents, those whose educational standards were low were not as dull as their attainments would appear to suggest, but rather that there was a distinct gap between their potential and their measured abilities.

The reasons for this state of affairs are various. Poor school attendance may be a direct result of parental irresponsibility—perpetually allowing children to 'oversleep' and miss school just as father misses work—or frequent changes of school. Emotional disturbance and consequent truancy may also play a part. But the problems of teaching children in large classes under far from satisfactory conditions cannot be excluded. In the not so recent past some Education Authorities have played down the idea that the 'blackboard jungle' school exists other than in the imagination of certain disaffected supply teachers. We now know that there is such a thing as the Educational Priority Area and that the conditions which have been highlighted by the presence of immigrant children have been there all the time.

It is entirely plausible to suggest that those boys who will drift through petty delinquency to more serious offences and finally enter the borstal system are more than likely to be found among those who have gone to the most socially disprivileged schools. They are likely to have had problems with authority and found themselves on the wrong side of the teacher, and have become bored during their last year when all that has been in their minds has been the anticipation of freedom from pedagogic restriction and the assumption of an independent wage earning role.

Both the Newsom and Plowden Reports have shown that a quarter of a century after the Butler Education Act, and a century since the introduction of state education itself, there is still much to be done. The borstal boy is, in the words of

Newsom, to be found in that 'other half of our future'—the half that has done pretty badly compared with the new élite of the swollen sixth form and the lavishly expanded university. But that some 60 per cent of the boys seen by Dr Stratta wanted to leave earlier than they did suggests that secondary education, as they perceived it, had no attractions for them, and indeed was actively disliked by some. In some of her interviews one can detect a sense of resignation on the part of both teacher and boy:

> They just didn't care. Whether you knew it or not. If you knew it you knew it. If you didn't you didn't. That was their attitude. If they thought you were a bit of a tearaway and didn't want to know, they didn't want to know you. I suppose it was reasonable.

Dr. Stratta's study has come at an interesting point in time. For in spite of the extravagant distortions of the recent so called 'Black Papers', it cannot be denied that in many aspects the whole of our educational system is in need of critical re-appraisal. What is perhaps more important for this group of boys is that the success rate of the borstal system—the lowness of it—gives just as much cause for disquiet of another kind. According to data recently published by the Home Office in *The Sentence of the Court*, about 38 per cent of first offenders and 71 per cent of previously convicted boys in borstal are again convicted within five years. The so-called 'decline in the quality of borstal receptions' has been a feature of the last decade. But is it fair to suggest that these depressing data are the result of inadequacies of the borstal system alone? The quality of delinquency has in an important sense changed too as have the opportunities for crime. All the same, Dr Stratta's account of the organization of educational facilities within borstal underlines the fact that there remains as much to be done here as in the schools outside. There is reason to think that in the period following the Mountbatten Report much that was good in informal practice has been sacrificed on the altar of the new God—Security. But long before the criminologically irrelevant escape of George Blake put the brake hard upon so many developments within the prison system, the relationship of the Tutor Organizer to the prison staff was problematic.

It is not, as Dr Stratta shows, just a matter of deciding where education fits into the borstal regime, but where the educationalist himself fits into the borstal community. The Tutor Organizer has status within the institutional hierarchy but little power to affect long term planning. There are arguments in favour of the present system whereby the Tutor Organizer is an outsider to the prison service, but others for the development of a genuine career structure for the educationalist within it. These are examined in useful detail in this book.

But one of the most important matters which she discusses relates to the way in which education must relate to the total training experience. At present it does not fit easily, but in any event it can be argued that the principles upon which borstal training is based may well be no longer wholly relevant to the needs of the contemporary borstal boy who bears little relationship to the ill-fed but basically respectful forelock-tugging working lad who characterized the Golden Age of Borstal.

Every research has its shortcomings, and this is no exception, but this is a book which will form a significant contribution to the borstal literature. Like any book about an institution, it will be read by some and talked about by many more—at least within the service itself. It raises issues which are not wholly confined to borstal. Is there reason, for example, to be sanguine about the state of education in other types of penal institution? Certainly there is nothing in this country to compare with the best of American practice (nor, mercifully, with the worst). How many young men who missed out at school have the opportunity to make up for wasted time and opportunity later? There is no substance in the theory that education by itself is an antidote to crime, although improvement in an individual's chances in the market may go a long way to breaking the cycle of unskilled work, unemployment and crime. There is a case for ensuring that every member of our complex and bureaucratically demanding society is at least minimally competent to meet its demands, and able to use his leisure critically and constructively. The tragedy of a borstal boy on licence whiling away his time in an amusement arcade lies not so much in the fact that he is again in the company of layabouts, but that his intelligence and ability are in many cases being insulted without his knowledge.

Acknowledgements

No study of this kind can be completed without help and advice from others. I would like, therefore, to acknowledge with gratitude the following people, who, in one way or another, have made it possible for me to complete this work.

The study could not have started had not the Home Office allowed me access to Wormwood Scrubs Allocation Centre and Borstal Institutions; and had I subsequently not received the co-operation of the staff within these institutions, the study could not have proceeded. I am, therefore, most grateful to the Administrators of the Head Office of the Prison Department, the Educational Psychologists, Governors and their Assistants, Discipline Staff, Vocational Training Instructors, Tutor Organizers and Teachers, who unstintingly gave of their time to provide facilities and information, and answer the many questions asked of them. Mention must also be made of the many borstal trainees who were willing to provide the material on which the whole study has been based.

Equally important to a study of this kind is the advice and encouragement of one's Supervisor. I should like to record my indebtedness to Dr Terence Morris of the London School of Economics and Political Science for his continuous support during the whole period of study.

Several people gave advice at crucial moments. I am grateful to Dr Josephine Klein of the University of Sussex for valuable discussions in the early stages, and in the later stages to the following staff of the School of Education, University of Birmingham: Mr W. Curr for advice on intelligence testing, Mr R. Lambourne for advice on statistical analysis, and Dr P. Platt for the services of the library.

I have been particularly fortunate to have had several invaluable discussions with Mr D. L. Howard of the College of

Acknowledgements

Education, Brighton. His experience, insight and deep understanding of the problems involved in dealing with delinquents, resulting from his work as Tutor Organizer in Dover Borstal, have been a source of inspiration to me.

Finally, I record my thanks to my husband, with whom I have frequently discussed the work. His support and understanding have sustained me at all times.

Needless to say the author herself must bear full responsibility for the study in its final form.

I

The Area of the Research

As a preliminary to the study of the educational experience of
a group of borstal boys in relation to the educational facilities,
as part of borstal training, it is proposed to examine the following areas:

(A) EDUCATION: ITS CONCEPTION AND
     DEVELOPMENT WITHIN PENAL INSTITUTIONS
(B) EDUCATIONAL PROVISION AS A PART OF
     BORSTAL TRAINING TODAY
(C) THE AREA IT IS PROPOSED TO EXAMINE IN
     THIS STUDY
(D) AN OUTLINE OF CURRENT RESEARCH INTO
     BORSTAL TRAINING
(E) THE METHOD CF SELECTION OF THE SAMPLE

(A) EDUCATION: ITS CONCEPTION AND
DEVELOPMENT WITHIN PENAL INSTITUTIONS

The need for educational provision within penal institutions has
long been recognized by some reformers. It has a history dating
back to the early nineteenth century. It is proposed therefore,
firstly to examine the origins of this early recognition, and
secondly to discuss the ways in which the role of education has
developed and changed during the course of the past 150 years.

The recognition in this country that education had a role to
play in penal institutions could be said to have its beginnings,
during the early nineteenth century, in the work of a devout
Christian, Sarah Martin. The conditions in Yarmouth Prison,
which Sarah Martin first visited in 1818, were described as
'filthy, confined, unhealthy, and its occupants were infested
with vermin and skin disease'. At this time no attempt was made
to segregate prisoners according to age; consequently the age

1

of the population ranged from nine to eighty. (The Religious Tract Society, 1872, pp. 44–7.)

As a result of what she saw, Sarah Martin was determined to try to improve the lot of the prisoner. She set prisoners to work making articles for sale, and with the money obtained, part was saved and given them on release, and part was set aside to buy religious books, which she used in teaching prisoners to read: 'Any who could not read I encouraged to learn; . . . whilst such as could write already copied extracts from books lent to them. Prisoners, who were able to read, committed verses from the Holy Scriptures to memory every day, according to their ability and inclination.'

In a *Prison Journal*, Sarah Martin kept records of the educational progress achieved by prisoners during their sentences, and from these records it is possible to see that, despite the appalling conditions, considerable progress was made under her tuition. 'Richard Conman, 23, Felony 6 months. Education: None. On leaving could read well. Brief remarks after departure: Temper frank and open. Attentive, answering well. Diligent, obedient. Not a corrupting one.' (Howard, 1960, p. 39).

The need for separate institutional provision for children sentenced to prison was recognized, in the mid-nineteenth century, by Mary Carpenter in her book *Reformatory Schools for the Children of the Perishing and Dangerous Classes and for Juvenile Offenders* (1851). She pointed to the needs of that section of society whom she described as the 'perishing and dangerous classes'. These were children who had either already broken the law, or, as a result of bad environmental conditions, were likely to do so. Mary Carpenter was concerned that these children should be prevented from following the criminal practices of their parents. In her opinion, many methods had been tried but 'none can prove effectual without setting right the main-spring of life, which can be done only by education. It is evident that a depth of ignorance . . . is consistent with crime, and doubtless in great measure the cause of it.'

Belief in the causal relationship between ignorance and crime resulted in the role of education being interpreted as that of prevention and reform. In Mary Carpenter's opinion, education could only carry out this function effectively if separate provision was made for this particular group of children, for

2

'the whole system of our good British Schools is utterly unfitted for them, and would not be endured by them'. For those children sentenced to prison, schools must be set up within the institution. Such schools would not only reform the children, but would also ensure that they were removed from the company of adult prisoners and given the kind of treatment suitable to their age.

The education provided in these Reformatory Schools would be one of 'sound moral and religious training' aimed at reform In addition, 'Industrial Training should form a part of all such Schools'. Mary Carpenter also recognized the importance of developing the intellects of her pupils in order 'to develop their powers and regulate their springs of action, as to enable them, if they use the opportunities afforded them, to become useful members of society'.

The methods used would be based on a belief in the importance of the individual, and the approach would be informal, using, when appropriate, the pupils' individual modes of expression; visual material would also be used. (It is interesting to note that educationists in the mid-twentieth century are becoming increasingly aware of the importance of the child's own use of language as a starting point in education, and of the value of visual material.) Children were to 'be treated with respect, with true Christian politeness, and they will give a ready response'.

In 1852, a Select Parliamentary Committee was set up with terms of reference to inquire into 'the present Treatment of Criminal and Destitute Children and what changes are desirable in their present treatment, in order to supply industrial training and to combine reformation with due correction of juvenile crime' (Select Committee, 1853). The Committee heard evidence from witnesses who had first-hand experience of prison conditions and of the few Industrial Training Schools, such as Parkhurst and Red Hill, already in existence as special institutions for the confinement of young offenders.[1] The Chaplain of Leeds Prison informed the Committee that 14 per cent of the total committals to Leeds were children under

---

[1] Parkhurst, an old military hospital on the Isle of Wight, was taken over in 1838 for the confinement of young criminals under twenty who had been sentenced to transportation or penal servitude. Red Hill was sponsored by the Philanthropic Society and was set up in Red Hill, Surrey, in 1849.

fourteen years of age; and of the adult population in the prison on charges of dishonesty, 21 per cent had started their careers as juveniles, and of those convicted of more serious crimes and sentenced to transportation, 35 per cent had started on a life of crime as a boy. This evidence indicated to the Committee that a prison sentence for juvenile crime was not a particularly effective deterrent. As R. M. Milnes, a magistrate, pointed out in his evidence, judging by the number of re-committals which some children had experienced, it would appear that the effect of a prison sentence was not to reform or even merely to deter but rather to increase their criminal habits.

Figures, such as those which showed that of 42 prisoners under seventeen admitted to prison on one particular day, 16 had never been to school and 17 had attended for not more than twelve months, together with figures as shown in Table 1, must have indicated to the Committee that the vast majority of juveniles committed to prison were illiterate, and seemed untouched by the provision for education existing at the time (Select Committee, 1853, p. 429).

TABLE 1

State of instruction amongst the juveniles in gaols
of England and Wales in the course of the year 1849

	Males	Females
Can neither read nor write	4,911	1,063
Can ready only	2,338	518
Can read or write or both imperfectly	3,506	308
Can read and write well	267	17
State of instruction not ascertained	28	1
Total	11,050	1,907

In the opinion of another witness, the Reverend Carter, who had been a prison chaplain for twelve years, the cause of crime amongst juveniles was 'a want of a correct sense of moral duty, and that this may be produced and promoted by a wider extension of real education'.

Another witness contrasted the treatment given to juveniles in prison with that given them in the voluntary industrial

4

schools. In prison, they were subjected to continuous solitary confinement, in a manner similar to adults, and were employed in oakum picking and stone breaking. For one hour a day, they were allowed to receive some instruction, entirely of a moral and literary character, and for this purpose the children were placed in separate boxes in the chapel. In an industrial school, however, a juvenile could learn a trade, such as shoe making, tailoring and mat making, and was also paid for the staple work of wood cutting. Here instruction was 'entirely of an industrial character . . . a child is a creature of habit, and he must be taught to work for his daily living, as well as taught to read and write'.

Even in a prison such as Parkhurst, an institution set up by the government to deal exclusively with young offenders, boys were 'placed in rigid seclusion for three or four months, as a probationary stage. During this period he . . . is not allowed to speak with or see, except at chapel, any of his fellow prisoners; and is instructed in the art of tailoring, or the mystery of knitting stockings' (Dixon, 1850, p. 180). Once out of solitary confinement, boys were taught a craft, or occupation, and alternated daily between work and school, where they were taught 'music, geography, geology, and generally speaking, all the elements of Science'. However, Annual Reports published throughout the years of its existence, 1838–64, showed that those in charge of Parkhurst were prepared to be flexible, and adapt their methods to the needs of the inmates. Considerable changes in the regime, suggested for example in the Annual Report of 1849, are evidence of this flexible approach (Carlebach, pp. 25–36, 1969).

It was evidence such as that outlined above, which on the one hand stressed the appalling ignorance amongst juvenile delinquents and the deleterious effects of prison sentences, and on the other pointed to the achievements of alternative methods of treatment, that resulted in the Committee's conclusions. These were that local prisons did not provide suitable means for the educational and corrective treatment of young people: 'That a great proportion of the criminal children of this country, especially those convicted of first offences, appear rather to require systematic education, care and industrial occupation than mere punishment,' and 'ought, when guilty of crime, to be treated in a manner different from the ordinary punishments of adult criminals'.

As a result of the Committee's recommendations The Youthful Offenders Act, 1854, was passed, recognizing offenders under sixteen as a distinct group, who would be sent to reformatory schools for corrective training. One of the consequences of this Act can be seen in the fact that, whereas in 1850 there were 15,000 juveniles detained in local prisons, by 1900 this number had dropped to 2,000 (B. and S. Webb, 1922, Introduction).

This Act was the first recognition that juvenile offenders required separate provision in penal institutions. It laid down the principle that juveniles should be trained rather than punished and that, as part of this training, there should be educational provision. Thus education was seen as a means of reform, and its content (not surprisingly as this was the mid-nineteenth century) was largely religious; the function of literacy was to acquaint delinquents with the scriptures.

So far as institutions for adults were concerned, an inquiry by a Select Committee into penal matters resulted in the Prisons Act of 1865. As a consequence of this, prisons were reorganized and security tightened; cells which had been unlocked during the day were now bolted and barred and the inmates left in isolation; the meagre attempts at group education, now in existence at Pentonville and Millbank, were stopped (B. and S. Webb, 1922, pp. 189–92). Under the Prisons Act of 1877, the responsibility for local prisons was transferred to the Central Government. Great emphasis was now placed on achieving uniformity throughout adult prisons, in the belief that this would result in an efficient and economic national prison system. Those industries, which were allowed to continue, had increasingly to be confined to work that could be done in separate cells. A uniform task upon the treadwheel, or crank, cellular confinement and the rule of silence between prisoners was introduced throughout the whole term of sentence. The Prison Commissioners introduced the Progressive Stage System whereby, as a result of docile and co-operative behaviour, a prisoner could improve in four distinct phases upon the dreadful conditions under which he had to exist. By the time a prisoner reached the second stage, which was after having served a minimum of one month of his sentence, he might receive some form of instruction and have the necessary books in his cell. But he had to wait until he reached the fourth stage before library books were permitted as well. The fact that in 1903, 61 per cent of men and 66 per cent of women were sent to prison for fourteen days or less, and only 2 per cent of the prisoners convicted to local prisons were sentenced for six months or more, meant that the great majority of prisoners were unable to benefit at all from the new system of prison education introduced under the Progressive Stage System. Thus, although the Prison Commissioners directed teachers to give instruction in reading and writing to illiterates, as the Webbs point out, 'we do not gather that there was any real improvement between 1878 and 1894 in the education imparted to the prison population as a whole'. During this period, however, it did become possible for inmates to obtain reading material, apart from religious tracts, in their libraries. By the end of the nineteenth century education in adult prisons had not even begun to approach the very limited practice to be found in institutions for juvenile offenders.

The *Report*, published in 1895, of the Departmental Committee on Prisons, challenged the principle of uniformity, which had, for the previous twenty years, infused the penal system; and in its place emphasized the principle of the individualization of treatment. The Committee recommended the establishment of separate reformatories catering for the needs of young offenders between the ages of sixteen and twenty-one on conviction. These institutions were to be 'amply provided with staff capable of giving sound education, training inmates in various kinds of industrial work, and qualified generally to exercise the best and healthiest kind of moral influence' (Cmnd. 7702, 1895, p. 30). In making such recommendations, the Gladstone Committee was advocating a completely new principle, for until this time, sixteen had been regarded as the age of majority and reformatories for adults had been out of the question. One of the influences behind the recommendation must have been the evidence received by the Committee on the successful and enlightened reformatory at Elmira in New York State (Cmnd. 7702, 1895, p. 526). However, as Roger Hood (1965, pp. 5–13) points out, the Prison Commissioners and the general public were not as convinced of the need for this kind of experiment in England.

The borstal scheme, which resulted from the recommendations of the 1895 *Report*, was started in 1900 by Sir Evelyn

7

Ruggles-Brise. Although he was prepared to adopt certain elements of the American system, these were not the most enlightened, and Borstal was certainly not an imitation of Elmira. Ruggles-Brise (1921, p. 93) described the borstal system as being 'one of stern and exact discipline, tempered only by such rewards and privileges as good conduct, with industry might earn: and resting on its physical side on the basis of hard, manual labour and skilled trades, and on its moral and intellectual side on the combined efforts of the Chaplain and the Schoolmaster'. It was believed that as a result of these methods, the inmate, a 'young hooligan advanced in crime, perhaps *with many previous convictions*, and who appeared to be inevitably doomed to a life of habitual crime' would become a 'strong, well-set-up, well-drilled handy English lad, with respect for authority, qualifying him to enter the ranks of honest, industrious labour'. Education seems to have consisted of 'exhortation and moral persuasion' together with 'physical drill, gymnastics, technical and literary instruction'. 'Lectures calculated to elevate and instruct . . . are given weekly during the winter months . . . and are frequently illustrated by lantern slides.' However, work as a disciplinary measure, seems to have been more important than work as vocational training (Cmnd. 7601, 1913–14, p. 107). Despite its obvious shortcomings, an institution run along these lines, with the main emphasis on training and reform, was in complete contrast to the regime in prisons at that time, and was a step forward in the development of education within the penal system.

The appointment in 1922 of Sir Alexander Paterson, as the Commissioner in charge of borstals, resulted in a different emphasis being placed on the principles behind borstal training. This was based on Paterson's belief that real change could only be the result of a conscious personal decision and not of any external pressures to conform.

Training a lad is to regard him as a living organism, having its secret of life and motive-power within, adapting itself in external conduct to the surroundings of the moment, but undergoing no permanent organic change merely as a result of outside pressure. So does Borstal look at him, as a lad of many mixtures, with a life and character of his own. The task is not to break or knead him into shape, but to stimulate some power within to regulate conduct aright, to insinuate a preference for the good and the clean, to make him want to use life well, so that he himself and not others will save him from waste. It becomes necessary to study the individual lad, to discover his trend and his possibilities, and to infect him with some idea of life which will germinate and produce a character, controlling desire and shaping conduct to some more glorious end than mere satisfaction or acquisition (Ruck, 1951, p. 97).

Paterson's beliefs influenced his thinking on every aspect of borstal training. Of education he wrote that its purpose was 'not to impart information or to make dullards into scholars, but to get rusty and ill-controlled brains to work, to enlarge the sphere of interest and to discover a point of contact with each lad . . . we are bent on discovering and developing the good, rather than flogging away at the bad'. The boys were encouraged to pursue 'cultural' activities for 'to discover and develop a love for music or letters, an interest in flowers or animals or stamps, is to foster the growth of something good, which will occupy the stage of interest in a lad's life, and oust the idle and unclean things that formerly held possession'. Although 'the syllabus . . . must be varied' for Paterson reform was the result of contact with, and emulation of, middle-class values. Education was conceived as a means of rescuing boys from their own culture and introducing them to what was 'good' in middle-class terms. Thus, although by now the approach may have been more enlightened and broader based, the main purpose of education was still reformative; its content was determined by the values of the middle class, whose influence in the hierarchical class structure of the time was powerful; its message was clearly to perpetuate the rigid class structure.

In keeping with the educational policies of the period, Paterson advocated the pursuance of 'literary subjects to a comparatively high standard' for the intelligent, whereas work with the hands was reserved for the less intelligent.

In teaching-methods, however, Paterson showed a much more enlightened attitude. He stressed the need to make the boys feel involved; they should be made to work and discover the information for themselves and not merely be treated as a receptive audience into which information is pumped. It was his leadership which created the conditions for the experiments, during the 1930s, of the open borstal.

It would appear that during the inter-war period, the main educational emphasis in borstal institutions was on industrial training

> as we believe that the youths committed to our charge have reached the age when they should be trained to work for at least eight hours a day at whatever trade is best suited to them . . . The instructional courses, which are worked in conjunction with workshop training, are a step in the right direction and they have undoubtedly created a greater keenness amongst the more intelligent lads (Cmnd. 5675, 1936, p. 27).

As part of a course in trade training, some boys were able to attend classes at local Technical Colleges, and in some cases Local Authorities provided teachers, who held classes in the institutions. However, with the exception of the provision outlined above, education was the responsibility of the borstal staff, which must have presented considerable problems so far as backwardness, for example, was concerned. As this Report points out, staff 'are severely handicapped by lack of experience and training and the need for specially trained teachers to deal with the education of backward lads becomes more and more apparent'. The result of education being the responsibility of the borstal staff was that, in the main, apart from vocational training, education was directed towards providing boys with a useful hobby 'such as would engage the leisure time interests of these lads in ordinary life'. This governor's Annual Report continues by indicating that: 'Rabbits, Pigeons, Cabinet-making, Fretwork, Rugmaking, Basket-making, Stool plaiting and Wireless are the principal subjects' (Cmnd. 4295, 1931, p. 52).

In 1947 an informal report by the Prisoners' Education Advisory Committee made the following major recommendations in respect of Borstals:

(i) that, for lads under eighteen, and more especially the backward and illiterate, education should form part of the normal working day;

(ii) that considerably more time than at present should be

devoted to evening education, with six hours as a minimum and with only a relatively short break during the summer;

(iii) that a Housemaster should be appointed to the staff of each Institution with specific charge of the educational side of the training:

(iv) that appropriate parts of the educational and recreational training should be concentrated in a distinct and separate part of the premises and organized on the lines of a club or community centre (Cmnd. 7777, 1948, p. 53).

The Commissioners accepted these recommendations in principle and 'will seek to give effect to them as and when conditions permit'. Considerable impetus was given, particularly to the second recommendation, by the transfer in 1948 of the major responsibility for education in borstals to the Local Education Authorities. One result was that: 'At several Borstals a full-time teacher has been appointed by the Local Education Authority, primarily to deal with the illiterates during working hours, but also to co-ordinate and help with the work of the evening classes.'

The gradual introduction of professional teachers into borstal institutions, in addition to the appointment of full-time educational advisers, Tutor Organizers, meant that the educational provision could be more broadly based and 'interpreted in its widest sense' (Cmnd. 645, 1959, p. 9). The effect of this change in emphasis, and the theoretical role of education in borstal training today, are discussed in the following section.

Despite an increasing recognition of the particular needs of certain sections of the prison population (for example, the setting up of borstal institutions) the educational provision in adult prisons, at the beginning of this century, continued to play a minor role, and did not aim to do more than 'teach the illiterate to read and write, and in the small space and opportunity given, to raise to a higher standard those who are just a little better than illiterates' (Ruggles-Brise, 1921, p. 126). This provision was limited, in the main, to those under twenty-five, for it was thought that it would be more effective with younger than older prisoners. Teachers were recruited from the discipline staff, who, having shown that they were sufficiently literate to enter 'the Schoolmaster class' had to teach for a probationary period of six months, under the guidance of the Prison Chaplain,

11

before passing permanently into the 'Schoolmaster grade' (Ruggles-Brise, 1921).

With the appointment of a new Chairman to the Prison Commission, however, the scope of educational activities widened. In 1923, an Adult Education Scheme was started, as a result of which evening classes taken by volunteers from outside the prison were established. In addition, a list of educational advisers to governors in local prisons was drawn up (Cmnd. 4151, 1930, pp. 58–9). Education in prisons continued to be organized in this manner until the Second World War, when the breakdown of voluntary arrangements, which resulted from the war, brought about a review of the future educational provision in prisons. This review, 'Recognizing the aim of prison education is "the making of better men and women" proceeded to consider the various elements, physical, vocational and social, of which each had its place in the system' (Cmnd. 7777, 1948, p. 39).

As with borstal institutions, the acceptance in principle by the Prison Commissioners, of the Advisory Committee's recommendations, in addition to the transfer of the major responsibility for education to Local Education Authorities, brought about considerable changes in educational provision in prisons. Thus, in 1953, Frances Banks was appointed to the newly created post of Tutor Organizer at Maidstone Prison, and, as a consequence of her experience was permitted by the Prison Commissioners to carry out a survey of education in prisons, excluding borstals and detention centres. This survey was subsequently the basis of a book about education in English prisons (Banks, 1958).

Frances Banks begins her book by stating her belief 'that the educational work of prisons was deep-set in the whole structure of the day's work, and that ultimately there must be a very close meeting-place between the voluntary work of the evening classes and the compulsory work of the day labour, so that every prison must be primarily a training institution—for work and for leisure, for vocation and for recreation, for family life and for citizenship'. In her opinion, we already have 'effective evidence of the civilizing force of education within the walls', but if education is really to affect reform in prison, it must be moulded into a cohesive scheme geared, on the one hand, to the individual's need for personal adjustment, and on the other to society's need for an economic use of man-power.

Much of what Frances Banks describes of the conditions under which classes are carried out in practice, tends to underline the impression that education has always been a secondary consideration. She describes how, in prisons, built in the nineteenth century, educational activities have to be carried out under improvised conditions. Sometimes cells may be converted for the purpose, but where there is already overcrowding this will not be encouraged. (In 1963 when the present author taught in the Allocation Centre in Wormwood Scrubs, several groups of boys, waiting for transfer, were taught around tables set up in the well of the prison block. Consequently four or five classes were carried on at once.) Frances Banks indicates that staff attitudes to the educational programmes vary between institutions; thus, in some prisons, she found that governors and officers tended to regard education as a threat to prison security, and by their attitude and behaviour were an inhibiting influence.

Frances Banks sees education in prison as having several functions. One of these is therapeutic, and this can be carried out through group discussions on topics such as those which could broadly be described as human relationships, or through writing, which she describes as being as 'cathartic, revealing and self uncovering' as the spoken word. (While discussing writing she also points out that her aim is to improve the literary ability of the prisoners.)

Other subjects which have a therapeutic role are drama and art. She also discusses the pre-release courses under this heading, which she describes as being a 'well developed instrument for social therapy in a few institutions'. In one such course, lasting two days, the following was the programme for half a day:

(1) *Finance and the Family*   *Speakers*

The cost of living and the family budget; how to   A Housewife and a
plan a budget; use and abuse of hire purchase,   Business Woman.
insurance, etc.
Questions and discussion.

(2) *The Home from the Wife's Point of View*

Present-day problems of catering and housekeeping.   The Governor's Wife.
Sharing responsibilities.

(3) *The Home from the Children's Point of View*

Children as individuals.   Wife of a Personnel
The child's place in the family.   Manager.
Questions and discussion.

13

For the purposes of the discussion, those on the course were divided into small groups led by the speakers. One cannot help feeling, however, that it would have been much more profitable to the individuals concerned if such topics as these had been part of a longer course and had been discussed at greater length throughout their sentences, rather than being dealt with as part of a two day programme prior to release. Finally, in the section on education as a therapy, Frances Banks discusses the function of group therapy. This she sees as a method of involving the prison officers in the educational programme. Volunteers guided and supported by psychiatrists would run therapeutic group discussions which would aim at deepening the members' understanding and enjoyment of the world in which they lived. Writing and painting might result from these group discussions.

Frances Banks describes the second function of education as being cultural and recreational. Subjects which are included here are music in both an active and passive capacity; lectures from specialists in various fields; hobbies; handicrafts; and the study of the sciences, which, as she points out, is hampered both by the environment itself and the lack of facilities within that environment.

The final function of education in prisons is vocational, which is catered for in the work all prisoners are obliged to do, and through vocational training schemes.

In her book, Frances Banks is not so much describing actual practice, but rather attempting to define theoretically the role of education inside prison, and supporting her theories with empirical evidence, based on her own experience as a Tutor Organizer, and from her knowledge of other prisons. If one regards the two main functions of prison education as being to satisfy the needs of the individual and of society to which he will return, Frances Banks has attempted to show how these two functions can be carried out.

Obviously if one believes in the value of education, one must agree with Frances Banks that education in prisons must 'be absorbed into the main stream of penal reform' and that it can no longer be 'merely a diversional evening occupation, consisting of a more or less haphazard collection of unrelated subjects'. On the other hand it would seem that in her analysis of the functions of education Frances Banks makes false distinctions in her grouping of particular subjects. For example, the function of discussion cannot only be conceived of as therapeutic; it is a means of improving self-expression, of articulating experience as one understands it, of learning to listen to, understand and perhaps sympathize with an opposite point of view; and art cannot only be concerned with achieving freedom of expression, but ought also to be concerned, among other things, with the development of an individual's creative ability, the stimulation of imagination and the heightening of visual awareness and sensitivity. Obviously the environment of a prison is not ideal for enlightened teaching, but with imagination and involvement on the part of the teacher, and flexibility on the part of the prison staff with regard to materials and facilities, much can be achieved. If real integration of all the activities in prison is to be brought about, then boundaries must be less rigid; everything must be geared to the over-all purpose of rehabilitating the prisoner towards a re-entry into society.

(B) EDUCATIONAL PROVISION AS A PART OF BORSTAL TRAINING TODAY

The conception and development of borstal institutions was very different from that of prisons for the adult population. Paterson stated 'that each lad shall be dealt with as an individual, and shall not be regarded as the same as any other lad, requiring the same universal prescription' (Ruck, 1951, p. 98). From its inception, the main emphasis of the regime has been on training. In 1959 (Cmnd. 645, p. 9) it was described as being 'essentially a remedial and educational system, based on personal training by a carefully selected staff. Its development since the Act of 1948 has been mainly in the extension of vocational training in skilled trades and of education in its widest sense.'

Prisons and Borstals (Home Office, 1960, p. 58) describes education in borstal as follows:

Education is a primary charge on the borstals. The Statutory Rules provide that:

1. At every Borstal provisions shall be made for the continued education of the inmates, by class teaching, individual study and all such cultural influences, including hobbies

15

and handicrafts, as may make for development of valuable interests and good use of leisure.

2. Facilities shall, so far as is practicable, be provided to enable every inmate to take part in such educational activities for at least six hours a week outside the normal working week, and where it is desirable in the educational interests of any inmate, particularly those under eighteen years of age, or those who are backward or illiterate, provision may be made for education within the normal working week.

It could be interpreted from the above that the Prison Department sees education in borstals today as having two main functions. Firstly, it is the means whereby a delinquent population can be brought into contact with various 'cultural influences', as a result of which they may acquire new interests and hobbies. Secondly, education is to provide facilities for that minority group who are sub-literate or illiterate, thereby enabling them to achieve a degree of literacy.

It might be argued that this is a rather narrow definition of educational aims, particularly within a training institution. The conception of education seems very similar to that of the thirties.

Examination of other aspects of training, for example work, suggests that the emphasis these aspects receive must severely limit any educational provision in borstal institutions. A further paragraph in *Prisons and Borstals* (1960) points out that 'the basis of every borstal day is eight hours work'. It could be argued that eight hours work of the right kind is truly educational, but if one looks at the ways in which many of the boys are employed, this can hardly be described as vocational, educational, or as teaching them 'respect for good craftsmanship'. The Prison Department Report for 1966 shows that of an effective daily labour force of 2,741 boys in closed borstals, 704 (26 per cent) are employed as cleaners, jobbers and labourers around the borstal, 206 (7·5 per cent) are employed in metal recovery and only 379 boys (14 per cent) are undergoing courses in vocational training.

In the open borstals, the largest group at any time of an effective labour force of 1,751 boys is the 422 boys (24 per cent) who are vocational trainees; the second largest group is the

328 boys (19 per cent) employed as cleaners, jobbers and labourers around the borstals; and the third largest group is the 264 boys (15 per cent) employed in farm work (Cmnd. 3408, 1966, pp. 52–4). It can be seen from these figures that for the majority of boys, the eight hours are spent in hard physical work, much of which is possibly unrewarding and boring. Furthermore, although a large group of boys is undergoing vocational training courses at any one time, these courses last only six months, as opposed to the average length of borstal training, which in 1966 was fourteen months. And many of the boys, selected to follow a course in trade training, are unable to be employed in related work for the remainder of their sentences, unless there happens to be a production shop in their borstal (*Report of the Advisory Council on the Employment of Prisoners,* 1962, pp. 15–16).

Considerable emphasis is also placed on physical training, and it is only after work and P.T. that the majority of boys are free for the education which is 'a primary charge on the borstals' (Home Office, 1960). After a day spent in this way, many boys must find it difficult to settle down to a concentrated span of mental work during the evenings.

In practice, it must also be difficult, in some institutions, to provide facilities 'to enable every inmate to take part in educational activities for at least six hours a week outside the normal working week'. In Hindley, for example, with an average population of 309 and an average of 10 boys per class, a programme of evening educational activities involving 186 hours per week would be needed to provide each boy with at least six hours. In practice, the educational programme for one term shows that the actual number of hours is 129 per week, of which fourteen hours is allocated to physical education, and a further six hours to providing related classes for boys who are following some kind of trade training during the day.[1] Thus, in this particular borstal, it is unlikely that every boy will be able to spend six hours per week in educational activities.

[1] This information was obtained from H.M. Borstal Hindley Programme of Educational Activities (Autumn, 1967), as a result of a private communication with the Home Office.

(c) THE AREA IT IS PROPOSED TO
EXAMINE IN THIS STUDY

As education in all institutions is a compulsory part of the training, it might be thought that relevant to the design of any programme of educational activities is some knowledge of the features in the educational experience of borstal boys prior to committal. This would seem to be essential if educational programmes are to cater for the particular needs of these boys. However, there has been no systematic attempt at discovering the educational experience of borstal boys prior to their committal, and consequently no evaluation of present day facilities in the light of this knowledge.

All educational provision must be geared to the needs of a particular population. The determinants of these needs come in part from within the individual population, being such factors as age, ability and attainment, and in part from the larger society of which the particular population is a member. In the case of borstal boys this is a group who are already 'educated' in the sense that they have reached the age at which full-time education is no longer compulsory; but to have been at school from five until fifteen does not necessarily mean that the education received has been effective or even welcomed. In addition, a boy committed to borstal training is entering an institution where once more education will be compulsory, but he may have ceased full-time education for anything up to five years. It is important then to try to establish what has been achieved so far, as a result of ten years compulsory education. One method of discovering this is to give a boy a series of tests. In actual fact three tests[1] are given on entry into borstal, and these are discussed more fully in the next chapter.

It was decided that another way of discovering what had been achieved so far was to question each boy himself about his own experiences at school. The picture that will emerge from his answers will be a personal one, of his school-days as he sees them in retrospect; it will probably be very different from the picture that would emerge if it were possible to question the teachers who had been responsible for teaching the boy.

Nevertheless, it is in the author's opinion very important to

[1] This is the minimum number. Some boys complete a maximum of six tests.

discover the attitudes of the boys to their education, as it is her belief that certain factors will emerge from amongst this population, which must be taken into consideration in designing education programmes in borstal institutions, if they are to serve the needs of the population for whom they are intended.

It was for these reasons that it was decided to question a sample of the borstal population about their educational experience, as well as extracting relevant data from their records. Previous research into similar populations had indicated that although there would be some boys of above average intelligence in this sample the majority would be below the median of average ability. In such a population there would also be a considerable degree of backwardness so that on the whole the boys' attainment would be below their potential.[1] It was thought that part of the explanation for this would be found in the fact that the majority of boys had experienced a disrupted school career because of truancy, or changes in their home circumstances, which may have resulted in their removal to Approved School or some other institution.

It might also be assumed that in a sample drawn from a borstal population very few of the boys would have attended a school which was selective on ability, such as a grammar or a technical school, although tests might reveal that more boys than the actual number who were selected, had the potential ability to follow the kind of courses provided in these schools. The majority would have left school at the earliest possible opportunity, without obtaining any tangible qualifications in the form of external examinations, and would take up jobs the performing of which was in some cases well below the individual's potential.

It might further be assumed that amongst a group of boys sentenced to borstal training there would be those who, looking back at what they had learnt at school, would feel it had little or no relevance to the life they were now leading; and in addition might not, at the time they were attending school, have been interested in what they were learning. There might also be boys who, when questioned about specific ways in which they had been prepared for life and work would remember little constructive advice. In addition, it might be expected that

---

[1] See Chapter II, Section B, for a full discussion on the subject of delinquency and intelligence.

a considerable proportion of the boys attended single-sex schools.

So far as staff is concerned, there might be boys who would feel that their teachers had shown no interest in them, or could not control them. The cane would be a form of punishment, and it is likely that some members of the sample would have been caned regularly during their time at school. It could be expected that boys would express interest in subjects which included some positive activity on their part.

So far as further education is concerned, it is probable that only a small minority would have attended any such courses since leaving school. If this fact emerges, it would be important to discover the boys' present attitudes to undergoing some form of education. It would also be important to discover in what areas, if any, they would now like to extend their knowledge. As a guide to planning educational programmes, it would be useful to know if any pattern of leisure activity emerges amongst the group and what kind of aspirations the boys have for the future.

Having analysed the answers to the individual questions, it will be interesting to see how far there is a consistent pattern of attitudes. It is likely that a consistent pattern will emerge. There will be boys who will indicate by their answers that they are very much against school and all it implies and who have no desire to learn anything new at this stage. Previous research has suggested that a consistent pattern of discontent about life generally is found amongst delinquents. The explanation of this attitude would appear to lie in the psychology of the individual (Willmott, 1966; Andry, 1960). What is important from the point of view of educational programmes is to establish the size of such a discontented group within a borstal population and to consider constructive ways of coping with it.

As with any interview of this nature, there are certain drawbacks to the collection of the information. Firstly there is the problem of recollection. A boy sentenced to borstal training may have finished his full-time education as much as five years previously. It is likely that both during and after the completion of full-time education he has experienced changes in his life, such as a sentence to an Approved School or a Detention Centre, which may make his pattern of educational experience confused, consequently impeding recollection. On the other hand he has spent ten years of his life undergoing full-time education, a fact which may help to impress experiences on his memory. What is important, however, to this particular study is the value of obtaining the boys' attitudes and opinions about their education in retrospect, especially since most of them have been out to work. How they assess what they learnt at school, and what their attitude to extending their knowledge in certain areas is, will be valuable to discover.

In addition, the boys' answers will reflect a perceptual bias both initially and in retrospect. This, however, is inevitable and would not be eliminated if the boys' teachers or their parents were to be asked for the same information. Part of this study is interested in the boys' opinions and attitudes and in building up a subjective picture as a result of this information. As has been stated earlier, it is thought to be important that these opinions and attitudes should be considered and evaluated if education is to be really successful in borstal institutions.

A third problem arises with difficulties over comprehension. In the case of the present *questionnaire* this problem was looked at very carefully during the pilot survey and boys were questioned about difficulties which arose in understanding a question. As a result of this, changes were made to the original *questionnaire*. As an additional safeguard, each question on the *questionnaire* was checked with the individual concerned, after he had completed his answers, so that any problems which he had encountered over comprehension could be clarified.

Finally, there is the consideration that the attitudes revealed here may be rather superficial, for they are based on an immediate response to a question, and in some cases this may be the first time a particular boy has thought about an issue.

However, the number of boys who have to be interviewed, so that the information obtained might be said to be representative, is a substantial figure, and this militates against depth interviewing. In addition, the actual number of questions in which boys are being asked to evaluate is very small. In an attempt to counteract the criticism of superficiality and to probe more deeply behind the responses to certain questions, it was decided to carry out a tape recorded interview with 39 of the boys from the original sample. The aim of this would be to get the boys to elaborate more fully on some of the answers which they had given to the written *questionnaire*. Thus, boys

C

would be asked to go into detail as to the reasons why they had left school or to say why they had disliked school, if they had indicated that they had truanted for this reason, and so on. They would also be asked to elaborate on the content of the various subjects taught to them, to say in what ways their school had prepared them for life and work and in what ways they thought their education had been inadequate. Although only a small number, these answers will help to supplement information from the whole sample.

Having obtained, from their records and their answers to a *questionnaire*, information about the sample's previous educational experience, it will then be necessary to evaluate this information against the existing provision for further education in borstal institutions. In order to do this, it will be necessary to visit a selection of borstals to obtain information concerning the education facilities, including vocational training.

Finally, some attempt will be made to assess the efficiency of education as a part of borstal training, and if necessary, to make recommendations as to its future role.

(D) AN OUTLINE OF CURRENT RESEARCH
INTO BORSTAL TRAINING

The need for research into education in borstal, an important aspect of the training, is given urgency by 'the gradual deterioration in the success rate of offenders discharged from borstal' (Little, 1965).

The Report of the Prison Department for 1965 (Cmnd. 3088, p. 26) states that 'study of the subsequent records of boys discharged from borstals in each of the years 1959 to 1962 shows that three years after the end of the year of discharge, a consistent proportion (32 per cent) had not been re-convicted'. That is to say 68 per cent of the boys discharged from borstals between 1959 and 1962 had been re-convicted within three years of their discharge; although of these, 23 per cent had only been re-convicted once. The Report comments that 'the rate of failure among boys discharged in the four years up to 1962 is disquieting'. This trend is confirmed by the most recent figures available at the time of the research, which show that of the latest group of boys to have been at risk a minimum of three years, 67·7 per cent have been re-convicted, and of these 41·6 per cent committed to prison or borstal as a result (Cmnd. 3304, 1965, p. 47).

The Prison Department continually makes the point that the deterioration in the success rate of borstal offenders is in part due to a decline in the 'quality' of boys who are being sentenced to borstal. In 1959 (Cmnd. 1117, p. 74), the Prison Commissioners observed that 'broadly speaking less good material for training has been received', and in 1960 (Cmnd. 1467, para. 6) pointed out that there had been 'further deterioration [of reception quality] in terms of the Mannheim-Wilkins prediction rating which seems likely to have an adverse effect on training'.

However, as a result of research based on a 10 per cent sample of receptions between 1950 and 1956, Alan Little (1965) suggests that, although there was a deterioration in 'reception-quality' during this time, 'the decline in success rates took place for receptions of similar "quality" [in Mannheim-Wilkins prediction terms] and therefore the decline in the Borstal success rate cannot be fully explained by "reception quality" '. That is to say, the gradual decrease in the number of boys who are not re-convicted after borstal training does not only reflect the fact that borstal now contains a higher proportion of boys who fall into the worst prediction categories, but also reflects a general decline in the effect of borstal training.

Roger Hood (1965, pp. 214–15) comments that this fact 'must mean that the prediction equation which was devised on the basis of data relating to pre-1950 boys is no longer related to success in the same way . . . that experience has changed, and that in general results are lower than before'. Thus, it cannot be argued that because boys are not responding as well as they did in the past to institutional training, they are intrinsically more difficult, 'but only that they are more difficult to train under existing methods'.

The modern borstal boy is not only more conditioned to institutional life than his predecessors, but is also likely to be more sophisticated. He is the product of a society which has called into question many of the social and religious principles upon which authority in borstal has been, and is still based; a society in which modern communications have enabled ideas and attitudes to reach a much wider audience than previously.

He is likely to be fare more affluent than his predecessors, and, as a result of modern advertising directed towards teenagers, he is likely to see himself as belonging to a separate group, with adolescence being thought of as an end in itself rather than as a stage of development in growing up.

In the light of the argument so far advanced, it might be argued that methods of borstal training need to be reviewed in the context of a rapidly changing modern society. Currently the Prison Department is making 'a comparative study of effects of different types of borstal training on boys of similar personality, social background and criminal sophistication' (Cmnd. 3088, 1965, p. 59). This comparative study is being carried out in three open borstals, each one using 'markedly different training methods (one with a group counselling regime, one with a case-work approach and one with a traditional approach). The allocation centre allocates boys to a pool from which they are distributed at random to the borstals concerned.' To be allocated to the pool boys must be of average or above average intelligence and 'be good open training material' which does not automatically exclude boys who have committed sexual or violent offences.[1]

The Prison Department's research is limited, therefore, to the extent that it is only studying training methods as they apply to a minority of the boys sent to borstals. The majority are in fact allocated to closed borstals. During 1965 boys sentenced to borstals 'included an increasing proportion found at the allocation centre to be suitable for closed conditions only' (Cmnd. 3088, 1965, p. 19).

The Cambridge Institute of Criminology is at present evaluating different methods of borstal training. As education plays an important part in this training, it will obviously be considered as part of this research (Cmnd. 3408, 1966, p. 50).

It is suggested, however, that there is also a need for the study of one aspect of borstal training, compulsory to all institutions and to all types of boys, namely education.

Research might profitably examine the following areas:

(a) the contribution education, as envisaged by the Prison Department, has in borstal training;

---

[1] This information was obtained in a private communication with the Home Office concerning their criteria for open borstals.

(b) how the role of education is interpreted within borstal institutions;
(c) how relevant the education provided is to the needs of the borstal population;
(d) how essential education is to the needs of all boys;
(e) how possible and desirable it is to formulate an over-all education policy within borstal training;
(f) the extent to which an over-all policy militates against important differences between individual institutions.

(E) THE METHOD OF SELECTION OF THE SAMPLE

From 1963 until April 1966, Wormwood Scrubs Prison in London was the allocation centre to which all boys sentenced to borstal training were sent. Here they spent a period of time undergoing observation and testing before being allocated to one of nineteen borstals. The entire future borstal population passed through Wormwood Scrubs. It was for this reason that it was decided to carry out all interviews at this allocation centre.

The sample size was fixed at 10 per cent of the annual average borstal population. As this figure fluctuated from year to year the mean of the last three years for which figures were available was calculated. The borstal population was taken as the annual number of boys sentenced to borstal training and the mean of the three years 1961, 1962 and 1963, was 3,627. The sample size was, therefore, set at 363 interviews. It was also decided to take 10 per cent of the sample number for an additional tape-recorded oral interview, in order to probe more deeply some of the written answers to the *questionnaire*. Thus thirty-nine depth interviews were carried out.

The sample was stratified on an area basis so that the number of boys interviewed from each area was in proportion to the total number of committals to borstal from that area.[1] This procedure was adopted after a pilot survey had been carried out. The pilot survey had shown that the selection of the sample on the basis of each boy's prison number was unsatisfactory, as boys were brought into the allocation centre in large numbers

---

[1] As the sub-sample was also stratified on an area basis, the number of interviews which could have been carried out, calculated to the nearest whole number, was thirty-four or thirty-nine. It was decided to take the larger of the two numbers.

from certain local prisons. This had resulted in boys from certain areas of the country being over-represented among the interviewees in proportion to the borstal population as a whole. As the borstal population is drawn from all over England and Wales, the sample was stratified on the basis of the Registrar-General standard regions (H.M.S.O. 1961).

All local prisons which accommodated borstal boys awaiting transfer to Wormwood Scrubs were grouped under the appropriate national region as listed in the 1961 Census. A boy's local prison was, therefore, taken as an indication of the area of the country in which he was now living and had been educated in the past.

The selection of the sample on an area basis was attempting to ensure two factors. First, that the sample was representative of the distribution of borstal committals throughout the country; selection of the sample in proportion to the committals from each local prison would ensure this. Second, that the educational experiences of the boys, throughout the country as a whole, were represented in proportion to the number of them who were committed to borstal from a particular area. Selection from local prisons, while ensuring this to some extent, does not take into account the mobility of the sample. A boy is tried and convicted in the area in which the crime was committed, but this may not be his home town. After selection on the basis of their local prison, it was found that 47 (12·9 per cent) boys in the sample were detained in local prisons not serving the area of their place of residence at the time of committal.[1] Obviously one cannot assume that the town in which a boy was living, at the time of his committal to borstal, was the one in which he was educated. If, however, his place of birth and his home town are both within the same area, this would suggest that the local prison might be taken as an indicator of the area in which he was educated. Of the boys interviewed, 236 (65 per cent) were, at the time of their committal, living in an area served by the same local prison as their place of birth. Of those boys who had moved away from the area where they were born, 32 were living at home and 26 in lodgings. (In the case of the remaining 22 boys the

---

[1] Of these boys 15 were absconders. The total number of absconders in the sample was 45, of which 43 were from Approved Schools and two from Detention Centres; 30 of the absconders were committed to local prisons serving their home town.

information was not available.) It is impossible to say whether these boys were educated in the area served by the local prison to which they were committed. However, despite these drawbacks, it was decided to use the local prison as an area indicator rather than the sentencing court or the home town.

It would have been very difficult to design a sample frame which would enable one to obtain a sample which was representative of both local area and educational experience. Local prison statistics were chosen because they went some way to satisfying these two demands, and they were more easily available.

The numbers of boys sentenced to borstal training for the years, 1961, 1962 and 1963, was again used to calculate the mean annual borstal population in transit through each local prison. From this the proportional representation of each local prison was calculated as a percentage of the total population of 3,627. The number of boys interviewed from each area is shown in the following table:

TABLE 2

The proportional distribution of the sample
on the basis of national regions

Standard Regions (England and Wales)	Number of boys interviewed	% of sample
Northern	24	6·5
North Western	71	19·6
Midland	40	11·1
London and the South East	107	29·5
South Western	24	6·5
East and West Riding	25	7·0
North Midland	24	6·5
Eastern	13	3·6
Southern	19	5·3
Wales	16	4·4
Total	363	100

It was arranged for the interviews to be carried out one half day a week. The pilot survey had shown that the maximum number of interviews which could be completed in that time was eight. It had also shown that it would be better to interview boys after they had been allocated to their borstal. This would help to diminish the natural connection that boys would make between this interview and the allocation procedure. It also meant that boys' records were completed and were more easily available, for they were returned after allocation to the Prison Record Office.

The Allocation Board, which informed boys to which borstal they were going, sat almost daily. It was decided to use their latest allocation list to select the boys who were to be interviewed each week. This was done by starting at the highest prison number on that list and working backwards in numerical order. The eight names taken from the list then were checked with the daily reception lists of borstal boys into the prison and the name of the local prison from which they had been sent was noted. It was decided to complete 100 interviews, within which each local prison was proportionately represented, before starting on the next 100. This ensured that local prisons which handled the smallest numbers of borstal boys were not left until the end of the total sample interviewing. The consequence of this was that after interviewing for some time, some of the boys amongst the last eight names on the allocation list were from local prisons whose representation in 100 interviews had been completed. In that case the next names in numerical order were taken from the list.

During the course of interviewing, which took place during 1965 and 1966, two problems arose concerning the local prison. Firstly, it was found that no borstal boys were being sent to Wormwood Scrubs from either Swansea or Dorchester prisons, although figures for both these prisons had appeared in the Home Office lists for 1961, 1962 and 1963. On checking with the Prison Department at the Home Office, it was found that borstal boys who had previously been sent to Swansea prison were now being held in the remand centre at Cardiff, and those who had been kept at Dorchester were now being sent to Winchester. Secondly, towards the end of the interviewing, which took nine months to complete, changes in prison administration resulted in boys, who earlier in the survey had been sent from local courts to Leeds or Liverpool prisons, being sent to Manchester prison. In both these cases, therefore, the sentencing courts serving the local prisons were used as the criteria for selection.

After the boys had been selected for interview, their records were obtained. Sometimes it was found that it was not possible to interview a particular boy when he had been selected. At this stage drop-out occurred in the case of 41 boys selected for interview. In 26 cases the reason was that they had already left the prison for their borstal, 9 of the boys were ill in the hospital block, one boy was in the punishment cell and for various reasons the records of the remainder were not available. When it was found that it would not be possible to interview a boy, the same procedure was adopted as before, in order to bring the interviews up to eight. There was drop-out later on in four more cases. One boy, after being asked to complete the interview, said he did not wish to do so. He was the only refusal. In the other three cases, the boys were interviewed before it was realized that their records were not available at Wormwood Scrubs. These interviews were, therefore, discounted. It will be seen in what way this drop-out affected the sample when comparisons are made between the boys interviewed and the borstal population as a whole.

Each boy's record was consulted in order to obtain the following information: the date and place of birth and information about his present living arrangements; the test scores he had been given during the allocation procedure; details as to his criminal and employment record; any information on his education and spare-time activities. A final heading provided for any additional information not included in the above.

There was unfortunately a great disparity between individual records as to the amount of information available. All the records contained detailed information on the boys' criminal activities; but this was not the case when it came to their employment record or their educational experience. The source of any information was noted, where this was available. For example, some records contained detailed reports from head teachers of schools attended by the boys; others only noted the age he had left school, even though this might have been an approved school.

The interviews were carried out between 6 and 8 p.m. This was a period of time when a large number of the boys in the Allocation Centre were out of their cells, either attending education classes or having their 'association'.[1] It was hoped

[1] 'Association' is the period of time during the day when the boys are allowed to relax in the company of other boys in their hall.

that this arrangement would cause the minimum inconvenience to prison routine. Boys who were called for interview would otherwise have been attending an evening class, having their 'association', or be locked in their cell. This obviously might have affected their responses to the interview situation, but none of the boys showed any outward resentment at being asked to spend time in this way.

The interviews were carried out four at a time in the office of a deputy governor. This was a large room containing a desk and three tables so that the boys could be quite separate when writing their answers. The first part of the interview was spent in discussing the content and purpose of the *questionnaire* and in explaining to the boys why they were being asked to complete the answers. It was pointed out that this was a private piece of research into the educational experience of a sample of people drawn from an area covering England and Wales. It was explained that the sample had been stratified on an area basis but that the selection of particular individuals for interveiwing was entirely random. Emphasis was always given to the fact that there was no connection between the information asked for in the *questionnaire* and the work of the prison authorities. It is obviously difficult to assess how much is understood and believed by people in this kind of situation. One indication, however, is the way the boys then approached what they had been asked to do. The boys were always given an opportunity to read through the *questionnaire* and ask any questions. Many of them did, the most frequent seeking an explanation of why the information was required. It was said in reply that it was thought to be important to get information on an individual's experience and opinions of this particular subject, in order to see what trends, if any, might emerge. It was always pointed out, during the discussion, that they could refuse to give the information, but in fact only one boy did so. The rest were all prepared to answer the questions, and in some cases took considerable care and thought over what they wrote.

The boys were asked to complete the interviews without consulting the opinions of other boys in the room. When they had finished, their answers were checked individually. At this stage, as a result of oral questioning, additional information in some cases was obtained and written on to the *questionnaire*.

Obviously, some of the boys who were interviewed were

unable to read or write. In these cases the questions were read to them and their dictated answers written down. It took approximately one hour to complete the four interviews.

ORAL INTERVIEW

The 39 boys who completed an oral interview were selected in the same way as the rest of the sample. They were, however, the last boys to be interviewed from their particular area. At the beginning of their interview it was explained that, in addition to completing the *questionnaire*, they would be asked further questions arising from their written answers, which they would answer orally on a tape recorder. At this stage they were always given the opportunity to withdraw, but in fact all the boys selected were prepared to undergo the oral interview.

In order to ensure that the same areas were covered in each interview, a skeleton outline was drawn up indicating the questions on which more information would be sought. It was decided to keep to this loose framework, basing further questions on the answers which were given to the initial question (See Appendix B).

Because of the extra time involved, it was only possible to complete three oral interviews in the two-hour period. After writing his answers to the questions, each boy was separately interviewed. After an initial embarrassment, the majority of the boys became accustomed to the tape recorder and talked very freely.

Later the tape was played back and the boys' answers were written down verbatim. It was hoped that in this way the tape-recorded interview would provide supplementary information to that obtained from the written answers.

II

A Description of the Sample

A description of the 363 borstal boys, with a view to establishing:

(a) Whether they could be considered representative of the borstal population as a whole.

(b) The characteristics of such a population which have relevance to education as part of borstal training.

The following aspects have, therefore, been covered:

(A) ENVIRONMENT
(B) INTELLIGENCE
(C) PREVIOUS EDUCATIONAL EXPERIENCE
(D) WORK RECORD
(E) CRIMINALITY
(F) PRESENT OFFENCE AND BORSTAL ALLOCATION

(A) ENVIRONMENT

In a sample derived from a delinquent population, it is likely that a considerable proportion of its members will have come from families which would be classified under the category of Social Class V; the determinant of class being the current occupational status of the head of the household (Morris, 1957, pp. 144 and 166). A more recent national survey based its classification 'on the education and social origins of *both* father and mother' (Douglas *et al*, 1966). Using this definition of social class, the survey indicated that there was a 'bottom heavy' distribution of delinquency. 'The lower manual working class stands out as having the highest incidence of all, approximately seven times that of the upper middle class.' In the case of serious delinquency, 'the social class differences are still further exaggerated'.

A description of the sample

With the present sample, it was not possible to classify the boys on the basis of either of the two social descriptions outlined above. It was, however, possible to examine their own occupational status. Basing the analysis on the last job held before the present conviction to borstal, it was found that 182 boys (50·1 per cent) had been employed in unskilled occupations, 74 boys (20·4 per cent) in semi-skilled, and 58 boys (16·0 per cent) in skilled occupations (Registrar-General, 1966). (The remaining 13·5 per cent had either not worked, or had been transferred from approved school, or there was insufficient information in their records.) If one accepts the findings of the research outlined above, and the fact that on conviction the majority of the sample was employed in unskilled work, it could be reasonably inferred that most of the boys came from the lower working class, or working class.

There are obviously other factors associated with social class which have relevance to delinquent behaviour. Unskilled work and consequent low incomes are to a great extent concomitant with inadequate housing. There has been shown to be a strong correlation between delinquency, overcrowding and social class (Morris, 1957, p. 169). Overcrowding and inadequate housing are likely to be two aspects of an underprivileged neighbourhood 'characterized by a long history of poverty, casual employment and bad housing. . . . In such areas educational attainments lag far behind those of the better-off districts and a lack of creative activities and healthy recreation are contributory causes for the general drift of children and young people into crime and delinquency' (Mays, 1954, p. 147).

The national sample, referred to earlier, was used to examine class differences in mental ability and school achievement. Comparison of the scores in 'non-verbal' and 'verbal' tests, administered at the age of eight and ten plus, showed that the performance of the children in the sample drawn from the lower-manual working class declined between the ages of eight and ten plus in relation to the other social groups in the sample. In addition, even when allowance was made for the differences between social groups in the level of their measured ability at the time of the selection examination, it was found that the chances of children from the lower-manual working class being selected for an academic education were low in comparison with those of the children from the middle class

33

A description of the sample

(Douglas, 1964, pp. 45–51). Jean Floud (1956, p. 114) discussing the whole question of education and social class, concluded that: 'It has now been established beyond doubt that there is a process of social as well as academic selection at work in the schools.' Basil Bernstein (1958, 1961) examining some aspects of language and social class, has suggested that because of restrictions in language ability, children from the lower working class are likely to come into conflict with formal education, especially in the secondary school, where the language norms of the teacher suggest a very different way of organizing and responding to experience. A consequence of this conflict is that children from the working class, and especially lower working class, are likely, especially in the secondary school, to be under-achieving to a marked degree.

Membership of a particular social class determines the pattern of child-rearing within the family grouping, and the amount of social control exercised by the family over its individual members. Thus, the working-class family is likely to have 'less interest in controlling the activities of its members, and because of this tends to be much less effective than its middle class counterpart as an agency of social control' (Morris, 1957, p. 179).

The incidence of broken families has been shown to exist to a considerable degree amongst delinquent populations. In his follow-up study of boys who had been discharged from borstal, A. G. Rose (1954, p. 55) found that of 471 boys 'almost exactly half came from families which were, at sentence, broken by death, desertion or separation'. On the basis of the same definition, of 321 boys in the present sample for whom information was available, 166 boys (45·7 per cent of the total sample) came from a broken family. One important fact to establish is the age at which disruption took place, as this will have implications for an individual's future experience; for example, the length of time he has spent in institutions up to the time of the present conviction. It was possible to establish that in the case of 72 boys (19·8 per cent) the break-up of the family occurred before the age of ten, and in the case of 50 (13·8 per cent) of these 72, it had taken place before the age of five.

In the absence of comparable figures for the population as a whole, it is not possible to make any correlation between a broken home and consequent criminality. It would seem important to point out, however, that although the defining of broken homes is a relatively easy matter, the question of stability in a home is far more complex. In the case of those members of the sample whose homes remain united in the technical sense, it cannot be concluded that their experiences were any less stressful as a result of this; or that the converse was true for those who had lost one or both of their parents. Broken homes, as defined above, does not take into account the fact that 103 members (28·4 per cent) of the sample had been sent to Approved School before the age of fifteen, an event which must have caused considerable disruption in their lives.

A further problem, related to the general disruption in the sample's lives, is that of homelessness, and this applies to about 8 per cent of boys released from borstal per year (Hood, 1966, p. 11). A boy is classified as homeless when there is 'virtually no chance of any effective reconciliation being made between any known home that he has lived in prior to conviction'. Examination of the background of boys classified under this heading showed that they divided into two distinct types (Hood, 1965, p. 196); those who, because of death or disagreement, had lost contact with their homes in the recent past—52 boys (14·3 per cent) in the present sample fell into this category; and those who had been without a home for many years, with the result that they already had considerable institutional experience—28 boys (7·7 per cent) fell into this category. In addition, there were a further 28 boys (7·7 per cent) who were either living rough or in lodgings at the time of their arrest, with no further explanation as to the circumstances which had led to this. Thus, it could be concluded that 30 per cent of the boys interviewed might be potential problems, so far as homelessness on release is concerned.

A final factor to be considered is the incidence of marriage among boys sentenced to borstal. In this sample, 20 boys were married at the time of committal, 12 of whom had the additional responsibility of a family to support. A further four boys were fathers but were not married. Four of the boys were already separated from their wives by the time they reached the Allocation Centre. Early marriage in itself is not necessarily disadvantageous, but problems will arise as a result of enforced separation.

(B) INTELLIGENCE

During the past fifty years, there has been a considerable shift in opinion amongst researchers as to the relationship between delinquency and intelligence.

Mary Woodward, reviewing the scene in 1955, wrote:

Forty years ago, on the basis of the results of delinquents in America on the early tests, it was thought that low intelligence was the most important single cause of delinquency and crime, and that 'every feeble-minded person is a potential criminal' (Goddard, 1914). Criticism by Burt (1925) and others of the interpretation of these results, and a decrease in the incidence of low IQs, led to the adoption of the view that low intelligence was one factor among many others. Further modifications of opinion followed the drawing of attention to the complicating effect of cultural influences on intelligence test scores and of the association of the same cultural factors with delinquency. Some American writers (Tappan, 1949; Reckless, 1950; Elliott, 1952) have concluded that low intelligence is only slightly related to delinquency, and Rouke in 1950 went even further and denied any relation at all, regarding this as so well established that no further research was necessary. In this country, in the last ten years, all varieties of opinion have been expressed, from Lewis (1944) attaching importance to low intelligence, particularly in recidivism, to Norwood East (1949) assigning mental deficiency an important but minor role, and Stott (1952), who argues for no causal relation at all (Woodward, 1963, p. 3).

Opinion seems still divided. A brief résumé follows of some of the significant findings of previous research, on the intelligence and attainment of delinquents, which seem to have relevance for the present sample.

Burt (1925, p. 296) concluded from the tests he administered to London delinquents that: 'The average mental ratio of the juvenile offender proves to be about 89 per cent. This means that at the actual age of ten, he has, on average, the mental growth of a child of barely nine; when he is grown up to manhood, his mental age will be that of a child of about thirteen.'

He pointed to 'the immense range of general intelligence over which the whole group is scattered', but added that in fact the great majority, 82 per cent, 'are below the middle line of average ability; 28 per cent are technically dull; and nearly 8 per cent are definitely defective'. So far as educational attainment of the delinquent was concerned: 'At every stage he is far more behind in knowledge than in capacity; and tends, all through his school career, to be a year or more beneath even the low standard of scholastic work, to which, with his intelligence, he should at least attain.' As a result of his entire analysis, Burt concluded that 'intellectual disabilities, such as backwardness or dullness' are one of several contributory factors to delinquency; and when considering the major causes he states:

Among personal conditions, the most significant are, first, the mental dullness which is not severe enough to be called deficiency, and, secondly, the temperamental instability which is not abnormal enough to be considered pathological. Among social conditions, by far the most potent is family life; and, next to it, the friendships formed outside the home. These four conditions are paramount. Between them, as main determining factors, they account for more than fifty per cent of juvenile delinquencies and crimes.

After matching delinquent and non-delinquent boys according to age and intelligence, the Gluecks (1950, p. 153) concluded that 'the delinquents were definitely more retarded educationally than were non-delinquents'. Part of the explanation for the greater degree of backwardness amongst delinquents than non-delinquents lay in the more frequent disruptions, one of whose results was broken schooling, which the Gluecks found in the lives of the delinquents. However, they did not feel that this was the entire explanation but suggested that delinquents possessed certain characteristics which also contributed to their backwardness. They found a prevalent dislike among the delinquents for subjects 'requiring strict logical reasoning and persistency of effort', and also for subjects 'dependent upon good memory'. They also pointed out that 61·5 per cent of the delinquents expressed a violent dislike of school, because in a large number of cases they resented the discipline or lacked interest in the school work. Only 10·3 per cent of the non-delinquents reacted this unfavourably to school, and their

D   37

reasons were mainly that they felt intellectually inferior and unable to learn. In their sample, the Gluecks also examined the differences in some of the elements which comprise general intelligence. After applying the Wechsler-Bellevue intelligence test, they concluded: 'On the whole, the delinquents average less in verbal intelligence than do the non-delinquents, but the two groups resemble each other in performance intelligence.' The results of a verbal intelligence test, however, would be affected by the environmental differences between the two populations.

J. Trenaman (1952, p. 59) examining delinquency in an army population, suggests that: 'The semi-illiterate (and a large proportion of all delinquents are semi-illiterate) tends to be slower in his responses and less capable of showing to advantage in any sort of paper test. He may, therefore, be at a disadvantage in a non-verbal test because of his inexperience at handling symbols, even picture symbols.' A comparison of the results obtained by a delinquent army population with the norms for that particular population in the non-verbal Raven Matrices Test showed the following:

TABLE 3

	I Very Bright %	II Above Average %	III Average %	IV Below Average %	V Dull %
			+ —		
Delinquents	7	19	21 26	21	6
Non-delinquents	11·5	22·4	22·8 20·8	17·3	5·2

'The significant thing about these results . . . is the great range of intelligence represented. Even if it were true that the delinquent is rather duller than his normal neighbour—though these figures suggest that he is not greatly so—the fact remains that a large number of offenders are more intelligent than the normal.' Trenaman pointed out that differences in the scores between the delinquents and non-delinquents could possibly be accounted for by 'two factors that influence intelligence levels in the population—size of family and social class'. And that: 'Taking these various factors into consideration, the intelligence figures for delinquents may well prove little different, if at all, from those of normal men of similar background.' He pointed out that this conclusion did not, however, support the findings of most investigators into the problems of delinquency.

Thus, A. G. Rose (1954, p. 145) writing of the borstal boys he examined, suggested that there was a 'general tendency to dullness' and 'delinquents are a little below average intelligence on the whole'. In the case of this sample, however, intelligence had been assessed on the basis of the Columbian Tests, which are dependent on literacy to complete.

Research has continued to draw attention to the complicating effect of cultural factors on intelligence test scores; the same cultural factors which have been shown to be associated with delinquency.

Basil Bernstein (1960), as a result of an experiment with two groups of pupils aged fifteen to eighteen years (one working class, the other middle class) into the relationship between language and social class, came to the conclusion that a score gained on a verbal test was a powerful indication of educational and occupational performance as well as intelligence; and that the relatively depressed scores in the verbal test by the working-class group would appear to suggest that the mode of expression of intelligence was a cultural factor.

In her review of the data on the subject of low intelligence and delinquency, Mary Woodward (1963, p. 9) concludes that the evidence today obtained as a result of adequate sampling and tests is 'that the average IQ of delinquents in this country is at least 90, and it may be the same as the American figure of 92'. After examining the studies which have tried to compare the intelligence of non-delinquents with delinquents, Mary Woodward points out that: 'Although no one of the controlled studies alone is conclusive, . . . taken together they indicate that with a completely controlled inquiry the difference between delinquents and non-delinquents would be small.' She further suggests that 'the application of non-verbal tests might produce an average IQ even nearer the general population of 100'.

If one accepts Mary Woodward's tentative conclusions that quantitative differences between the intellectual functioning of delinquents and non-delinquents would appear to be slight, if existent at all, one must still note that the global concept of intelligence expressed as an IQ score, obscures the individual component abilities which are combined in this score. It would seem important then to try to isolate specific intellectual abilities which it is known are differentially related in certain personality traits, to see if there are qualitative differences in intelligence between delinquents and non-delinquents.

The Wechsler-Bellevue Intelligence Scale, which consists of eleven sub-tests and provides a Verbal IQ, a Performance IQ and a Full Scale IQ has been used in much of the research on qualitative intellectual functioning amongst juvenile delinquents (Caplan, 1965, pp. 106–13). Wechsler, as a result of a study of adolescent psychopaths, found that they had three outstanding sub-test scatter diagnostic signs, which distinguished them from normal adolescents. Firstly, in almost every case their Performance IQ was superior to their Verbal IQ, Secondly, within the battery of Performance sub-tests, 'the subjects tended to do better on items requiring visual-motor co-ordination and social understanding than on sub-tests involving perceptual and analytical abilities in addition to visual-motor co-ordination'. Finally, Wechsler found that the sub-test scatter pattern was significantly different from that of normal adolescents.

Subsequent research, using the Wechsler-Bellevue Intelligence Scale, has corroborated the finding that delinquents tend to obtain higher Performance than Verbal IQs (S. and E. Glueck, 1950, p. 207). Results, so far as the more subtle differences in sub-test achievements are concerned, are less conclussive (Blank, 1958; Foster 1959). However, a poor performance on verbal tests has been shown to be associated with membership of the lower socio-economic class (Bernstein, 1960; Jahoda, 1964). In the light of this fact, Caplan concludes that: 'It is likely, therefore, that factors related to class differences could account, at least in part, for the weak verbal IQs generally found among delinquent samples.'

Thus, the evidence seems to suggest that there are likely to be some qualitative differences in intelligence between delinquent and non-delinquent groups.

Any discussion of intelligence and its relationship to a particular group, in this case delinquents, must take into consideration certain fundamental shifts in opinion on this subject which have emerged in recent years. Examination of tests of intelligence show that they are based on different concepts about the nature of intelligence, and that in the absence of any 'generally accepted definition of what is being tested . . . intelligence tests . . . are built upon views of the nature of intelligence peculiar to the individual test constructor (Stones, 1966, pp. 280–2).[1]

> Thus, an individual's intelligence may vary with the test he is asked to perform, for it is only partly true that different intelligence tests measure the same thing. They do overlap or correlate fairly highly with one another, but somewhat different results will certainly be obtained from say Moray House and National Foundation [for Educational Research] tests, more different from a verbal group test and individual Terman-Merrill, and still more different from verbal tests and non-verbal ones based on pictures, diagrams, or practical materials (Vernon, 1958).

Many educational psychologists now no longer believe that it is possible to devise an intelligence test which will reveal an individual's innate intelligence irrespective of his acquired scholastic attainment. P. E. Vernon (1956, p. 156) has suggested that: 'The good or poor intelligence which we observe in every-day life, at school or at work, and which we try to measure by our tests, is the product of innate factors and environment.' And E. Stones argues that: 'whichever test is used the behaviour which it samples can only be expressed through the medium of such complex social attainments as speech, writing, the ability to manipulate numbers or symbols, and so on. All of these are acquired abilities which depend to a great extent on the social environment and cultural stimulation.' Arguments such as these would suggest that certain cultural factors associated with delinquency are likely to have an adverse effect on an individual's intellectual development and consequently on any test designed to measure that development.

Allied to this rejection of the view that it is possible to compute a score which is indicative of an individual's true intelligence is the rejection of the concept of the immutable nature of intelligence. It is no longer accepted that a score on an intelligence test (IQ) indicates a ceiling of ability, and, as a consequence, the level of attainment. Investigations into the stability of IQ have shown that IQ can by no means be considered

[1] For a summary of various definitions of intelligence, see Peel (1956, pp. 123–6).

stable when 'the average or median child alters by about 7 IQ points up or down on re-testing. Many are more stable than this, but a few show larger gains or losses of 30 or more points, . . . and 17 per cent are liable to alter 15 or more points either way' (Vernon, 1956, p. 157).

Yet a further rejection of the over-simplified attitude to intelligence is that of J. P. Guilford (1959, pp. 234–7) who, in discussing the structure of intellect, suggests that: 'With about fifty intellectual factors already known, we may say that there are at least fifty ways of being intelligent.' The implication of this, so far as the assessment of intelligence is concerned, is 'that to know an individual's intellectual resources thoroughly we shall need a surprisingly large number of scores.' Furthermore, 'If education has the general objective of developing the intellects of the students, it can be suggested that each intellectual factor provides a particular goal at which to aim.'

Finally, it should be borne in mind that a global IQ score says little or nothing about the real potential of individuals. All that can be said for certain about a person scoring, say, 100 on a Verbal IQ test is that in any random sample, he will be one of many who score 100, and that there will be less numbers scoring, say, 130. As yet, there is no knowledge about the ceiling achievement level of an individual who scores 100. Consequently, in the absence of this knowledge, it is better to discover empirically what an individual can achieve in a good learning situation, rather than predetermine his ability, based on the knowledge of the global IQ score.

THE PRESENT SAMPLE

All boys sentenced to borstal training undergo a series of psychological tests. These provide 'a basis for the assessment of intelligence and other aptitudes and attainment in certain educational areas'. They also contribute information useful in connection with guidance as to vocational training (Cockett, 1967). Testing may be carried out either at a Remand Centre or on arrival at the Allocation Centre. So far as the present sample was concerned, it was found that the actual number of tests completed was affected by where a boy had been tested. Thus, forty-six records contained details of only three tests; yet boys tested at Ashford Remand Centre had completed six tests, whereas only five tests were administered at Wormwood Scrubs.[1] No explanation was given of the reasons for these discrepancies.

As only three tests had been administered to the whole sample, and because it was felt that these tests were the most broadly based, it was decided to examine the scores of the sample in these three tests only, which are as follows:

(a) Test O, the Raven Progressive Matrices

The test used is the 1933 version (Revised Order, 1956). 'This test may be broadly designated as a non-verbal test of general intelligence' (Cockett, 1967) and has been designed so as to find out 'a person's capacity at the time of the test to apprehend meaningless figures presented for his observation, see the relations between them, conceive the value of the figure completing each system of relations presented, and, by so doing, develop a systematic method of reasoning' (Raven, 1956, p. 1). Correlations between scores gained on Progressive Matrices and tests of reading, spelling and elementary arithmetic indicate that an individual's total score on the Progressive Matrices 'provides an index of his intellectual capacity, whatever his nationality or education'.

The norms of the particular version of the test used at the Wormwood Scrubs Allocation Centre do not appear in the 1938 guide. The test used is a timed 20-minute version, although Raven has pointed out that: 'It cannot be given satisfactorily with a time-limit and takes up to 45 minutes to complete.' The 20-minute version was first used on an Army population during the war[2] and its norms were standardized 'on very large National Service intakes to the forces, and consequently can

[1] The tests, details of which are outlined in this section, are still completed by boys allocated at Wormwood Scrubs. A different set of tests is given to boys allocated through the Manchester Allocation Centre. In this the Educational Test is divorced from the battery of psychological tests, for 'we think that we have taken the further step necessary to deal with the great number and the growing complexity of pressures put upon borstal boys'. (Private communication with the Governor of Manchester Allocation Centre.)

[2] The Educational Psychologist at Wormwood Scrubs Allocation Centre points out, however, that 'a correlation between the 45-minutes and the 20-minutes versions was once made over a limited number of Service men and that there was no significant difference between the scores on the two versions'—unpublished paper produced for the information of members of the Prison Service.

be regarded as based on the late adolescent and very early twenties' population of the country at large' (Cockett, 1967). The subsequent use by the Prison Service of these norms and population percentiles means that inmates are assessed 'on intelligence, in terms of the ordinary population' (Cockett, 1967). The scores and population percentiles, which are grouped into five grades on this 20-minute version, are as follows:

TABLE 4

Raven's Progressive Matrices (1938) 20-minute
version (revised order, 1956)

Test Grade	A	B	C+	C−	D	E
Score	48–60	42–47	38–41	34–37	26–33	5–25
Population percentile	10%	20%	20%	20%	20%	10%

Before examining the scores of the sample of borstal boys interviewed, it seems important to re-emphasize the point that there is no global definition of intelligence. Thus, although the Raven's Matrices may be considered to be a test of general intelligence, this is nevertheless only 'an average of whatever abilities the tester likes to include' (Vernon, 1958). Raven's definition has been quoted earlier.

In Vernon's opinion, however, 'Non-verbal or pictorial group tests, and individual performance tests, are much inferior to verbal ones in predicting educability (except, possibly in predicting ability for science and technical courses among older pupils) . . . they do not yield a better index of "innate potentiality" ' (Vernon 1958). Consequently, differences in an individual's performance between verbal and non-verbal tests may be considered to be an indication of differences in an individual's ability to perform the particular intellectual function involved in the tests rather than anything else. This point has relevance to any comparison between the Raven Matrices and the Abstractions Test, referred to later.

The score distribution of the sample interviewed, in comparison with a random sample of 1,000 borstal boys tested at

Wormwood Scrubs Allocation Centre between May 1966, and February 1967, is given below.[1]

TABLE 5

Score distribution of samples of borstal boys
in Raven Progressive Matrices

Grade	A	B	C+	C−	D	E	Total
Sample of 363 boys	69	106	72	42	49	24	362*
%	19·1	29·3	19·9	11·6	13·5	6·6	100
Sample of 1,000 boys	206	328	184	114	108	60	1,000
%	20·6	32·8	18·4	11·4	10·8	6·0	100

$\chi^2 = 3 \cdot 638$ for 5 d.f. P between 0·90 and 0·10 (not significant).

* In the case of one boy interviewed no test scores were available in his record.

It would appear that the score distribution of the sample interviewed is not significantly different from the sample of 1,000 boys tested over a nine-month period immediately after this research was carried out. Comparison of these two score distributions with the norms shown in Table 4 indicates that in the past twenty years, since these norms were standardized, there has been a considerable shift and that the number of boys who are scoring in the top two percentiles has increased from 30 per cent to approximately 51 per cent. One explanation of this shift might be that it simply reflects a trend which has taken place as a result of improved educational opportunities, in the population as a whole. Alternatively, it might indicate that the proportion of more intelligent boys receiving sentences of borstal training has increased, in relation to the borstal population as a whole. It might, however, be a combination of these, and other factors as yet unknown.

(b) C.P. Test 1. The Abstraction Test (See Appendix A)

This is a test of general intelligence, 'using verbal and numerical material, and consequently having some slight educational loading' (Cockett, 1967). It was originally standardized 'on

[1] This score distribution of 1,000 boys was obtained from the Allocation Centre at Wormwood Scrubs. For the purpose of comparison with the present sample, the score distribution of the 1,000 boys is assumed to be representative of the total borstal population at this time.

very large National Service intakes to the forces, and consequently can be regarded as based on the late adolescent and very early twenties' population of the country at large'. It was 'developed and used extensively by the armed forces in their selection procedures during the war', and afterwards came into use by the Prison Service.

The norms and population percentiles for this test are as follows:

TABLE 6

Abstractions C.P. Test 1

Test Grade	A	B	C+	C−	D	E
Score	32–40	28–31	24–27	19–23	13–18	0–12
Population percentile	10%	20%	20%	20%	20%	10%

The following table shows the score distribution of the present sample in comparison with the same 1,000 borstal boys referred to earlier.

TABLE 7

Score distribution of samples of borstal boys
in Abstractions C.P. Test 1

Grade	A	B	C+	C−	D	E	Total
Sample of 363 boys	50	60	68	76	56	52	362
%	13·8	16·6	18·8	21·0	15·5	14·3	100
Sample of 1,000 boys	191	179	174	168	164	124	1,000
%	19·1	17·9	17·4	16·8	16·4	12·4	100

$\chi^2 = 8\cdot881$ for 5 d.f. P between 0·90 and 0·10 (not significant)

Again there would appear to be no significant difference in the score distribution between the two samples. As with the Raven Matrices, comparison with the original norms indicates that there has been a shift, but it would appear to be more marked in the top percentile than in the top two. Tentative suggestions as to the reason for this shift have already been advanced; similarly, tentative suggestions regarding conclusions to be drawn from differences in individual performances on the Raven Matrices and Abstractions C.P. Test 1 have also been advanced. A comparison of these performances is given in Table 8.

TABLE 8

Comparison of grades obtained by the sample in the Raven Progressive Matrices* and the Abstractions Test C.P. 1

Intelligence Test	A	B	C+	C—	D	E	Total
Raven's Matrices	69						69
Abstractions C.P. 1.	38	18	10	2	1	0	69
Raven's Matrices		106					106
Abstractions C.P. 1.	9	22	33	28	12	2	106
Raven's Matrices			72				72
Abstractions C.P. 1.	3	15	15	21	12	6	72
Raven's Matrices				42			42
Abstractions C.P. 1.	0	1	9	12	12	8	42
Raven's Matrices					49		49
Abstractions C.P. 1.	0	3	1	12	17	16	49
Raven's Matrices						24	24
Abstractions C.P. 1.	0	1	0	1	2	20	24
							362

* Raven Progressive Matrices (1938) 20-minute version (Revised Order, 1956).

181 boys obtained a lower grade in the Abstractions Test C.P. 1 than in the Raven Matrices and 57 a higher grade.

It is interesting to see these grades in terms of IQ scores. Comparisons between IQ and the Centre's test grades are, however,

a little complicated for two reasons: (a) it depends on how the IQ tests are standardized; (b) the fact that non-verbal and verbal tests may not give the same grades for a particular lad (because they are not exactly the same ability) means that there are two grades for comparison with IQ. Usually one makes one's judgment taking both tests into account.

47

A description of the sample

However, it is published information that the standard deviation of IQs obtained by the Terman-Merrill Scale is 17, that for those obtained by the Wechsler Adult Intelligence Scale 15. Using this information and statistical tables, it is then possible to draw up the following comparisons, for the convenience of anyone interested[1] (Cockett, 1967).

TABLE 9

Comparison between the Test Grades and IQ

| Test Grade | Equivalent IQ Grouping | |
	Terman-Merrill	Wechsler Adult Scale
A	122 or more	119 or more
B	109–121	108–118
C+	100–108	100–107
C−	92–100	93–100
D	78–91	82–92
E	77 or less	81 or less

Comparison of Table 9 with the details of the grades in the Raven Matrices and Abstractions in Table 8 shows that based on a combination of the scores in these two tests 163 boys (45 per cent) had IQs of 100+. Of these, 87 (24 per cent) had an IQ of 108+, and 38 (11 per cent) an IQ of 119+. On the other hand, only 20 boys (6 per cent) had an IQ of 81 or less.[2] These figures would certainly seem to disprove the statement that: 'About 45 per cent of borstal boys . . . are likely to be of subnormal intelligence' (Wolff, 1967, p. 71), and the conclusion, which is a consequence of this belief, that: 'Many of the boys, by reason of their low intelligence, or for causes stemming from physical or mental incapacity, are unable to take up any skilled or semi-skilled tasks.'

[1] Although Dr. Cockett does not actually specify the two tests by name, it is assumed that he is referring to the grades from the Raven Matrices and the Abstractions. They are the tests of general intelligence used and have been standardized on a normal population. Furthermore, the only non-verbal test used is the Raven Matrices.

[2] These conversions are all based on the Wechsler Adult Scale and would be slightly higher or lower in the case of the Terman-Merrill.

(c) Test C.P. 102 Literacy (See Appendix A)

This is a comparatively recent test 'of literacy requiring ability to read and knowledge of vocabulary of the material involved. This test was developed under our own auspices' and has 'been standardized on Remand Centre and borstal samples', and, 'Some account has been taken of the known fact that such populations are usually a little depressed in educational standard' (Cockett, 1967). Its purpose is to differentiate those boys who are either illiterate or semi-literate. Boys who fall into these categories are interviewed by an Educational Psychologist who obtains their reading age from a Schonell test, and also gives them an analytic Arithmetic test, in order to provide a more detailed diagnosis of their problems in this area. A report on each boy interviewed is included in his record as a supplement to the test scores.[1]

The grading and population percentiles in this test are the same as in the Raven Matrices and the Abstractions C.P. Test 1.

Once again, the following table shows the score distribution of the present sample in comparison with the same 1,000 borstal boys referred to earlier.

Unlike the previous two tests, there would appear to be a significant difference in this test between the score distributions

TABLE 10

Details of the Literacy Test C.P. 102

Grade	A	B	C+	C−	D	E	Total
Score	25–26	23–24	21–22	19–20	12–18	0–11	
Norms %	10	20	20	20	20	10	
Sample of 363 boys	10	59	121	72	67	33	362*
%	2·8	16·3	33·4	19·9	18·5	9·1	100
Sample of 1,000 boys	32	257	296	176	168	67	996*
%	3·2	25·8	29·7	17·7	16·9	6·7	100

$\chi^2 = 15\cdot180$ for 5 d.f. P <0·01, significant at 1% level.

* This was the total number of scores in this test.

[1] This information was obtained as a result of a private communication with the Educational Psychologist at Wormwood Scrubs responsible for this testing.

of the two samples. This is probably as a result of discrepancies in the second percentile only. Comparison with the original norms indicates once again that there has been a shift, although on this occasion in the opposite direction to that shown in the Raven Matrices and Abstractions C.P. Test 1. It is unlikely, however, that this indicates any real change, as the scores are to undifferentiated at the top end of the scale (as can be seen from the above table), the purpose of the test being to differentiate at the bottom end of the scale.

(d) Further Tests

In addition to the three tests which have been outlined in detail, the majority of borstal boys (87 per cent of the present sample) complete the Bennet Mechanical Comprehension, which is a test of mechanical knowledge and was standardized in the same way and at the same time as the Raven Matrices and Abstractions C.P. Test 1. A fifth test, completed by the majority of boys sentenced to borstal, is an Arithmetic Test C.P. 101A, which is an internal test having been standardized on a borstal population. Boys tested at Ashford (approximately 15 per cent of the population) complete an internal test of space perception C.P. 103. This is seen as a useful adjunct in assessing practical capability, for example in vocational training and in 'avoiding misinterpretations of the non-verbal intelligence test' (Cockett, 1967).

The available test scores are used as guide lines by the Vocational Guidance Officer at Wormwood Scrubs in his selection of boys for trade testing. As a result of his interview, the Vocational Guidance Officer recommends boys for particular trade courses during borstal training.

(C) INFORMATION, CONTAINED IN THE RECORDS, ON PREVIOUS EDUCATIONAL EXPERIENCE

On the subject of school reports, Mannheim and Wilkins (1955, p. 97) observed that they 'were not available in more than half the files studied', and that those which did exist 'were in large measure unguided and unsystematic'. Thus, information might have been omitted on, for example, truancy, as no specific question was asked on that topic. Since the completion of their research, however, Mannheim and Wilkins point out that 'the pattern of the files has been standardized', and as a consequence 'school reports . . . now form a standard part of every Borstal file'.

It was disappointing to find, on consulting each boy's file, that there were still considerable differences between individual records in the amount of information available; for example, a copy of the form, to be completed by the school or approved school, was still not to be found in the majority of the files. There appeared, moreover, to be no logical explanation of the differences between records. Boys who had previously spent a period of time in an Approved School or Detention Centre did not necessarily have more information in their records on the subject of their education and attainments, than those for whom it was the first time in an institution.

There are obvious difficulties to obtaining information about secondary education, in view of the fact that all boys sentenced to borstal are beyond the statutory school-leaving age. However, 260 boys (71·6 per cent) in the sample, had been convicted at least once by the time they were fifteen (see Table 13). Their reports were no fuller than others, which would suggest that, even before they had completed full-time education, it had often not been considered important to obtain a report from the school.

It was found that, apart from containing test scores, 38 of the 363 records consulted had no reference whatsoever to a boy's ability or his previous educational experience, unless he happened to have been sentenced to an Approved School, when this fact appeared under a list of his previous convictions; 147 records gave only details of the kinds of school and age on leaving (some gave only one of these pieces of information); the remaining 178 did contain some comment on the boy's educational experience. (Furthermore, it was possible to tell from the records of only 181 boys that they had been able to leave school at the earliest opportunity, and that 11 had chosen to stay on.) The following information (Table 11) regarding the type of state school attended by the sample was obtained from their records.

Of the boys who were listed as having attended special schools, nine had attended schools for educationally subnormal children and two for maladjusted. (A more complex situation

TABLE 11

State Secondary Schools attended by the sample

	Sec. Modern	Gram- mar	Compre- hensive	Tech- nical	Special	All Age	No infor- mation	At Approved School
Number	243	9	6	4	17	7	69	8
%	66·9	2·5	1·7	1·1	4·7	1·9	19·0	2·2

Total Number = 363

will be revealed by the boys' answers in Chapter III, Section B.)

Of the 178 records containing comments, 34 were made by social workers as a result of an interview with the boys at the Allocation Centre. The information was, therefore, supplied by the boy himself, although obviously the social worker was free to add her comments to these statements in the light of further information available to her. Typical of the information provided by a social worker was 'liked school, truanted very occasionally' or ' "B" stream, truanted occasionally', 'always truanting, said he did not like school'. The information was vague, and being divorced from the context of the individual school, some of it was meaningless; in addition, because of the nature of the interview, it could also have been distorted. As information which would supplement the test scores, it was of doubtful value.

In 11 other records the comment was by someone such as the police, a psychologist or a doctor, who had interviewed the boy for the first time at some stage between his arrest and his allocation to borstal. One hundred and thirty-three of the records consulted did, however, contain a report from either a school the boy had attended, or a probation officer.

Thus, only 36·6 per cent of the records consulted contained a report from someone who had known the boy over a period of time, either while he had attended school or after. Seventy-four of these were from schools.

Of the 74, only 28 were of any value in the limited sense that they made a comment on the boy's aptitude and ability which supported or supplemented the test scores (assuming that these are an accurate and objective measure). Some of the 28 records also supplied additional information on the boy's background (for example, truancy, home conditions) which offered some explanation of the test scores attained by the boy. An example of such a report was one which contained the following information: 'He has a very low IQ (77) and was in the remedial class throughout. He was always late for school although he lived less than a quarter of a mile away. There was truancy and in fact his attendance at school was less than 75 per cent. There was no participation in school life, his only interest was watching television.'

The remaining 46 records contained comments which in some cases described the boy in a way which sharply contradicted the test results (possibly indicating that the school was unaware of his ability). Thus, a school wrote of a boy who obtained a raw score on the Raven Matrices which corresponds to an IQ of 114: 'His ability is below average, in the bottom stream.' Or commenting on a boy who obtained a raw score in the same test corresponding to an IQ of 75, the school wrote: 'He is of average ability but he does not use it.'[1] Some reports were so lacking in detail as to be meaningless, using one word such as 'fair' or 'average' in answer to a question asking for details of ability or attendance. Others gave information, in particular about streaming, which unless it is set in the school context, means nothing: 'In the "B" stream of a secondary modern', 'in the "C" stream'. To anyone who is ignorant of the catchment area of a particular school, the criteria used for streaming in the school, and the number of streams in each year, the mere fact that a boy was in a certain stream provides very little information about his ability.

It would appear then that there was not much valid information in individual records concerning the previous educational experience of this group of borstal boys. This might have serious repercussions for Tutor Organizers, for without adequate information, they will have difficulties in providing really effective individual courses.

[1] The IQ Equivalents are Deviation Quotients based on a mean of 100 and a S.D. of 15. The Deviation Quotients were fitted by transforming the percentile points given in Raven's *Guide to the Progressive Matrices* (Revised version, 1956) into the corresponding quotients on the assumption of a normal frequency distribution of Raven Scores. Intermediate values, IQs corresponding to Raw Scores lying between those corresponding to the percentile points calculated by Raven, have been obtained by a straight line interpolation.

TRUANCY FROM SCHOOL

Previous research has indicated the likelihood of a considerable degree of truancy amongst the present sample (S. and E. Glueck, 1950, p. 148; Trenaman, 1952, p. 162; Stott, 1952, p. 9). Forty-eight of the records (13·2 per cent) contained details, from either probation officers or teachers, on the incidence of truancy at school. In the light of other findings, this would seem to be a rather low percentage. The fact that, in the majority of files, there was no information on truancy cannot be taken to indicate that truancy did not take place, so far as the remainder of the sample is concerned.

Finally as there seemed to be no systematic and objective collection of information relating to education and attainment, this seems to suggest the need to decide whether its collection from source has relevance to the education carried out in borstal institutions. It may be that the boys themselves could adequately perform this function. If this information is considered essential to the training of delinquents, then there is a need to decide on what areas are relevant, and how this information should be collected.

(D) WORK RECORD

Investigations into delinquent behaviour all tend to support the conclusion that delinquents tend to be characterized by poor work records (Rose, 1954, pp. 71–2; Mannheim and Wilkins, 1955, p. 100; Little, 1965). Of the present sample, 168 boys (46·3 per cent) were recorded as being out of work at the time of their arrest. This information, however, gives no real indication of employment experience. In order to make an objective and comparable assessment of the sample's work experience, it was decided to use a shortened version of the Mannheim and Wilkins classification. Figures were obtained from the sample as to the number of boys who had held one job for at least a year, and for those boys who had never held a job for more than two months. Table 12 below shows those figures in comparison with Mannheim and Wilkins' original study, and with figures for the years 1950 to 1956 produced by Alan Little.

TABLE 12

The longest period in any one job: a comparison of the present sample with two other similar samples

Longest period in any one job	Mannheim & Wilkins original		Alan Little study						Present sample
	1946–7	1950	1951	1952	1953	1954	1955	1956	1965
One year or more %	37·0	38·4	35·0	32·5	34·5	31·4	36·6	40·2	32·2
Less than 2 months %	3·5	4·8	4·4	3·4	2·4	8·1	3·6	2·4	4·9
Mean Score %*	22·0	28·9	29·0	32·6	23·8	32·6	22·8	23·5	20·11

*The 'mean score' is the percentage of the sample who have had no work experience (in the present sample this is mainly boys who have come direct from Approved Schools) or about whom there is not sufficient information on their employment record. Alan Little comments that there has been a significant decline in the number of boys about whom there has been 'no information'. In 1950, 93 per cent of all 'mean score' cases were from this category. By 1956, it had dropped to 57 per cent. In the present sample 79 per cent of the 'mean score' cases had 'no information'. This fact will obviously affect, to some extent, changes in the table.

This table indicates that the pre-institutional work record of boys sentenced to borstal has not fluctuated greatly from the time of the original study to the present sample. Looked at together with Alan Little's more detailed table, the above table suggests that the work record of a large proportion of boys sentenced to borstal is one of constantly changing jobs.

(E) CRIMINALITY

In 1965 (Cmnd. 3088, p. 19), the Prison Department commented on 'the increasing number of boys who have had other forms of treatment before reaching borstal. A borstal sentence tends to be used as the last resort rather than as a form of training which may well be appropriate, and more likely to succeed if given earlier in a boy's criminal career.' In 1965 (Cmnd. 3408, p. 15), 38 per cent of the boys sentenced to borstal had already been in a Detention Centre.

This would suggest that contrary to the intentions of the Criminal Justice Act of 1948, the number of previous convictions, rather than the need for training, has become an important determinant of a borstal sentence. In 1965, the average number of previous convictions per boy was 7·5, and in 1966 only 128 boys of a total of 4,953 sentenced to borstal had no previous recorded offences. Roger Hood (1965, pp. 70–4), commenting on the effects of the Criminal Justice Act of 1948 upon the sentencing policy of the courts, points out that: 'The detention centre has become to some extent an alternative to long-term training, and the use of sentences of imprisonment of greater length than the detention sentence has persisted as a real alternative to borstal.'

There were further implications for the borstal population arising from the Criminal Justice Act of 1961, which, among other provisions, removed the power of the courts to sentence offenders between seventeen and twenty-one to prison, except for the most serious offenders, and lowered the minimum age of sentence to borstal to fifteen. Lowering the minimum age was introduced in order to provide closed training for boys in this age group who were considered completely unsuitable for Approved Schools.

It would appear then, that changes in the law, and subsequent sentencing policy, have considerably altered during the past twenty years, the population received into borstals. Borstals are now having to cater for a larger proportion of criminally sophisticated boys, and a proportion of younger boys.

In this section, it is proposed to examine some aspects of the criminality of the present sample and to compare this, wherever possible, with the borstal population as a whole.

1. AGE AT FIRST CONVICTION

The following table shows the breakdown of the sample into age groups at first conviction.

These figures reflect the national situation, in which the age group thirteen to seventeen contains the highest number of persons found guilty of indictable offences; and in which fourteen is the peak age (Cmnd. 3332, 1966, p. li). Forty-nine per cent of the boys in the sample had made at least one court appearance before the age of fourteen; the fact that, in a

TABLE 13

Age at first conviction of the boys in the sample

Age	8	9	10	11	12	13	14	15	16	17	18	19	20	Total
No. of boys in the sample	14	26	25	34	80	50	46	35	47	25	23	5	3	363

sample of boys discharged from borstal between 1941 and 1944, this number of boys was 32 per cent, is an indication of the increasing proportion of boys, with early criminal experience, now being sentenced to borstal (Rose, 1954, p. 67).

2. AGE ON CONVICTION

The table below shows the age on conviction of the present sample in comparison with the figures for the total borstal receptions in 1965 (Cmnd. 3304, p. 26). Although there is a significant difference between the two samples, it would seem that the reason for this is that there is a larger proportion of boys in the age group fifteen to seventeen in the sample, than in the borstal population as a whole.

TABLE 14

Age on conviction of the boys in the sample in comparison with the borstal receptions in 1965

	15	16	17	18	19	20	Total
Receptions 1965	102	374	982	1,076	863	526	3,923
% of total	2·6	9·6	25·0	27·4	22·0	13·4	100
Sample	18	46	84	90	70	55	363
% of total	5·0	12·7	23·1	24·8	19·3	15·1	100

$\chi^2 = 13·09$ for 5 d.f. P is between 0·05 and 0·02 (significant at the 5% level).

3. PREVIOUS CONVICTIONS

The incidence of previous convictions is another factor giving an indication of the increased criminal sophistication of boys sentenced to borstal. Figures for the total borstal receptions for 1965 indicate that 45·9 per cent of the boys had five or more previous convictions, in comparison with 25·8 per cent in 1956 (Little, 1965). Conversely the percentage of boys being sentenced to borstal with no previous convictions has steadily declined from being 12·5 per cent in 1950 to 3·2 per cent in 1965. The figures for the present sample, in comparison with the borstal receptions for 1965, are shown in the table below (Cmnd. 3304, p. 26).

TABLE 15

Number of previous proved offences of the boys in the sample in comparison with borstal receptions in 1965

	None	1	2	3	4	5	6–10	11–20	Over 20	Total
Receptions 1965	124	259	439	612	684	605	1,131	68	1	3,923
% of total	3·2	6·6	11·2	15·6	17·5	15·4	28·8	1·7		100
Sample	11	20	33	62	67	59	106	5		363
% of total	3·0	5·5	9·0	17·1	18·5	16·3	29·2	1·4		100

$\chi^2 = 3·0574$ for 7 d.f. P is between 0·90 and 0·10 (not significant).

4. PREVIOUS INSTITUTIONAL EXPERIENCE

An increase in the proportion of boys with long criminal records is consistent with an increase in the proportion of boys who have had previous institutional experience. It is a further indication of the degree of penal sophistication of boys sentenced to borstal. As can be seen from Table 16, 71·1 per cent of all borstal receptions in 1965 had previous institutional experience, compared with 44·5 per cent in 1956 (Little, 1965). The figures for the present sample, in comparison with the total borstal receptions, are given below (Cmnd. 3304, 1965, p. 26).

58

TABLE 16

Number of boys with previous institutional experience

	Approved School	Borstal Training	Detention Centre	Imprison- ment	None	Total
Receptions 1965	1,450	224	1,451	161	1,337	4,623
% of total	31·4	4·8	31·4	3·5	28·9	100
Sample	145	19	127	16	112	419
% of total	34·6	4·6	30·3	3·8	26·7	100

$\chi^2 = 2\cdot20121$ for 4 d.f. P is between 0·90 and 0·10 (not significant).

In the present sample, 52 boys (14·3 per cent) had had experience of more than one type of institution, prior to the present committal to borstal.

(F) PRESENT OFFENCE

The following figures refer to offences and not to individuals who committed them. The reason for this is that the method of recording information in the boys' records makes it difficult to distinguish those who have committed a single type of offence from those who have committed a combination of offences of different types.

TABLE 17

Offences committed by the sample which resulted in the present sentence of borstal training

(A)	Offences against the person	Number of offences	% of total
(a)	Manslaughter	1	
(b)	Causing death by dangerous driving	1	
(c)	Assault with intent to commit grievous bodily harm	5	
(d)	Assault occasioning actual bodily harm	23	
(e)	Assault on a policeman	6	
(f)	Intimidation	1	
(g)	Sexual offences	6	
		43	7·3

(B)	Offences against property with violence	Number of offences	% of total
	(a) Breaking and entering	189	
	(b) Robbery	22	
		211	35·8
(C)	Offences against property without violence		
	(a) Larceny	218	
	(b) Receiving	8	
	(c) Fraud	4	
		230	39·0
(D)	Taking and driving away motor vehicles	94	15·9
(E)	Other offences		
	(a) Malicious injuries to property	3	
	(b) Forgery	5	
	(c) Affray	2	
	(d) In possession of dangerous drugs	1	
	(e) Causing a breach of the peace in conjunction with motoring offences	1	
		12	2·0
	Total number of offences	590	100

It was felt that the type of crime a boy had committed would be an important determinant in the allocation procedure. Crimes involving some form of violence against either another person or property, for example, would carry more weight than any other consideration. As this has relevance to educational provision, it was decided to look at the scores in the Raven Matrices intelligence test of those boys who had committed an offence involving any form of violence. (The limitations of any single test of intelligence have been discussed in Chapter II, Section B.)

Of the 43 boys who were convicted of offences of violence against the person, the breakdown was as follows:

TABLE 18

Intelligence rating in the Raven Matrices of boys convicted of crimes of violence against the person

Grades	A	B	C+	C−	D	E	Total
Number of boys	6	15	3	7	7	5	43
As a % of rating in the sample	8·7	14·2	4·2	16·7	14·3	20·8	

Of the group as a whole, 4 boys only were allocated to an open borstal, and were drawn from all ranges of intelligence. In an examination of the Raven Matrices intelligence test scores of the 201 boys whose only violent offence was one against property, the following emerged:

TABLE 19

Intelligence rating in the Raven Matrices of boys convicted of a crime involving violence against property

Grades	A	B	C+	C−	D	E	Total
Number of boys	39	61	42	23	25	11	201*
As a % of rating in the sample	56·5	57·5	58·3	54·8	51·0	45·8	

* Nine boys had committed offences involving both violence against the person and property. Their scores and allocation have, therefore, already been taken into account. In the case of one other boy in this group, test scores were not available.

Of this group, almost half (97) were allocated to open borstals. A comparison of the test scores with allocation showed that of the 100 boys who scored above average on the Raven Matrices test, 44 were allocated to open borstals, whereas of the 36 who scored below average, 13 were allocated to open borstals.

If, however, one takes the evidence of both tables together, on the basis of this sample, violent offences would appear to be distributed fairly evenly throughout all ranges of ability. Although only small numbers, the evidence would tend to suggest that a higher proportion of less intelligent boys, who have committed crimes of violence, are likely to be allocated to closed borstals.

A description of the sample

As the allocation process is the determinant of the population within particular borstals, it was decided to examine its implications for the sample, with particular emphasis on the role intelligence plays in this process.

R. L. Morrison (1957) writing on borstal allocation, described the process as taking a period of six weeks, after which there would be: 'A further period ranging from a few days to a few weeks, depending on vacancies, before a lad is finally dispatched to his training institutions.' It would appear that, owing to pressure of numbers (which have increased by two and a half thousand since R. L. Morrison's article was written), the process of allocation is now much more streamlined; yet time spent between conviction and arrival at borstal for the majority of boys had lengthened, by the end of 1965, to a period of between two and four months, this time being spent in local prisons or Wormwood Scrubs (Cmnd. 599, 1966–67, p. 44). In April 1966, the Senior Psychologist of Wormwood Scrubs Prison commented that:

> During the last five or six years I have watched the increasing tide of borstal receptions destroy most of the sophistication that ever existed in allocation practice. It has become necessary to distribute the boys at all costs, sometimes with only cursory examination and to rely increasingly on the more obvious signs (generally the negative ones which have required closed allocation). (Holloway, 1966).

At the time of this research, allocation had become a nine-day process. During this time, boys completed aptitude and ability tests. If a boy's results in the intelligence tests indicated that he had the ability to benefit from a trade training course, he would also undergo a practical test, as further verification, and to indicate which trades would be most suitable. If it was also felt that further information, in addition to the test scores, was needed about a boy's intelligence, he would be interviewed by an Educational Psychologist. A developmental interview was also carried out with every boy, by a woman social worker. In addition, certain boys, who presented an allocation problem, were interviewed by a member of the prison administrative staff and/or a psychologist.

To assist with allocation, and to correlate the views of all
those who take part in the process, a primary allocation form
was made out for each boy. On this were entered details, from
the boy's record, as to his age and home town; plus information,
where it applied, of absconding, violence, sexual deviance or
unlawful sexual behaviour, either currently or in the past.
If a boy's record contained evidence of any of the latter forms
of behaviour, the number of borstals to which he could be
allocated is immediately reduced; a boy's age and location of
his home town in the north or south of England also affected
the number of borstals to which he could be allocated. It was
on the basis of the information on the primary allocation form
that a preliminary selection of possible allocations was made,
and it was from this selection that the interviewing team was
asked to make its choice. Each member of the Allocation Board
was asked to indicate whether he considered the boy could be
sent to any, some, or none of the borstals from this preliminary
selection.

It can be concluded from this that, in the case of some boys,
borstal allocation was on the basis of narrow behavioural
criteria, and did not take into account other considerations,
such as ability and interest in following a particular trade
course, with the result that boys were allocated to borstals
which did not provide the trade course they had opted
for.

In the case of those boys who have not shown evidence of
violence, absconding, sexual deviance, or unlawful sexual
behaviour, the choice of borstal was less rigidly defined, and
other criteria were taken into consideration.

It can be seen that allocation conducted in this way will
result in certain borstals housing populations of boys with long
criminal records, some of whom have shown themselves to be
security risks.

So far as allocation of the present sample was concerned, 209
(57·6 per cent) of the 363 boys were allocated to closed borstals.
This compares to a population proportion of 63·6 per cent in
closed borstals during 1966[1] (Cmnd. 3408, p. 45). So far as
individual borstals were concerned, some, such as Portland and
Lowdham Grange, were under-represented in the present

---

[1] Observed differences in the proportions can in part be accounted for in the
opening of a closed borstal at Stoke Heath since the completion of interviewing.

sample, in comparison with their daily average populations as a proportion of the borstal population as a whole.

As a result of the allocation process, it would be reasonable to suppose that the population of a closed borstal would cover all ranges of ability. A breakdown of the scores in the Raven Matrices test, of the boys in the sample allocated to three closed borstals, showed the following:

TABLE 20

Intelligence ratings in the Raven Matrices
test of boys allocated to three closed borstals

Borstal	Scores		
Everthorpe	*A B*	*C+ C−*	*D E*
Number of boys	19	8	5
% of daily average population	5·8	2·4	1·5
Wellingborough			
Number of boys	15	9	5
% of daily average population	6·7	4·0	2·2
Rochester			
Number of boys	17	8	6
% of daily average population	6·2	2·9	2·2

A further point emerges when the figures for these three closed borstals are compared with those for the two open borstals, Hatfield and Gaynes Hall (which specialize in dealing with boys of average and above average intelligence, and have a special emphasis on trade training).

TABLE 21

Intelligence ratings in the Raven Matrices test of boys
allocated to two open borstals

Borstal	Scores		
Gaynes Hall	*A B*	*C+ C−*	*D E*
Number of boys	12	3	0
% of daily average population	7·6	1·9	
Hatfield			
Number of boys	8	6	0
% of daily average population	6·1	4·6	

$\chi^2 = 0\cdot0328$ for 1 d.f. P between 0·90 and 0·10 (not significant).

A description of the sample

A comparison of these two tables indicates that, although Hatfield and Gaynes Hall do not have the same spread of intelligence within their populations as the three closed borstals referred to, in the experience of the sample, there is no significant difference in the number of boys who obtained a score of C— or above on the Raven Matrices being allocated to the open or closed borstals. Although the numbers are small, this comparison seems to suggest that the number of boys of average and above intelligence allocated to three closed borstals is similar to the number allocated to two open borstals specially catering for this type of boy.

Examination of the Raven Matrices scores for the whole sample indicated that all the closed borstals received a cross-section of ability. In the case, however, of the open borstals, no boy in the sample, who had received an intelligence rating of D or E in the Raven Matrices test, was allocated to any of three borstals which made up the 'pool', or Hatfield or Gaynes Hall. This would imply that there are less opportunities for boys of low intelligence to be allocated to open conditions. In the remainder of the open borstals, there was found, in the sample, to be a cross-section of intelligence amongst the boys who were allocated to them.

III

Previous Educational Experience

This chapter is an analysis of the *questionnaire* completed by the sample, together with extracts from the oral interviews with a small sub-sample of 39 boys (see Appendix B). The aim is to supplement the information in the preceding chapter, by obtaining further information from the boys themselves, and by so doing adding a new dimension to a study of education in borstal. The information from the boys is of two kinds: firstly, quantitative data on such matters as type and number of schools attended, amount of absence, experience of Further Education; and, secondly, qualitative data relating to their interests and attitudes. Some of the problems in obtaining information in this way have already been indicated. However, despite the problems, it was felt to be fundamental to any study of the role of education, as part of borstal training, to obtain detailed and varied information from boys sentenced to borstal training, on their previous educational experience, as they perceive it themselves.

The boys' answers have been grouped under the following headings:

(A) AGE ON, AND ATTITUDES TOWARDS, LEAVING SCHOOL
(B) INFORMATION ON SCHOOLS ATTENDED
(C) EXAMINATIONS
(D) ABSENCE FROM SCHOOL
    1. *Truancy*
    2. *Further reasons*
(E) SUBJECTS WHICH HAVE BEEN USEFUL SINCE LEAVING SCHOOL
(F) SUBJECTS WHICH WERE INTERESTING AT SCHOOL
(G) PREPARATION FOR LEAVING SCHOOL
(H) ATTITUDE TOWARDS LEISURE; LEISURE ACTIVITIES
(I) FURTHER EDUCATION
(J) FUTURE PLANS AND AMBITIONS

Previous educational experience

Question 1: At what age did you leave school?

Analysis of the answers to this question showed that the sample fell into three main groups:

TABLE 22

Age on leaving Secondary School

	Boys sentenced to a penal institution before 15	Left at statutory school-leaving age	Stayed on voluntarily after statutory leaving age	Total
Number	100*	245†	17	362‡
%	27·6	67·7	4·7	100

* Of these 100 boys, 96 were sentenced to an Approved School and 4 to a Detention Centre.

† Seven of these boys had spent a period in an Approved School but had returned to a state school before the age of fifteen. This group includes those boys attending Special Schools (see Chapter III, Section B, Table 26(a)), and who, therefore, left school at sixteen.

‡ In the case of one boy, it was not possible to place him in any group. The boy's record and *questionnaire* stated that he had left school at sixteen. He had difficulty with reading and writing and was of low intelligence, but there was no indication that he was attending a Special School.

As had been anticipated, the majority of boys had either chosen to leave or been removed from their state schools by the time they had reached the minimum school-leaving age. A sentence to an Approved School or a Detention Centre places the decision as to age at which an individual is allowed to leave the institution in the hands of an outside authority. It was, therefore, decided for the next three questions, to omit the answers of the 100 boys who had been sentenced to a penal institution, as this fact would obviously very much influence the answers they would give to these questions.

Question 2: Why did you leave then?

Of the remaining 262 boys, their answers fell under the following headings:

67

TABLE 23

Reasons for leaving School

Reasons for leaving school	Number	%
1. To start work	69	24·5
2. To earn money	22	7·8
3. Had to leave	20	7·1
4. Wanted to leave	23	8·2
5. Lacked confidence in own ability	5	1·8
6. Disliked some aspect of school	28	9·9
7. School had nothing more to offer	6	2·1
8. Everybody left at that age	83	29·4
9. Other reasons	20	7·1
10. No reason given/Don't know	6	2·1
Total	282*	100

* Twenty boys gave more than one reason for leaving.

An interesting point to emerge from these answers is the fact that the largest proportion (29·4 per cent) were those boys who replied: 'that was the normal age of leaving', 'it was the school leaving age', or words to that effect. This seems to imply a negative attitude to school on the part of the respondent; the kind of attitude which Peter Willmott (1966, p. 93) found to exist amongst boys he talked to. 'School was just a part of life; something they did not feel strongly about one way or the other.'

Boys were asked to elaborate on their written answers, during the tape-recorded interviews, and some of the reasons behind their negative attitude to school emerged:

Unless you had taken the scholarship or something like that you left at fifteen. Could stay for a year I think until the age of sixteen but you've got to be pretty bright for that; just to further your education for a job or something . . . Point of fact nobody asked me to stay on.

Well you had to leave at fifteen or you could stay on you know and try the G.C.E. or something like that . . . I had to leave at fifteen . . . The teacher said you are leaving you know and I asked if I could stay on and do a test, some other test. And she said you can't. I don't know—that's what they told me so I had to leave.

Well all the others had passed some scholarship or something who were staying on. But I never passed any so I left when I was fifteen.

Only a few stayed on; you know that took G.C.E.s.

These answers suggest that school was a place one attended between the ages of five and fifteen, but it was only the most intelligent (which by implication did not include oneself) who stayed on after that time. For others, however, staying on at school presented a real problem.

I was in a Children's Home and I wanted to get out into digs. I needed money to stay in digs so I had to leave school. If I had stayed on I would have been in the Children's Home.

Question 3: Did you want to leave school at an earlier age than you did?

From the boys' answers to this question, a dislike of school becomes more apparent.

TABLE 24

Did you want to leave school earlier than you did?

	Number	%	Dislike of school		To go out to work	
			Number	%	Number	%
Yes	122	46·6	73	59·8	29	23·7
No	140	53·4				
Total	262	100				

Thus, of that group of boys who had not been compulsorily removed from secondary school before they were fifteen, almost half (46·6 per cent) wanted to leave school before they did.

A complete breakdown of the answers to Question 3 and Question 4 which was: 'Did you want to leave school at a later age?' is shown in Table 25.

The fact that 110 boys (42 per cent) seemed not to care whether they stayed or left might further suggest that school had no particular attraction for them.

F

69

TABLE 25

Attitude towards leaving school

		Wanted to stay on longer than they did	Wanted to leave earlier than they did	Did not want to leave or stay on	Total
Number		30*	122†	110	262
%		11·5	46·5	42·0	100

* This figure includes 7 boys who had already stayed on beyond the minimum school-leaving age.

† This figure includes 4 boys who had stayed on beyond the minimum school-leaving age.

(B) INFORMATION ON SCHOOLS ATTENDED

Question 12: What kind of school did you go to after 11?

TABLE 26

Type of Secondary School attended

	Compre-hensive	Gram-mar	Sec. Modern	Tech-nical	Special	Approved School or Deten-tion Centre	Other	Total
Number	12	12	301	10	22	107	28	492*
%	2·4	2·4	61·2	2·0	4·5	21·8	5·7	100

* 121 boys attended more than one type of Secondary School: 113 two types; 8 three types.

TABLE 26(a)

Types of Special School*

E.S.N.	Maladjusted	Asthmatic	Open Air	Not known	Total
11	2	8	1	1	23†

* Eleven of these schools were residential.

† One boy attended two Special Schools.

TABLE 26(b)

Other

All age	Abroad	Boarding School	Naval School	Not known	Total
11	7	6	1	3	28

TABLE 26(c)

Number of Secondary Schools attended*

	One	Two	Three	Four	Five	Total
Number	213	113	28	8	1	363
%	58·7	31·1	7·7	2·2	0·3	100

* In the case of the 4 boys sentenced to a Detention Centre in their last year at school, this was not counted as an additional school.

Tables 26(a), (b) and (c), compiled from the answers to the *questionnaire,* provide a more complex picture of school experience than that which was obtained solely from information contained in the borstal records. The tables indicate that a considerable number of boys attended more than one secondary school, and/or spent a period of time in residence while they were at school. Disruptions of this kind, which must affect progress, are an indication of the sample's disturbed school career. A change in school was not, in the main, the result of family mobility, some indication of which has already been given. Attendance at more than one school meant, for the majority, a removal to Approved School.

The tables confirm that only a small minority of the sample attended schools which were selective by ability.

1. TYPE OF SCHOOL ABOUT WHICH INFORMATION
   WAS GIVEN IN THE QUESTIONNAIRE

In order to ensure that a consistent picture emerged of one school attended, those boys who had attended more than one school were asked to choose the one they had attended longest and answer the subsequent questions on that. The actual numbers of each type of school, about which information is given, is shown below:

71

TABLE 27

Secondary Schools on which information was obtained

	Compre- hensive	Gram- mar	Sec. Modern	Tech- nical	Special School	Approved School	Other	Total
Number	9	10	256	6	15	49	18	363
%	2·5	2·7	70·5	1·7	4·1	13·5	5·0	100

The relatively small number of boys who chose to give details of their Approved School experience is understandable in view of the fact that only 37 boys in the sample had spent two or more years in an Approved School before they were fifteen.

2. POPULATION AT THE SCHOOL

Having indicated the particular school about which they were going to give information, the boys were then asked to state whether this school was mixed or single-sex. Their answers showed that 192 boys (53 per cent) had attended single-sex schools.[1] Of those who attended mixed schools (170 boys), the majority (148 boys) attended Secondary Modern Schools. With regard to those schools other than Approved, there is no reason to believe that the experience of the sample, concerning mixed as opposed to single-sex schools, was any different from the school population as a whole at that particular time (*Report of the Central Advisory Council for Education*, i, 1960, 19).

Thus, over half the sample, segregated according to sex at school, had not been encouraged to regard membership of a mixed community as normal, nor been given the opportunity of learning to live in a mixed community within the more controlled environment of a school.

In addition to this, many of the boys went from school to spend periods of time in single-sex residential schools, and were about to embark on a further period of time in borstal, a similar single-sex institution. All this experience seems inadequate preparation for life in a mixed community, and could be, in part, instrumental in creating problems in establishing a stable and mature relationship with a member of the opposite sex.

[1] One boy omitted to answer this question.

It would also suggest the need to introduce more women into borstal institutions, and an appropriate opportunity is through the teaching staff. By means of this contact, boys have an opportunity of forming relationships with members of the opposite sex, which are based on respect for them as individuals.

As Madeleine Smith (1967) observed, after working as a Marriage Guidance Counsellor in a borstal institution:

It is all important for the group leader to be a woman. It is, after all, by seeing and hearing how a woman thinks and feels and reacts to them, how they in turn do the same towards her, that they can begin to understand what a relationship with a member of the opposite sex can mean. It is probably a great deal more difficult for them to do this with a woman than a man but if they begin to understand what is taking place it must be of some value to them.

The importance of understanding the woman's point of view is obvious in any discussion of marriage and mature relationships between the sexes. The opportunity to discuss a variety of subjects with women could contribute to this understanding and help to heighten an individual's awareness.

The author has, in fact, also taught borstal boys and found most of them willing to discuss intelligently a variety of topics with her. In her experience the discussions seem to have had a wider dimension, for she was able to put forward a woman's viewpoint on topics which needed this, and which, without her presence, would have had a lopsided slant.

3. TEACHERS

As can be seen from Table 28, 269 of the boys felt that their teachers were able to control them, and for the great majority of these (212) control had seemed fair and reasonable. There was no significant difference between the answers of the boys describing their Approved School experience and the remainder of the sample. When boys were asked to elaborate on their answers, fairness in control implied that in many of the boys' opinions one received the treatment one deserved:

If you did something wrong you got caned. There were some who could cane and some that couldn't. Some could lay it

TABLE 28

Question 20: What do you remember about your teachers at secondary school? Were at least three-quarters of the staff:

	Able to control you and fair and reason-able	Able to control you—but unfair	Inter-ested in you	Unable to control you	Not inter-ested in you	Other answer	Total
Total sample	212	57	130	64	71	5	539
% of total	39·3	10·6	24·1	11·9	13·2	0·9	100
Sub-group describing Approved School	27	9	15	6	11	1	69
% of total	39·2	13·0	21·7	8·7	15·9	1·5	100

$\chi^2 = 1\cdot4211$ for 5 d.f. P between 0·95 and 0·90 (not significant)

on and some couldn't. They could control us . . . They were more or less all young. If they needed to knock us about they could do. Anyway, apart from that we used to get ón with them all right.

They would tell you if you were messing about and give you the stick. You had to write out 400 lines or something like that. 'I must not mess about.' If you were all right with them they would be all right with you . . . Mess about when it's all right and as soon as he tells you to pack up—pack up.

When one examines the boys' comments on those teachers who could control them but seemed unfair, it was not the treatment they resented but the fact that, in their opinion, punishment was often unmerited. Thus one boy said of the staff at his Approved School:

You didn't know what was going to come next with them you know. They have you—used to keep you on parade four or five hours a day like, sometimes. The next day they don't worry you like. Keep away from you . . . Put you on parade for anything. When they blew the whistle, if someone didn't move or didn't walk into the hall that would be an excuse for it.

Similar attitudes towards teachers' behaviour were expressed by the sample interviewed by Carter (1962, p. 69).

Approximately a third (130) of the boys felt that their teachers were positively interested in them. This belief seemed to stem from the fact that teachers had been prepared to take that extra bit of trouble, either with them individually:

There was one or two of them that tried to make me read and write better you know. Used to ask me, would you stay in a bit longer you know. Now and again I used to stay in a bit and try and read and write a bit better.

Or, with a whole group:

After school they'd take you for games in their own time. Organize things like that. Woman teacher take you for dancing if wanted you it. Hobbies, anything like.

Although the number of boys who actually stated their teachers were not interested in them was small, their reasons for saying this were quite perceptive:

Well they used to tell us what to do and if I didn't do it they never bothered, so I'd do nothing about it. So I used to go my own way . . . They would have said something about it wouldn't they if they had been interested at all.

Here again some felt that their behaviour justified this treatment:

They just did not care—whether you knew it or not. If you knew it you knew it. If you didn't you didn't. That was their attitude. If they thought you were a bit of a tearaway and did not want to know they did not want to know you. I suppose it is reasonable.

Question 22: Do you feel most of your teachers really knew what you were like or tried to find out?

The majority of the sample (62 per cent) said 'yes' in answer to this question. During the oral interview, the interviewer tried to probe more deeply on this, by specifically asking boys about the amount of informal discussion they had had at school on such topics as their life outside the school. A few boys suggested they had had such discussion with their teachers:

> The games master I particularly got on with him. Out of school he talked to us you know. When we had these basketball matches for instance we'd go in the staff room after and he'd chat to us about things other than school.
>
> Yes, I used to talk to a teacher about that you know. When I'd been in trouble and I went back to school, the teachers, well the Headmaster used to talk to me about it; keep out of trouble and what are you going to do when you leave school and things like that, but I took no notice of him. I just thought I've got to do my own life and I will do you know. Do my own life.

This last comment emphasizes the sensitive handling, arising out of a real relationship, that needs to be built up, if constructive advice is to be given.

More frequently the boys' answers indicated there was little informal discussion and mutual understanding, which might suggest ignorance of the full implications of the question. Alternatively, their fuller answers could be interpreted as contradicting the majority opinion:

> No. Only going to church on Sunday. On Monday morning they asked you [if you had been to church].
>
> I don't think so. You would get now and again after you came back in the summer. They would ask you how you spent your holidays . . . Made a change. They seemed human.

Several of the boys referred to an atmosphere of distrust, which made them suspicious of such enquiries and conditioned the answers they gave. Thus a boy, describing his Approved School, said of the teachers that after he had been home:

> First of all they always asked us what we had done at the night time. When I used to go in our home I used to stay in most of the night time . . . They'd want to catch us out. See what we'd be like if we went outside. I used to think that anyhow so I never used to say much.

Others had obviously not wanted to communicate with their teachers:

Did not like them. I would not have discussed it. If they had said to me what clubs do you go to I would tell them to find out and mind their own business. I was too big-headed when I was at school. I should have known better.

Another boy, when asked if he would have liked to have had a more informal relationship with his teachers, said:

I suppose if they want to know about it they've got to ask the questions. I would not have welcomed it. I keep myself to myself. I never talk to nobody like the probation officers.

Boys were also asked during the oral interview, if they had been in trouble with the police while they were still at school. If their answer was in the affirmative, they were asked if the school knew about this, and if so, what the teachers' reactions had been. Their answers to these questions suggested that there had been little constructive policy for dealing with the problem of delinquents:

I was in trouble once when I was in secondary modern school . . . I don't think they did know because I got a conditional discharge. I didn't get put on probation or anything.
None of the teachers said anything. It was the Headmaster. He said I was a silly boy to do it and I had to watch myself. Catch hold of myself. I was really never any bother at school you know like.
One or two of them you know tried, was interested in that way. Tried to get me out of trouble, you know. One or two of them asked me to take on a club when they found out I was in trouble you know. The rest, you know, they used to say, 'Oh, here he is trouble-maker', that's all.
The Headmaster usually dropped a hint when we'd go on holidays. He says, he doesn't want to see any more of the white forms on his desk when he comes back . . . I had an idea he knew, the way he used to go out in the playground. He said, 'Keep still yobs'. That's what they used to call us . . . That was me and my mates.

Here again the relationship between teacher and taught would seem to be crucial if confidence is to be won and advice given. An interview with the Headmaster, often a more distant figure than the subject teacher, may not be the best way to gain trust and confidence when information about delinquency becomes known to the school. One boy said of the methods used in his school:

> Everyone knew—all the school. When we used to get together in the hall we used to get punished publicly . . . They'd cane us. They'd say such and such a person was in trouble this week and we are going to give him a public caning. Then you'd get four or six, whatever it was.

Question 23: What did your teachers think about you?

When it came to analysing this question, it was decided to group the answers into three broad categories outlined in Table 29. In the column headed 'remainder' were grouped those boys who knew their teachers' opinions and indicated that this was not an unreservedly poor one.

TABLE 29

Teachers' opinions

	Not known	*Poor opinion*	*Remainder*	*Total*
Number	119	90	154	363
%	32·8	24·8	42·4	100

What is surprising about the answers to this question is that almost a third of the sample were ignorant of their teachers' opinions of them. When questioned about the reason for this, the individuals concerned replied that pupils could not be expected to know them, as opinions about pupils were the teachers' private affair. Attitudes such as this would tend to support the impression that there was a lack of open discussion and rapport (between teachers and taught), already evidenced by the oral interviews quoted above. Of those boys who were aware of their teachers' opinion, the great majority (75 per cent) felt that in the light of their behaviour this was quite fair.

These tables, looked at together with the extracts from the oral interviews, suggest that the boys interviewed were reasonable in their opinions, and despite the fact that only 130 boys stated that their teachers were interested in them were, nevertheless, prepared to see positive attributes in their teachers. It would seem that only a minority were really antipathetic

78

towards school, and some of these may have been given little encouragement to be otherwise.

Despite the conclusions arrived at in the previous sections, suggesting that the majority of the boys had little regard for school and education, the analysis of this section could lead one to more hopeful conclusions. It indicates that there is common sense, fairness and goodwill amongst the sample, which might be tapped, provided the approach and circumstances were right. Their dislike of school may well be the result of other factors, such as the dullness of school life, lack of support and interest at home, the glamour of teenage culture, and so on.

4. CORPORAL PUNISHMENT

TABLE 30

Question 21: Was the cane or other form of corporal punishment used in your school?
  If yes:

	Often used by most of the staff	*Often used by some of the staff*	*Often used by only the head/ deputy head*	*Rarely used by only the head/ deputy head*	*Other answers*	*Total*
Number	141	75	92	40	7	355
%	39·7	21·1	25·9	11·3	2·0	100

Only 8 (2 per cent) of the 363 boys interviewed said there was no form of corporal punishment at the particular school they had chosen to describe. One of these 8 boys was referring to an Approved School.

Of the boys who said there was corporal punishment at the school, the majority (60·8 per cent) indicated that it was administered by the staff as a whole; 37·2 per cent stated that its use was confined to the head and deputy head. The answers of the boys describing their Approved School experience did not, however, conform to the pattern of the sample as a whole. Of the 48 boys who stated that corporal punishment was used at their Approved School, 34 said its administration was limited to the head or deputy head.

79

In view of the widespread use of the cane among the schools attended by the boys, it was not surprising to find that 91 per cent of the sample said they personally had been caned whilst at school. Of the 25 boys who said they were never caned at school, 6 were describing Approved Schools. Of the 91 per cent caned, just over half (52 per cent) said they were caned at least once a week. Here again the experience of the boys describing Approved Schools did not conform to the pattern for the sample as a whole. Of 42 boys who said they were caned at Approved School, only a third said they were caned as frequently as once a week.

Of the 170 boys who said they were caned at least once a week, it was interesting to note that in answer to an earlier question only 32 of them had stated that they felt the staff were unfair in their control, and 56 had indicated that their teachers had been interested in them and their future. These figures would tend to support the impression that caning was not, in the main, resented or felt to be unjust.

Boys who were caned fairly frequently, when questioned about its efficacy during the oral interview, commented:

There's nothing in the cane. Everybody got caned now and again. I don't think it stops anyone. It hurts you for a minute then you forget all about it.

The boys used to boast about how many times they had had it in a week. The Headmaster could not hit you hard at all. It should have learned me but I did not want it to. If anyone starts pushing me around I always turn round and start pushing back instead of trying to keep out of it . . . There was one teacher who never used to push me about, never say anything to me. The two of us got on O.K. . . . . He used to try and understand you when you went in there . . . He'd come up and talk to you and have a laugh and joke with you. The other teachers would say, 'Shut up!' and 'Get back' and all that.

This boy was answering a further question about alternative methods which could be used to maintain discipline. Others, whilst pointing out that caning had not been effective, so far as they were concerned, were unable to suggest an alternative method, other than caning harder.

Although there might be some exaggeration regarding the

80

extent of caning, corporal punishment does seem to have loomed large in the sample's school experience and to have been frequently administered.

The figures in Table 30 suggest that the majority of the sample had attended schools where corporal punishment had been widely used to maintain control, and as a deterrent to anti-social activities. This experience might have serious repercussions for borstal training, for if this training is regarded by the boys as being synonymous with punishment, and punishment has been understood, in the main, to be of a violent kind, namely corporal punishment, boys may well be confused at first by a more liberal approach. As the main emphasis in borstal is, or should be, on training, as opposed to deterrence, it is important for the boys to have some intellectual grasp of liberal methods, if these methods are not to be misinterpreted as weakness by the boys.

Many of the answers given to the question: Why were you caned? were vague and general, but 64 of the boys gave as the reason an offence which comes under the broad heading of truancy; the group ranged from those boys who said they had been caned for opting out of particular lessons, to those who were caned for running away from a residential school. Behaviour of this kind is motivated by a variety of reasons, ranging from a desire to escape from an intolerable situation to simply preferring to spend the time in some other way. It is doubtful whether use of the cane will bring about any real change by getting at the root cause of the problem, and caning for this offence would seem to be particularly inappropriate as a corrective measure. As one boy, who had been strapped for non-attendance at school, observed:

> That's when I was at school they used to strap me . . . It made me go away, worse. They did give me the strap and so I said, 'All right, I won't be coming tomorrow', because they gave me the strap, just to show them.

(c) EXAMINATIONS

Question 11: Did you sit an examination at the age of eleven?

In order to get information on their examination experience, the sample were asked if they had sat an examination at the age

81

of eleven. Thirty-two per cent of the sample said they had not. Of the 243 boys who said they had sat the examination, 30 said they had passed it. Of the boys who said they had passed the selection examination, 20 continued their education in schools which provided courses for the higher ability ranges. Ten, however, attended a secondary modern school. When questioned about this, the reason given was usually that they had not wanted to attend a grammar school, or, more rarely, that the nearest grammar school was a long way from their home.

Question 5: Did you pass any examinations before you left school?

In abstracting the number of subjects passed in examinations before leaving school, it was decided to omit those boys who said they had passed subjects in an internal school-leaving examination. Only subjects passed in public examinations were noted, as standards in these examinations are known, and comparison and assessment is therefore possible.

The total number of boys who had any success in external examinations is small. As shown in the table below, 10 of the boys interviewed said they had passed at least one subject in a public examination before leaving school, and a further 6 passed examinations whilst at Approved School.[1]

When questioned about staying on at school in order to sit examinations, the largest proportion of replies were those which were broadly in agreement with this comment:

> Well actually at the time I didn't think it was necessary, if you know what I mean, because I wasn't particularly interested in the school and the only thought I ever wanted to do was to be able to get out of it . . . you know all my brothers were at work and I thought well you know, so I wanted to get out and do it as well. And they seemed to have roughly the same education and they got on all right so I thought I could do the same.

Others felt that they did not have the ability:

> I was in a lower form, too low for that, 'C' stream and 'B' stream usually. I went in a 'B' stream in the first two years and then went down to the 'C' stream in the third.

[1] Their performances in the two tests of general intelligence, indicated that all the boys listed in Table 31 had the ability to pass examinations at this level.

TABLE 31

Number of subjects passed in public examinations

	City & Guilds	U.E.I.	College of Preceptors	R.S.A.	'O' Level	ULCI	London Ass. Eng. Studies
Boys at State Schools							
(1)			3†				
(2)				4†			
(3)					7*		
(4)			5	2*			
(5)				5*	4		5
(6)				4	1		
(7)		6			3		
(8)					5		
(9)					5*		
(10)					1*		
Boys at Approved School							
(1)				3	1		
(2)				1 (Maths. part 1)			
(3)				1		3	
(4)				2			
(5)				2		3	
(6)	1*			2			

* The fact that boys had passed this number of subjects was confirmed by their records. The *questionnaire* was the only source of information for the remainder.

† Both boys stated that they had left school at the end of their fourth year.

In conclusion, it is important to realize that the criteria of examination success is no real indication of the sample's ability. The results of the sample's performance in intelligence tests, administered at the Allocation Centre, suggest that a much larger proportion of boys have the ability to pass examinations at G.C.E. 'O' Level, and possibly at a higher level.

(D) ABSENCE FROM SCHOOL

1. TRUANCY—QUESTIONS 6, 7, 8 AND 9

It has been suggested in Chapter II, Section C, that information relating to truancy obtained from the boys' records probably considerably underestimated its existence amongst the sample. In an attempt to get a more accurate picture of its extent the boys were asked to state how frequently they were absent during their time at junior and also secondary school and to indicate the reasons.[1] The form of the *questionnaire* made the assumption that absences would be short, spread evenly over a period of time, and caused by two reasons: dislike of school and/or illness on the part of the boys. It could be argued that these two reasons for absence were not comprehensive; that frequency of absence is not necessarily evenly distributed throughout a school career and truancy may take the form of continued absence from school over a long period of time. The *questionnaire* was designed, however, to provide a general rather than detailed picture of absence at school as the boys recalled it; it is doubtful whether individual recall could provide anything more accurate than this. A later question attempted to obtain information on long periods of absence and reasons for them.

Another possible difficulty in obtaining information on truancy is that some boys may not have been prepared to admit having truanted, because of their belief that it is regarded as unlawful behaviour. Caning for truancy would emphasize this belief. The wording of the question attempted to alleviate any fears that might arise, but obviously the fact cannot be ruled out that some boys may not have admitted to truancy.

As truancy has been shown to be associated with delinquency, it was considered to be of relevance to compare the absence admitted by boys who were sentenced to Approved School before fifteen with the remainder of the sample.

It would appear that boys sent to an Approved School or Detention Centre before they were fifteen, were absent more frequently at their junior school, than those who remained at state schools. For both groups, however, the number of boys

---

[1] A boy was assumed to have truanted if he indicated that he had stayed away because he did not like school. Some boys may have feigned illness, or become ill, because they disliked attending school, but this could not be taken into account.

TABLE 32

Absence at Junior School

Time Absent	Termly	Monthly	Weekly	Never	Cannot remember	Other	Total
Boys sent to Approved School/ Detention Centre before 15	36	26	31	4	2	1*	100
Boys not sent to Approved School/ Detention Centre before 15	137	62	51	9	3	1*	263
Total	173	88	82	13	5	2	363
%	47·6	24·2	22·6	3·6	1·4	0·6	100

$\chi^2 = 8 \cdot 405$ for 2 d.f. P between 0·02 and 0·01 (significant at the 5% level).

* Two boys stated that for various reasons they had not attended junior school for almost the entire time.

who said they were absent weekly from school is quite considerable. Of the 82 boys who admitted to weekly absence, 41 gave dislike of school as the only reason; and of the 88 boys who admitted to monthly absence, 22 gave the same sole reason. The reasons for absence are given in Table 33.

It would appear from the figures given that dislike of school was more frequently a reason for absence amongst the group of boys, who were sent to an Approved School or Detention Centre before 15, than the remainder of the sample. As frequency of absence was directly related to dislike of school, it can be concluded that the degree of truancy at junior school amongst this sub-group was higher than for the sample as a whole.

When compiling the figures for absence at secondary school, it was decided to group together those boys whose *questionnaires*, which were checked with their records, indicated that they had spent at least two years of this time in a residential school. The period of time was fixed at two or more years as this represents at least half of the time normally spent at a

TABLE 33

Reasons for absence at Junior School

Reasons	Ill	Did not like school	Both reasons	Other reasons	Total
Boys sent to Approved School/Detention Centre before 15	33	30	27	3	93
Boys not sent to Approved School/Detention Centre before 15	126	44	75	5	250
Total	159	74	102	8	343
%	46·4	21·6	29·7	2·3	100

$\chi^2 = 9·872$ for 2 d.f. P less than 0·01 (significant at the 1% level).

secondary school. Removal to a residential school must affect absence and the reasons for it, and prevents truancy of the kind which can take place at a day school. It was for this reason that the explanations for absence given by boys resident at school (Approved School or otherwise) for at least half their secondary school career were discounted.

The figures for absence at secondary school (Table 34) show an over-all increase in frequency, although the fact that the 43 boys attending residential schools are no longer at risk does invalidate any real comparison with figures for absence at junior school.

Once again those boys who were to be sent to an Approved School or Detention Centre before 15 were absent more frequently at the secondary stage than the remainder. Of the 91 boys who admitted to weekly absence, 59 gave dislike of school as the only reason; and of the 94 boys who admitted to monthly absence, 32 gave the same sole reason. Reasons for absence are given in Table 35.

It would appear, however, that the reasons for absence at secondary school were not significantly different between the two groups.

During the tape-recorded interviews, boys, who had indicated that they absented themselves frequently from school because they did not like it, were asked what action had been

TABLE 34

Absence at Secondary School

Time Absent	Termly	Monthly	Weekly	Never	Resident	Total
Boys sent to Approved School/ Detention Centre before 15	21	20	27	–	32	100
Boys not sent to Approved School/ Detention Centre before 15	105	74	64	9	11*	263
Total	126	94	91	9	43	363
%	34·7	25·9	25·1	2·5	11·8	100

$\chi^2 = 5\cdot261$ for 2 d.f. P between 0·05 and 0·02 (significant at the 5% level).

* This figure includes five boys who had spent over two years of their secondary schooling in an Approved School. They had returned to a Secondary School before they were 15.

TABLE 35

Reasons for absence at Secondary School

Reasons	Ill	Did not like school	Both reasons	Other reasons	Total
Boys sent to Approved School/ Detention Centre before 15	17	27	21	3	68
Boys not sent to Approved School/Detention Centre before 15	97	73	68	5	243
Total	114	100	89	8	311
%	36·7	32·1	28·6	2·6	100

$\chi^2 = 3\cdot532$ for 2 d.f. P between 0·90 and 0·10 (not significant).

taken by the school. It seemed clear from their replies that many had been able to absent themselves from school for considerable periods of time without any really constructive action being taken by any of the staff. The following replies indicate the scope of that action:

They did not like it but they did not say very much. Once they found out that I was writing my own notes they did not like it then so they started to give me the cane for it every time . . . all they done . . . .

Only send the school attendance officer around to tell my mother that I didn't attend school, but half the time she didn't know I was away from school because she was working. Then I'd go for a couple of weeks, then I wouldn't go anymore.

You used to get caned if they found out. They used to write home to your parents.

It was apparent that some boys absented themselves regularly from school, whenever they wanted to, without any action being taken at all:

I was always off like on a Wednesday afternoon, well that's when Geography used to come up. Every time she used to come in I used to be off somewhere, you know.

I sometimes used to go up the school get ticked off on the register. I used to slide out then and go home. Didn't know I was gone.

It is obvious that this kind of situation can in no way get to the heart of the problem or provide any long term solution. Furthermore, a school's ineffectiveness may even reinforce an individual's tendency to opt out of situations when he feels he can get away with something. And in later life, because there might be less opportunity to get away with something, lax measures, such as these, might help to establish a pattern of behaviour which manifests itself in constantly changing jobs interlaced with periods of unemployment.

2. FURTHER REASONS FOR ABSENCE—QUESTION 10

An analysis of additional reasons for absence or disruption at school, showed that, in the sample's experience, they fell into three main categories: the removal of a boy from his home into a residential institution which did not include a school; a long illness; a change of home circumstances resulting either from a move made by the boy's own family or a change of foster home. It was found that 126 boys (35 per cent) had experienced an interruption in their education for one or more of these reasons.

TABLE 36

Further reasons for disruptions in education

Into an institution other than a school	Illness	Moved house with family/ into a foster home	Total
34	58	50	142*

* Sixteen boys had experienced more than one kind of interruption.

The periods of time boys were absent from school and/or away from home varied considerably.

TABLE 36(a)

Period of absence from school and/or removal from home

	Up to 3 mths.	3–6 mths.	6 mths. –1 yr.	1 yr.– 2 yrs.	2 yrs.– 3 yrs.	3 yrs. +	Unknown	Total
Number	44	23	17	18	5	17	2	126

In the case of those boys who had experienced a removal, alternative arrangements for their education would be made, and they might not have missed as much education as those who had experienced a long illness. However, a change of school can be disrupting, as can a change in the boy's whole environment caused by the removal.

(E) SUBJECTS WHICH HAVE BEEN USEFUL SINCE LEAVING SCHOOL

Question 15: Write as much as you like in answer to the following questions:

Which of the subjects you learnt at school have you found most useful in life and in what way?

This question was asked in order to try to get the boys to evaluate what they had learnt at school in the light of their experiences since they had left. An analysis of their answers showed the following:

89

TABLE 37

The number of subjects which have been useful
since leaving school

	More than one subject useful	One only useful	None useful	Never worked	No answer/ Don't know	Total
Number	63	173	89	19*	19	363
%	17·4	47·7	24·5	5·2	5·2	100

* This was a group of boys who, whilst attending an Approved School, were sentenced to borstal training. None of them had been free at any time after the statutory school leaving age.

With those boys who had found at least one subject useful, these were grouped together as shown below:

TABLE 37(a)

Subjects which have been useful since leaving school

	English/ Maths	Craft	P.E.	Science	Languages	Music	Humanities	All subjects	Total
Number	124	103	47	12	4	7	15	5	317
%	39·1	32·5	14·8	3·8	1·3	2·2	4·7	1·6	100

As can be seen from the table, the choice of subjects was very disproportionate and concentrated in the main in four broad areas: English, Mathematics, Craft subjects and Physical Education. A variety of reasons could be given for this emphasis. It may reflect a limited employment experience; or the fact that the sample's abilities have been channelled into practical rather than academic outlets (Maddock, 1967, elaborates on this); or an inability to relate what has been learnt at school to life outside school. A possible example of this last point is the small number of boys who say that they have made use of the Science they learnt at school since they left. The demands of modern technology and the opportunities that are available for people with scientific knowledge would all indicate that potentially this figure should have been much larger.

The same three reasons suggested above might account for the 89 boys who replied that they had found nothing had been useful since they left. Alternatively, it could be argued that this is a group which is consistently resentful and discontented. If this is the case, one might expect to find that the group contained a disproportionately larger number of boys who had said in answer to an earlier question that they had wanted to leave school before the statutory leaving age. An examination of their answers to these earlier questions of school-leaving, showed that their replies were not significantly different from the remainder of the sample.[1] So far as school-leaving was concerned, this group did not contain a higher proportion of boys who had wanted to leave before the statutory school-leaving age, than the remainder of the sample.

The ways in which the sample had found subjects useful were grouped as shown in the following table:

TABLE 38

Ways in which subjects had been useful
since leaving school

	Work	Apart from work	Further education	No reason given	Total
Number	119	167	34	3	323
%	36·8	51·7	10·5*	1·0	100

* This heading included boys who said that a knowledge of a subject had helped them in an apprenticeship and vocational training during an earlier borstal sentence.

The interesting figure to emerge here is that the largest group is those who have found what they learnt at school useful in ways apart from in their work. This might suggest that many of the boys saw their jobs as making few intellectual demands on them. Alternatively, it might suggest that what they were taught had little relevance to this important aspect of life as they later experienced it.

The answers to this question might suggest the need to widen the sample's intellectual horizons, and also the need to indicate ways in which subjects, not necessarily those which they already have experience of, can be related to life and work generally.

[1] Twenty of the 89 boys had been removed to an Approved School before they were 15. A comparison of the answers of the remaining 69 with the remainder of the sample showed that $\chi^2 = 1·585$ for 2 d.f. and P was between 0·90 and 0·10.

Previous educational experience

(F) SUBJECTS WHICH WERE INTERESTING AT SCHOOL

Question 19: What subjects did you enjoy most at school and why? Please give as full an answer as possible.

An analysis of the answers to this question showed the following:

TABLE 39

The number of subjects which were of interest at school

	More than one subject interesting	One Only	None	No answer/ Don't know	Total
Number	150	180	24	9	363
%	41·3	49·6	6·6	2·5	100

With those boys who had found at least one subject interesting, the distribution between the various subjects is shown in the following table:

TABLE 39(a)

Subjects which were interesting at school

	English/ Maths.	Craft	P.E.	Science	Langu- ages	Music	Humani- ties	Total
Number	119	162	130	40	9	11	61	532
%	22·3	30·5	24·4	7·5	1·7	2·1	11·5	100

Comparison of the figures above with those in the previous section, indicates a greater amount of interest, amongst the sample, in subjects (learnt at school), than subsequent use for them. Forty-one per cent of the sample had found more than one subject interesting, as opposed to 17 per cent who had found more than one subject useful to them since they had left. Only 7 per cent of the sample said they had found nothing interesting. This information is encouraging for educational programming, as it suggests interest exists and could probably be aroused if imaginatively encouraged.

The number of boys who said they had found a subject

interesting and were subsequently able to put this interest to some use on leaving school was small. In all subjects, except English and Mathematics, less than half the boys who had found them interesting also found them useful.

TABLE 40

Number of boys who found a subject interesting and useful

	English/ Maths.	Craft	P.E.	Science	Langu- ages	Music	Human- ities	Total
Number	66	74	13	4	2	3	7	169

The situation revealed by the tables in this section would seem to point to a failure in the area of work to engage the boys' interests and possibly further suggests that the leisure activities of these boys engages only the hedonistic side of their personalities. Thus, of the 40 boys who said they had been interested in Science at school, only 4 had found any use for their interest since they left.

The figures for English and Mathematics are more difficult to understand; a good grasp of both would appear to be essential to life in our complex modern society. The fact that only just over half the boys (53 per cent) who said they enjoyed these subjects at school said they had had any use for them since they left might suggest some failure on the part of the individual. However, it might also be a failure on the part of the educational system to relate the content and teaching methods in these two subjects to life as these boys have so far experienced it. It is apparent, however, that whatever ways the boys were taught, whether in a pedestrian or imaginative manner, interest does exist; what might now be needed is to develop this interest further, indicating ways it can be put to use by relating content more directly to life and living in a complex industrial society.

Some of the teaching methods they had experienced, as described by the boys during the oral interviews, did not seem to be those which would arouse or maintain interest in a particular subject:

I enjoyed looking at backward things but there was a lot of trouble in history. You would gradually be coming up through the ages then you'd get another teacher taking you. In the same school but they used to change round classes and they would carry on with something else. You used to be interested in doing something and then all of a sudden you would be doing something completely different.

We'd get a textbook and he'd give you so many to do and you'd set about doing them. If you hadn't done by the end you used to have to stay in at dinner or at night-time till you finished them.

We used to do a lot of hand writing, hand-writing tests. We used to write from books or the teachers would put something on the board. We used to have to copy it or write the alphabet up. Write it out backwards.

Most of the time it was written work and we used to read it out of a book you know. We used to do a test on it every week. What we'd learnt in the week. No I never saw any films.

You usually had to write about things about Science. He would tell us about something and then you would write it down. I can't ever remember doing an experiment.

When the reasons for their enjoyment of a particular subject were examined, it was found that the largest group were those who could not be more specific than giving their reasons as pure enjoyment or their own ability at the particular subject. The remainder were more perceptive about the reasons for their enjoyment, which were classified as follows:

TABLE 41

Reasons for enjoying a subject

	Enjoyed own ability	More freedom	Could see the point	The teacher	Had something to show for it	Total
Number	117	21	104	26	62	330
%	35·4	6·4	31·5	7·9	18·8	100

It is interesting to note that one of the largest groups was those boys who said they enjoyed a subject because they could see the point of learning it; how it might be applied either vocationally or generally. This reason for enjoying a subject was given for the whole range. On the other hand, reasons such as the greater freedom enjoyed and the fact that the individual had produced something tangible tended, as might be expected, to be confined to the more practical subjects.

The boys' enjoyment of a particular subject, and some of the reasons for this, emerged from their descriptions of how they were taught:

> That was another good subject. I was good at it at school. I made a coffee table, a standard lamp, an ironing board and when I got into the fourth year there were five of us made two canoes. I still do it now. I wanted to be a carpenter.
>
> He always seemed able to make things interesting. He wouldn't just give us something and say get on with it. Like we'd study *Merchant of Venice* first, the book you see and then we'd go and see the play after, or *Hamlet* and see the film after.
>
> It gave you the chance to do something you wanted to do. You know Science from the book, it gets a bit boring. You can do it at home any time, but it's the practical you can't do at home. You haven't got the equipment at home, microscopes and so on.
>
> We used to paint and make boats and things like that. A couple of us made a big aerodrome. It was not only something to do. You could get a prize for them. We used to put them in for competitions.
>
> We used to sit in class like and sing these folksongs. It was great that. We used to have a real laugh with it you know. The teacher was great that one.

The fact that the boys were able to be so specific about why they had enjoyed a particular subject, might suggest that the reasons they gave are fundamental. If this is the case it would seem important to try and incorporate them into the teaching of all subjects.

(G) PREPARATION FOR LEAVING SCHOOL

Question 16: How did the school prepare you for when you left?

Preparation for leaving school and going out into the world, as described by the Newsom Report, is a complex and detailed process (*A Report of the Central Advisory Council for Education,*

1963, pp. 72–9). The aim of questions 16 and 17 was to obtain information on two particular aspects of this preparation: availability of jobs within an area, and methods of applying, for particular jobs. These two aspects were chosen, because it was felt that they are fundamental covering 'the more formal processes of vocational guidance operated jointly by the schools and the youth employment service'. The fact that a boy has been given this information does not necessarily mean that he has been adequately prepared for leaving school, a point elaborated on later.

Analysis of the answers to this question shows that of the whole sample, 155 boys said they had been given no information on availability and methods of applying for jobs. Table 42 presents a comparison of the answers of those boys who were at Approved School when they reached working age, with the answers of the remainder of the sample. This shows a significant difference in the experience of the two groups, which is almost entirely as a result of the greater number of boys going out to work from Approved School who said they had been given none of this information. Removal to an Approved School must make it difficult to acquaint every boy with the opportunities for work in his home area; in addition, a period in such an institution creates problems with regard to returning to live and work in the community.

For this reason it would seem even more important to try to ensure that boys are aware of the opportunities available to them and know how to go about getting a particular job.

It is obviously not adequate simply to know that the boys were given the information in Table 42. What is also important is to know how the boys were given the information, and by whom. From their answers, it was possible to ascertain that there were three main groups of informants (Table 43).

Although some boys said they had been given the information by more than one group, the great majority (208) mentioned only one group.

The answers of the 86 boys who said they were given the information by teachers were then grouped under four headings as follows (for supporting evidence see Carter, 1962, pp. 101–6):

(i) Those boys who indicated that this had been part of a comprehensive preparation for leaving which took place over

96

TABLE 42

Preparation for leaving

	(i) All available work	(ii) How to apply for a job	Both (i) and (ii)	No informa- tion	Total
Boys leaving from a State secondary school	21	31	113	98	263
Boys who reached working age whilst at Approved School/ Detention Centre	5†	10	28†	57*†	100
Total	26	41	141	155	363
%	7·2	11·3	38·8	42·7	100

$\chi^2 = 11·745$ for 3 d.f. P is $< 0·01$ (significant at the 1% level).

* Fourteen of these boys were absconders from Approved School which perhaps accounts for their not having received this information.

† These figures include the 4 boys who were removed to a Detention Centre in their last year at school. As the sentence was imposed shortly before they could have left school and was for a three month period their answers refer to the preparation they received at school. One boy had received no information; two had been told about available work only and one was given information under both headings.

TABLE 43

Main groups of informants

Teachers	Youth Employment Officers	Head Teachers	Others	Total
86	130	24	20*	260

* The majority of this group were boys going out to work from Approved School who said they were given this information by some agency outside the school, such as a Welfare or Probation Officer.

a period of time and involved such items as visiting speakers, and outside visits as well as general class discussion.

(ii) Those who indicated that this had been part of a general discussion in certain lessons, over a period of time.

(iii) Those who indicated that they had been given the information as a result of an interview or series of interviews, either individually or in groups.

Previous educational experience

(iv) Those who indicated that the information had arisen informally; examples of this were those boys who said it might arise in the context of a lesson or at the end, if current work had been completed. It also included those boys who said they had been given the information as the result of an individual inquiry to a member of staff.

TABLE 44

Advice from teachers

(i)	(ii)	(iii)	(iv)	Total
16	30	17	23	86*

* The answers of the 24 boys who gave the head teacher as their informant are not included in this table. Four of this group were also given information by teachers. In the case of 22 of the group, the information from the head teacher was given in the manner outlined in (iii).

As can be seen from this more detailed table, only 16 of the boys interviewed remembered receiving a preparation for leaving school similar to that recommended by the Newsom Report which suggests that 'the school programme, in the last year especially, ought to be deliberately outgoing. This means taking the pupils mentally and often physically beyond the school walls. It also means bringing men and women from the world outside the walls into the schools.'

This fact gives even more cause for concern in the light of the comment: 'All boys and girls need guidance, but the youngest and less well endowed school-leavers need it especially.' As has been shown in an earlier section, the majority of those boys in the sample, who were free to do so, left school at the earliest opportunity.

TABLE 45

Advice from Youth Employment Officers

		Form of interview			
One individually	One in a group	More than one individually	More than one in a group	More than one individually and with a group	Total
70	32	14	5	9	130

Detailed examination of the way in which the boys received information from Youth Employment Officers indicates that, in the main, this took the form of a single interview. For 83 of the above boys (23 per cent), an interview with the Youth Employment Officer was the only advice and help they remembered being given with regard to future work before they left school, and the majority (67 of this group) said this advice was given in a single interview. In the light of this information, it would seem quite inadequate for the schools to place the responsibility for vocational guidance on the Youth Employment Service.[1]

It is the school which has the essential role to play in vocational guidance. Not in what appears to be the haphazard manner experienced by many boys in the sample, but through a process involving courses which have been designed to suit the 'particular patterns and profiles of abilities' of the pupils concerned (Wiseman, 1964, p. 151). Thus, vocational orientation is a process which continues throughout the school career, and its success 'rests firstly upon the whole teaching force being sensitive to and aware of the child's personal needs, and secondly, on the establishment in our schools of Counsellors trained in educational psychology, who would be responsible for both educational and vocational guidance' (Raynor, 1967, p. 210).

It has already been indicated that many boys sentenced to borstal training have a poor work record. It might be argued that the kind of preparation which has been outlined in this section would tend to accentuate this tendency. If a boy has a chance to discuss the opportunities available in his area, and if possible get an idea of what the conditions are like in different jobs, a more constructive attitude to work is likely to be encouraged, than if there is little or no discussion during his time at school.

Lack of discussion might be taken to imply a derogatory attitude to certain kinds of work on the part of educational establishments. It is inevitable that many boys who leave school at fifteen go into jobs that are unskilled, boring and lack

[1] Research findings suggest that the Youth Employment Service does not have an extensive influence on the choice of job. For a discussion of the Youth Employment Service in comparison with other factors affecting job choice see: Logan and Goldberg, 1953; Carter, 1962, pp. 88–129, 160–77; Willmott, 1966, pp. 105–8.

prospects. It is important that everything is done to make them aware of this state of affairs.

TABLE 46

Question 18: Did you discuss and learn about the following things at your school? Answer Yes or No.

Topics	Yes	No	Total
Claiming of benefits if unemployed or sick	77	286	
Disposal of money deducted in tax and insurance	90	273	
Hobby or interest apart from work	186	177	
Interest in foreign countries, their people and foreign travel	112	251	
An understanding of news and current affairs	201	162	
An understanding of local politics	86	277	
An understanding of national politics	105	258	
			363

It was indicated earlier in this section that a further question would attempt to obtain information on whether other topics, considered essential aspects of a preparation for leaving, had been covered before the boys left school.

The topics selected were not intended to be in any way comprehensive. Some might only be introduced in a final year, others would seem applicable at every stage in the secondary school curriculum.

It was obviously difficult to reduce the complexity of some topics into a single phrase, so worded that it would be intelligible to the entire sample. Despite this, it was felt that the meaning implied by the phrase was apparent, and a 'yes' or 'no' could be taken to indicate whether or not a boy had discussed a particular area.

Seventy-six of the boys interviewed said they had not discussed any of these topics whilst at school; and except for two topics, negative replies were always in the majority. The fact that the two topics which had the widest coverage were hobbies and day-to-day news was predictable. They would seem to fit most easily into the secondary school curriculum, and opportunities for acquiring an interest in a hobby at school are fairly numerous, for example sport. The analysis of this aspect of the sample's school experience would appear to indicate that what is needed is a more widespread recognition

100

of the importance of discussion of certain important topics before school-leaving age is attained.

When the boys were asked during the oral interviews if they felt that their total school experience had prepared them for going out to work, and life generally, the majority answered 'no'. When invited to elaborate on this, their reasons were diverse. There were those who felt that their education was unsuited, even unnecessary, to the kind of work they found themselves doing.

> When we had school we were sat down and had lessons, writing and all that. When we went to work it was not like that. You just had to work, you know what I mean. Didn't have to use your brain at all, just work . . . Well it's not very nice. It wasn't what I expected. I couldn't get a good job.

> I can't think that there is anything worth doing. What good is Maths. to you unless you are going to go in for trade where Maths. will be some use? Geography—what is the point in learning that unless it is going to be some use? Me I knew I would be a labourer.

One boy who had stayed on at a grammar school and obtained several 'O' levels commented:

> I don't think so, where I was at school they just prepared you for the next stage of education; it didn't prepare you for leaving and going outside to work at all. The whole emphasis was on going on with education and that. There was nothing very practical given to you at all.

Another said of his secondary modern:

> I don't think they did at all. As I left school I bought a motor bike. I used to go out in the fields and I just started to learn about engines on that engine, which was something I had never done at school. And after that I went into that class of work—learn it all from there. What I learnt at school I never used at all at work.

Another boy said of his Approved School:

> They should have asked us questions so we could answer when we got out. I never knew anything. We used to get cards coming to the house. Sign these cards for income tax. I never

knew how to sign them. I just used to put them on the mantelpiece . . . He was asking us what kind of job we would like and all that but you couldn't find a job that you wanted very much and we never had any of our cards stamped. They should have put us right on the lot. About what would happen when we got outside. They never said anything about that. They just said to go to the Labour Exchange.

Others felt that the school was not to blame for the fact they were not properly prepared:

I didn't take school really seriously like you know. I was getting the education that the other boys were getting but it was just going in one ear and out the other. You know what I mean.

Those who felt they had been fully prepared tended to interpret the school's function rather narrowly:

If I did not have enough money [in my wage packet] Maths. would come in handy. If I had to fill in a time sheet— English. We were working on contract work and had to read the details through. It came in useful then.

I could always read and write ever since I went to school. Could always spell and add.

Others singled out a particular aspect of the school curriculum, such as visits to places of work.

These extracts would appear to underline the suggestion made earlier, of a failure in the educational system to relate the subjects taught to the life and work of pupils outside school. They further suggest a narrow interpretation of the function of education on the part of both teacher and taught, in that the teachers seem not to have regarded the giving of certain kinds of essential information about life outside school as part of their job, and the pupils tended to have considered useful only those aspects of their education which had an immediate, practical application to their life at work.

While it is recognized that education should be for the whole person, and not merely in terms of the areas discussed above, it does seem a serious indictment of our schools, if subjects such as these are not fully discussed with the pupils prior to their leaving school.

(H) ATTITUDES TOWARDS LEISURE; LEISURE ACTIVITIES

It was considered important to obtain information on attitudes to leisure and the way in which leisure time was spent. The majority of the boys in the sample had been employed in unskilled or semi-skilled work, which demands little ability either mentally or in terms of a particular skill. The conclusion which emerges strongly from recent studies is 'that for the great mass of industrial workers and for many white collars too, work is not a significant area of life'. Consequently the ways in which leisure time is spent cannot be looked at in isolation from the work situation. The work one does 'sets limits on the kinds of leisure which are possible and seem to be desirable, and profoundly influences non-work activities, beliefs and attitudes' (Cotsgrove and Parker, 1963). Thus, although one might expect the sample to attempt to find in leisure some compensation for their lack of satisfaction at work, their choice of leisure activity might not always take a constructive or desirable form. Choice of leisure activity is likely to be determined by several factors, some of which are outlined in the discussion which follows.

Provision for imaginative and constructive use of leisure is unlikely to be found in the working-class areas which most of the boys have been brought up in. Their home backgrounds have probably been limiting in the sense that their parents might never have actively encouraged their sons to widen their horizons through new experiences. It is, for example, unlikely that many of their parents are even first generation grammar school.

The home background may impose further limitations because it restricts language growth, and consequently growth through language. Basil Bernstein, in several theoretical and experimental papers, has developed the argument that sensitivity to the way in which one organizes and responds to experience depends to a great extent on the language codes one habitually uses:

Language is considered one of the most important means of initiating, synthesizing and *reinforcing* ways of thinking, feeling and behaviour which are functionally related to the social group. It does not, of itself, prevent the expression of specific ideas or confine the individual to a given level of conceptualization, but certain ideas and generalizations are facilitated rather than others. That is the language use facilitates development in a particular direction rather than inhibiting all other possible directions (1959).

He argues that people from the working-class, and lower working-class especially, habitually use a restricted language code (originally called public language). Thus their language tends to be 'short, grammatically simple, often unfinished sentences, a poor syntactical construction with a verbal form stressing the active mood'. It tends to have: 'Simple and repetitive use of conjunctions (so, then, and, because)' . . . and a: 'Rigid and limited use of adjectives and adverbs.' There is: 'Infrequent use of impersonal pronouns as subjects (one, it)' and: 'Symbolism is of a low order of generality.'

Bernstein also argues that:

As the structure of a public language reinforces a strong inclusive relationship, the individual will exhibit through a range of activities a powerful sense of allegiance and loyalty to the group, its forms and its aspirations, at the cost of exclusion and perhaps conflict with other social groups who possess a different linguistic form which symbolizes *their* social arrangements. In addition, curiosity is limited by the low level of conceptualization which is fostered by this form of language use; the concern with the immediate prevents the development of a reflective experience; and a resistance to change or inherent conservatism is partly a function of a disinterest in processes and a concern for things.

If Bernstein's theories are correct, it is likely that the restricted language code will be the norm for the majority of the boys in the sample, and will reinforce social solidarity. Thus, the tendency for these boys, so far as leisure is concerned, will be to restrict their activities to the norm of their social class, rather than explore and experiment in different and unusual leisure activities.

In addition, early leaving may have provided these boys with far more undirected free time than their contemporaries, who attend selective schools, and/or stay on at school after the statutory leaving age. Their employment, making few intellectual demands, does not encourage a feeling of involvement, and leads to what David Downes (1966, pp. 236–43) has described as a process of 'dissociation'; that is an opting out of the system which regards work and upward mobility as all important, and a consequent channelling of aspirations into non-work activities.

Downes' observation of delinquent sub-cultures in Stepney and Poplar led him to the conclusion that freedom from parental domination and the educational experience of the groups affected their leisure activities to the extent that

> the only non-work area to which he [the delinquent] is unequivocally attracted is straightforward, uncluttered leisure. In the absence of work-orientation and job-satisfaction, and lacking the compensations accruing from alternative areas of non-work, such as home-centredness, political activity and community service, the 'corner boy' attaches unusual importance to 'leisure'. [The main outlets were the] commercial milieu, the caff, the cinema, the dance-hall.

It would be reasonable to expect that similar characteristics would be exhibited by the boys in the present sample.

Question 27: Are you ever bored during your leisure time?

In answer to this question 235 boys (64·7 per cent) replied that they were rarely bored. Of the remainder, 67 (18·5 per cent) said that they were frequently bored. Boys who had indicated on their *questionnaire* that they were bored, either frequently or moderately, were asked during the oral interview what they thought might be the reasons for this. Some blamed the lack of entertainment facilities in the areas in which they lived.

> You get a lack of entertainment. In our town you've got so many youth clubs. It seems these youth clubs and dance halls open on the same night. You've got to find somewhere to go. Just hang about. It's boring staying in watching television.
> Well round our way they've got nothing in the sense of, you know for youngsters. They've got no pictures, no dances; they've got nothing. When you have time to yourself, it was either stick indoors or you were just walking and after a while you get bored stiff with it.

Others were half aware that the panacea was not more cinemas, youth clubs, dance halls, pubs:

It's something I can't understand myself. I don't know why it is. I don't like staying at home even though I like painting something like that. I can never stay at home because I get bored stiff sitting at home. I always get out of the house and go to the town the first chance I get. Now I get bored stiff when I'm in town.

It's because I don't do anything. I work overtime at night to pass the time away. I go home. There's nothing to do at home. Well there is if I wanted to do things but I have got no interest in gardening or anything like that.

These boys, although very much in a minority, seemed to be questioning their own resourcefulness, and the quality of their lives.

The majority, as will be seen from the answers to the next question, appeared to regard leisure as an activity antithetical to work, and to seek in it some of the experiences and satisfactions which they did not appear to get from their work. Thus it would seem that their leisure pursuits are confined by this attitude, and boredom, in their opinion, arises when there is an inadequate supply of these limited pursuits.

Question 28: How do you like to spend your leisure time?

In order to tabulate the information on the sample's leisure activities these activities were grouped under three broad headings, which were defined as:

(a) Anti-social activities such as stealing and drug-peddling.
(b) Passive/hedonistic/self-centred activities—which includes gambling, drinking, watching TV and films, attending commercial clubs and cafés, driving around in cars, going to parties, with women, playing records, hanging about.
(c) Activities involving creativity/active involvement on the part of the participant, which includes sport, mending motor bikes and cars, walking, mountain climbing, youth club activities, dancing.

It is obvious that in the case of certain activities it would be difficult to categorize them definitely under either of the last two headings. For example, the differences between some of the activities, such as dancing, at a commercial club, from those at a youth club, are fine ones. As the answers to this question were quite full, it was possible to get a better idea of what the activities involved, than it would appear from the headings listed above. If, however, there was any doubt, they were listed under the 'no information' column. Many boys indicated that they spent their time both passively and actively and were placed accordingly under both headings.

TABLE 47

Ways in which leisure time is spent

Anti-social activities	Passive activities	Active activities	Not enough information	Total
12	135	261	14	422

The table above shows that the largest group was those who indicated that they spent their free time either wholly or partly in what has been defined as active leisure pursuits; a sizeable minority, 88 boys, indicated that they spent their time solely in what has been defined as passive and/or anti-social activities. David Downes' (1966, pp. 247–50) description of the delinquent sub-culture in Stepney and Poplar suggests that the leisure activities of the majority would have come under the present definition of passive. However, the present definition of active leisure pursuits does include one aspect of Downes' commercial milieu, i.e. dancing. In addition, although several kinds of pursuit are grouped under the heading 'active', the most frequent examples were sport, mending motor bikes and cars, and dancing. Only a very small minority of boys spent their leisure time walking or mountaineering, or in any other activity which might be thought somewhat different.

Further factors which need to be taken into account when making comparisons are firstly, the difference between the sample frames, and, secondly, differences in the age structure. As the amount of time spent pursuing a particular leisure activity varies with age, proportional differences between two populations in particular age groups may affect the predominance given to certain activities in a particular group (Willmott, 1966, pp. 28–33).

Examination of the answers to this question indicates that the sample's range of leisure activities is very limited. This fact would tend to support Basil Bernstein's theory of the effect of language ability which, whilst not inhibiting development in all possible directions tends to facilitate development in a particular direction; thus, in the case of the present sample, their restricted language code may tend to reinforce their social solidarity and may help to confine their leisure activities to the norms of their social class and inhibit different and unusual pursuits.

(i) FURTHER EDUCATION

Question 25: Did you attend any further education classes after you left school?

If further education is defined as any course of study pursued after leaving school, then as a result of their committal to various penal institutions, the further education experience of the present sample is likely to be considerable.

Of the boys interviewed 126 were in attendance at Approved Schools after the statutory school-leaving age of fifteen. In addition, 123 boys were sentenced to a Detention Centre and 19 to borstal training after they had left school. At all these institutions, education courses are provided and boys are given every encouragement to enrol on them. It was, however, decided to omit the educational experience in penal institutions from a consideration of further education; the fact that education is part of a compulsory period of training in an institution must affect the response to it.

In addition to this experience inside penal institutions, 95 boys in the sample had continued their education after leaving school.

TABLE 48

Details of further education apart from that pursued in Approved Schools, Detention Centres and Borstals

	Evening	Type of Course Day/Block release	Full-time	Correspondence course	Total
Number	68	43	2	1	114*

* Nineteen boys who were on day or block release courses also attended classes in the evening.

Further analysis of the answers on this subject indicates that the majority of courses of study pursued were in connection with either a particular job or trade. For example, a boy might be following an apprenticeship and be released from his work to attend courses at the local Technical College. Some of the boys indicated that they had been released by their firms for the purpose of general study. However, a change of job, which has been shown to be quite frequent, might mean the end of a course of study. Although release from work must make further education more attractive and accessible, 68 of the 95 boys stated that they attended classes in the evening, which requires more determination to pursue. However, of the 95 boys who attended further education classes, 55 indicated that they had not stayed to complete their course.[1] Thirty-two boys had attended for less than six months, although 38 had continued for at least a year. In addition, only 21 had managed to obtain a qualification as a result of this further education. In the case of 17 boys this was a vocational qualification but only 4 of them had actually completed their courses; for the remainder the qualifications were part of a full qualification. Although the purpose of further education is not solely to obtain additional qualifications, this must be an important consideration and is often the reason for study. The evidence here indicates that although just over a quarter of the sample were interested enough to continue their education after leaving school, the majority attended for less than a year and many failed to complete their courses.

During the oral interviews boys explained why they had not completed a course and obtained the qualifications for which they had been working:

> I was working for an apprenticeship, but I packed it up because I got fed up with the wages. I was earning £5 to £6 per week. My friends were earning double.

Another boy who had been studying full time for his 'A' levels at Technical College said:

> I left home and left the area.

Others commented:

---

[1] Although this is a high figure, it must be borne in mind that the *Report of the Central Advisory Council for Education* (1960), Vol. ii, p. 66, showed that the failure rate in all part-time courses was 66 per cent.

I did used to do a bit of weight-lifting but I packed that up after four months. We did not have proper instructors. I was getting nowhere.

I took up a draughtsmanship but it didn't appeal to me. I found it was just like back at school again going to classes . . . I thought they'd just put me in an office and I'd earn some money . . . Every two days out of the week they sent me to classes.

Boys who had never voluntarily undertaken any further education explained:

I don't like going to classes; I like to get out and enjoy myself. I spent all my time like in the evening going to dances and that, messing around with girls.

I started on a job in the construction. I could have went to night school, but I was never there long enough. You had to be there a year before you went on an apprenticeship. I left before then.

I was teaching myself things that I had missed; if I went out to another school most of them would have taken the mickey out of me. They'd say, 'Oh, he's not educated and I am educated', and all that jazz . . . Not much but I taught myself how to read much better.

It is obvious from these quotations that the reasons why the boys in the sample did not take advantage of the existing opportunities in further education are complex and varied. It is also interesting to observe that in their replies to the question on leisure pursuits, no boys included attendance at an academic kind of evening class as a leisure pursuit. This may suggest that this kind of evening activity is not equated with leisure.

Question 26: With the wider experience of life you now have what subjects would you like to know more about? You need not limit yourself to normal school subjects.

It would appear from the figures opposite that the majority of the sample (76 per cent), at the time they completed the *questionnaire*, stated that they would be interested to pursue a course of study in at least one subject. Faced with the prospect of a period of time in an institution, providing educational facilities, many boys, who had never previously enrolled for

TABLE 49

Attitudes to further education at the
time of completing the *questionnaire*

Would like to study further	*Not interested in further study*	*Don't know*	*Total*
276	81	6	363

further education class, might want to take advantage of this provision. It would seem important to capitalize on this attitude; to use the institutional environment as an opportunity not only to take full advantage of further education during borstal training, but also to stimulate an interest which will have some carry-over on release.

A significance test showed that the group of 81 boys, who said they were not interested in further study, contained, in comparison to the remainder of the sample, a higher proportion of boys who had stated that they had found no subject interesting at school.[1] This group of boys might manifest a real antagonism to any form of education, and would probably need very careful handling in the initial stages, if they are to benefit from educational programmes provided in borstal. Of the majority who stated that they were interested to study further, the greater part mentioned subjects with which they were already familiar. This is hardly surprising, but emphasizes yet again the obvious need to widen horizons by means of, where and when possible, new areas of knowledge.

(J) FUTURE PLANS AND AMBITIONS

In answer to the question in Table 50, over half the replies (57·7 per cent) made some mention of work after borstal training. It is obvious that this would be an important consideration to many of the boys, and this concern must in part arise from the fact that they have been sentenced to a period of borstal training with all the implications that this may have for job prospects in the future. A further 12·9 per cent of the replies

[1] $x^2 = 6 \cdot 0248$ for 1 d.f. P between $0 \cdot 02$ and $0 \cdot 01$ (significant at the 5 per cent level)

TABLE 50

Question 29: When you leave here what would you really like
to do and become? Answer as fully as possible.

Return to previous job—skilled	39 ⎫		
Get a new job—skilled and/or with some		185 ⎫	
form of responsibility	146 ⎭		251
Return to a previous job	29 ⎱		
Get a new job	37 ⎰	66 ⎭	
Travel	44		
Make a lot of money	5		
Unrealistic ambition	18		
Obtain security and independence	56		
Anti-social activities	4		
Don't know	25		
Other answers	14		
Nothing	18		
Total	435		

mentioned a desire for security and independence. Thus, a
large majority of replies (70·6 per cent) showed concern about
employment and security, as compared with 6·2 per cent of the
replies which mentioned anti-social, hedonistic and unrealistic
ambitions. The figures suggest that the boys have a realistic and
responsible attitude to their futures.

It is further interesting to note the emphasis placed on obtaining a job involving skill and/or responsibility. Some boys gave
their reasons for this:

> My old man he's got just a labouring job. Any time can come
> up and kick him off the site and say they don't want him.
> With a bricklayer if they throw you off can go anywhere and
> pick up another job.

> I have seen my brothers. One has a trade and he is picking
> good money up; the other hasn't and he's on practically
> what he started with, whereas if he had a trade he would be
> picking better money up.

An apprentice fitter earning half as much as his friends said
what he liked about the job was:

> The variety. I used to like going about different things all the
> time. I would hate to be stuck in the one place all the time
> doing the same old thing.

Previous educational experience

A boy who wanted to return to steel erecting said:

> I can get on well with the blokes I went with and it seems to pay all right and I like the work I'm doing. You feel like you've got like responsibility . . . Well every man's got his own life in his own hands you see. It's dangerous work.

In the light of the sensible and responsible comments above, it is unfortunate that the boys' job prospects are likely to be considerably affected, as a result of their criminal records, not least by the period of time spent in a borstal institution. Educational programmes whilst attempting to improve the situation, for example by establishing good contacts between borstal inmates and future employers, must at the same time give the boys a realistic appraisal of the world they will enter on release. This would suggest that the educational programme should try to hold a balance between, on the one hand, an emphasis towards vocational training, and on the other an emphasis on personal and emotional development, to help boys understand the setbacks and personal difficulties they will meet on release.

The comments of a small minority gave less reason for optimism:

> I don't really care what I do, whether I stay a labourer or travel . . . I am lazy really. I don't see any interest in a trade. In times to come there's going to be no trades. There's going to be pressing buttons and things like that.

> I expect I shall get a job and carry on till I come in again or something like that. I have not got anything in mind.

IV

Education as a Part of Borstal Training

The two previous chapters have contained a detailed analysis of the educational experience, prior to the present committal, of a sample of boys sentenced to borstal training. This chapter is an examination of the educational provision, including vocational training, in nine borstal institutions. These nine institutions were selected so as to provide a representative cross-section of borstals. It is assumed that the conclusions which will emerge will have general application.

The section examines the following areas:

(A) INSTITUTIONS VISITED
(B) INSTITUTIONAL DIFFERENCES
(C) THE TRAINING PATTERN IN BORSTAL INSTITUTIONS
(D) ORGANIZATIONAL STRUCTURE
(E) THE FUNCTION OF THE TUTOR ORGANIZER
(F) EDUCATIONAL PROVISION

(A) INSTITUTIONS VISITED

Once information had been obtained on the educational experience prior to their present conviction, of a representative sample of borstal boys, visits were carried out from October 1967, to January 1968, to a number of institutions. The purpose of these visits was to obtain information on the educational provision, including vocational training, as part of borstal training; and subsequently, to attempt an evaluation of this provision, and its relevance to the needs of the particular population.

As has been indicated earlier, it would appear that the most obvious differences between borstal institutions result from the importance of criminal criteria in the allocation decision, as these are the main determinants of boys being sent to a closed,

114

as opposed to an open borstal. Within this broad division, between open and closed, it is possible to differentiate further on the basis of age, mental and emotional maturity, and medical needs. Consequently, the selection of institutions to be visited attempted to reflect the diversity which exists within them as a whole.

From a total of 19 borstal institutions (10 open, 8 closed and one semi-closed), visits were made to 9, which included one preliminary, pilot visit. The table below gives details of the borstals visited, together with the Prison Department classification of inmates.[1]

TABLE 51

Details of borstal institutions visited

Type of boy	Age range
Closed Borstals	
1 and 2. With bad records needing secure conditions.	15–18
3. Mature and tougher with bad records.	18–20
4. Needing a full-time Medical Officer. Weak and inadequates of low intelligence. Takes psychological and disabled cases.	15–20
Open Borstals	
5. Controlled treatment 'pool' allocation borstal. Intelligence rating not below C—. Sex and violence cases not automatically excluded. Good open training material.	16–18½
6. Average intelligence, mature with fairly good records. No sexual offenders or cases involving bad violence.	17–20
7. Average to low intelligence.	17–19
8. Above average to average intelligence and maturity. Good records; emphasis on trade training. No violence or sex cases.	18–20
*Semi-closed Borstal**	
9. Immature and inadequate boys not in need of a full-time Medical Officer. No sex or bad violence offenders.	16–19
Numbers 1–9 represent Institution.	

* This institution was where a preliminary pilot visit was made.

[1] Details as to the classification of inmates in individual institutions were obtained as a result of a private communication with the Home Office, who point out that these are broad categories and not a description of every inmate. At their request, the names of institutions have been omitted.

In order to obtain, within each institution, the required information on the educational provision as part of the training pattern, Tutor Organizers were interviewed; and in all cases but two this was a tape-recorded interview (see Appendix C). As many instructors as possible of the various trade courses were also interviewed individually; and a selection of classes in each institution visited were observed, and where possible, the content of the lessons was discussed with the teachers concerned. In order to establish a picture of the total pattern of training within each institution visited, an effort was made to talk informally to the Governor or his Deputy, Assistant Governors, and members of the Discipline Staff.

(B) INSTITUTIONAL DIFFERENCES

It was decided to examine the differences between institutions, with regard to two areas which have particular relevance to the present study.

1. RANGE OF INTELLIGENCE

On the basis of this particular criterion, it was found that the institutions visited divided into three main groups. There were those borstals which, because of the weight given to other criteria in the allocation procedure, had in their populations a wide range of intelligence. Their educational programmes had, therefore, on the one hand, to cater for boys who had the ability and knowledge to pass public examinations at the level of the GCE and beyond; while, at the same time, making provision for a sizeable proportion of boys with low reading ages and even total illiteracy. Also, as a result of the allocation procedure, there were other institutions, as in the case of those in the 'pool', which had had their intellectual range deliberately limited to mainly average or above, and which, therefore, did not have to make such a wide range of provision. A third group were those institutions where the Tutor Organizers were of the opinion that the incidence of certain characteristics among the boys was reflected in the levels of intelligence they had subsequently to cater for. Thus, in a borstal taking a preponderance of immature boys the Tutor Organizer was of the opinion that this characteristic tended to be associated with low intelligence, whilst an increase in a borstal population of boys convicted of drug offences was thought to be directly associated with an increase in the proportion of more intelligent inmates.[1]

2. OPPORTUNITIES FOR VOCATIONAL TRAINING

As has already been indicated, a proportion of the boys are given trade tests. On the basis of these tests, the Vocational Guidance Officer makes a recommendation for a particular trade course during borstal training.[2]

Commenting on the effects of the allocation procedure, the Advisory Council in 'Work and Vocational Training in Borstals' (1962, pp. 11–12) points out that: 'Since there are so many other factors to be considered, however, it commonly happens that the borstal most suited to him does not run a course in the appropriate trade.'

Thus, having shown an interest and ability in a particular trade at the Allocation Centre, many boys will find on arrival at their borstals, that although there are opportunities for trade training, it is likely that 'the course will not be in the trade of his choice or that for which he is most suited'. Interviews with Tutor Organizers and Trade Instructors confirmed that this situation applied to a greater or lesser degree in the institutions visited. In the case of one institution this did not apply, as the boys had not completed tests at the Manchester Allocation Centre.

Opportunities for trade training were provided in all of the borstals visited, the number of courses ranging from a minimum of three to a maximum of eight. The number of places on trade courses was not necessarily in proportion to the size of the population; thus, in the borstal visited with the third largest daily average population, provision was made for only three trade courses. Nor were the number of courses provided in an

---

[1] As has already been pointed out, the measurement of intelligence is very complex (see Chapter II, Section B). It would, therefore, seem unlikely that there is the direct correlation between certain personality characteristics and levels of intelligence suggested here.

[2] Although this still applies to boys who are allocated at Wormwood Scrubs, at the time visits were made to institutions there was no Vocational Guidance Officer at the Manchester Allocation Centre, which has been opened since the completion of the interviews with the boys. Consequently, trade tests were not administered at Manchester.

institution necessarily related to the ability of their inmates to complete a course in trade training, at least in terms of the Allocation Centre criteria. The Tutor Organizer at one institution which ran seven trade courses, pointed out that the great majority of boys allocated to the borstal had not been recommended for trade training. This had applied in the case of every boy in the last two groups received from the Allocation Centre prior to the interview. The Trade Instructors confirmed that many of the boys enrolled on their courses had been considered by the Allocation Centre to be unsuitable for trade training. They pointed out, however, that despite this fact, their failure rate in the examination set by the Prison Department was low and that some boys went on and obtained external qualifications during their training, in examinations such as the City and Guilds.

In another institution, an instructor showed from his records, that of the boys who had been recommended by the Allocation Centre to follow his particular trade, 64 per cent passed the Prison Department examination at the end of the course, and in the case of those not recommended the percentage was 58 per cent.

The Trade Instructors pointed out, however, that the trade recommendation at the Allocation Centre was also affected by the individual's reaction to the situation on arrival at his training borstal. A tour of the workshops, and/or the knowledge that a course in the trade of his choice was not starting for another four or five months, might result in a boy changing his mind and asking to be considered for another course.

The present situation with regard to trade testing and the allocation procedure, plus some discrepancies between the Vocational Guidance Officer's recommendation and the actual performance, once a boy enrols on a course at the training borstal, would appear to call into question the value of trade testing at the Allocation Centre. It suggests that it might be better to carry out trade testing at the training borstal where it would appear that: 'The final decision whether a boy is to take a vocational training course is made' (*Report of the Advisory Council on the Employment of Prisoners*, 1962).

At the moment, the present system, by raising a boy's expectations which, in practice, may not be realized, can only undermine confidence in the whole process.

(c) THE TRAINING PATTERN IN BORSTAL INSTITUTIONS

In 1960, the Prison Department referring to the writings of Paterson for a description of the essence of the present system of borstal training, pointed out that the primary assumption underlying borstal training, is 'that the young person under training is to be regarded as "a living organism" . . . with a life and character of his own . . . Further, it requires that each lad shall be dealt with as an individual, and shall not be regarded as the same as any other lad, requiring the same universal prescription' (Home Office, 1960, p. 56). It is also clear that this is one of the more important principles behind the whole process of borstal allocation which 'recognizing the uniqueness of the individual Borstal lad . . . concentrates on his needs, how adequate are the present resources which he can draw on to meet these needs and how severe are the personal limitations and defects which would impede this' (Morrison, 1957).

This emphasis on the individual approach might tend to be reflected in the individual institutions and to result in differences between them. The borstal rules (1964, p. 4) allow that: 'Methods of training may vary as between one borstal and another, according to the needs of the inmates allocated to them.' R. L. Morrison (1957), pointing to some of the more obvious distinguishing characteristics between institutions, suggested that there was variation in 'size, geographical and physical features, security, training facilities (vocational, educational, etc.), staff, including the availability of specialists such as doctors, and in the range and quality of inter-personal relations fostered by their separate cultural traditions'.

Differences, such as those listed above, were found to exist in the institutions visited, as has already been indicated in the case of two particular areas in the previous section. There were, however, in all the borstals visited, certain fundamental elements of training which are common to all institutions, namely:

(a) The eight hour working day;
(b) The indeterminate sentence ranging from six months to two years;
(c) The grade system whereby increasing trust, responsibility

Education as a part of Borstal training
and ultimately freedom are dependent on an individual's reaction to training;

(d) The provision of vocational training for a proportion of the population;

(e) A minimum of six hours educational activity a week 'outside the normal working hours'; (Borstal Rules, 1964, p. 9).

(f) Compulsory attendance at religious services.

Although in practice the content and approach towards these basic elements of training have changed since their introduction, the principles on which they are based were first advocated by the Gladstone Committee of 1895 (Cmnd. 7702, p. 30) and later embodied in the 'Prevention of Crime Act', which gave official legal recognition to Borstal Institutions. They have been, and still are, the basic elements of borstal training.

Thus, despite the emphasis on the need for individual treatment within borstal training, and consequent differences between institutions, there does exist a common training pattern within which each institution has to function.

Examination of the actual content of this common pattern, of which a major part is eight hours work per day, indicates the importance attached to manual work as 'one of the most vital factors in Borstal training' (Cmnd. 10, 1955, p. 96). This emphasis, which has been a major element since the inception of Borstal, would seem to be based on a middle-class conception of the working-class delinquent. 'What they require, and get, as far as possible, is a severe course of drill, gymnasium and hard work, together with a strict attention to discipline' (Cmnd. 7601, 1913–14, p. 107). The fact that for the majority of boys the major part of the day is still spent in hard manual work suggests that this rationale still applies. Eight hours work per day is seen not only as a means of instilling good work habits, but also as providing 'excellent opportunities for training character' (*Report of the Advisory Council on the Employment of Prisoners*, 1962, p. 6). Character training, however, would seem to be a complex of many things, not merely the individual's ability to cope with hard work. Furthermore, the existence of this common training pattern assumes that it is essential to the training of all boys sentenced to borstal. It is now proposed to consider the effects of this common structure on the one aspect of training which is being examined, in this study.

120

EFFECTS OF THE COMMON STRUCTURE
ON THE ROLE OF EDUCATION

As a result of the insistence on the eight-hour working day for the majority of boys, education during training is an evening activity, associated therefore with recreation, as opposed to work which is done during the day. The only boys who can spend time during the day in an educational activity are some of those in need of remedial work in the basic subjects, the vocational trainees, and a few boys who are preparing for external examinations. In four of the institutions visited, boys who were backward in remedial subjects, that is with a reading age of eleven or less, were placed on day classes. A small group of boys in three institutions spent a proportion of the week, ranging from one to three and a half whole days, preparing for external examinations, and one boy was attending full-time at the local Technical College.

The fact that vocational training is carried out on a full-time basis creates an artificial distinction between it and the educational activities. This arrangement suggests that trade training is identified with work, as opposed to education, which, in the main, takes place after work has been completed. By singling out trade training and remedial teaching as the only educational activities allowed to take place on any scale during the day, the Prison Department of the Home Office clearly reveals its educational priorities; it would appear to regard the main function of education in borstal as a means whereby borstal inmates are brought up to a minimum level for effective functioning at work in society, rather than seeing education as a means whereby a real attempt could be made to develop latent ability.

Teaching-staff in borstals are, in the main, employed on a part-time basis. They attend the institution perhaps a couple of hours a week, having already completed a day's teaching elsewhere. The only teachers to be employed full-time in the institution are the Vocational Training Instructors, the Tutor Organizers (although in two of the borstals visited they were part-time), and occasionally a full-time teacher, who takes the day classes. Two of the institutions visited had one or two full-time teachers. Thus, the conditions of employment for the majority of teachers in borstal institutions determine that their role is mainly one of instruction, comparable to that carried out by teachers in evening institutes. The limited amount of time a teacher has with a group inhibits any wider interpretation, such as an attempt to build up an understanding between the teacher and individual members of the class, and consequently to some kind of more personal relationship.

When questioned about the influence of the teaching-staff on the training as a whole, two Tutor Organizers felt that the contribution from their teachers was a stimulating one as they were completely outside the institution. The remainder, however, stated that their teachers had little influence on training as a whole. Even within their own particular sphere of education, it was apparent that there was little opportunity for discussion amongst themselves. In only one institution was the Prison Department prepared to pay teachers when they attended a staff meeting once a term. In the remainder teachers were paid only to attend a staff meeting once a year. The Tutor Organizers carried the main burden of co-ordination in a situation where teachers, some of whom were taking the same individuals for the same subjects as other teachers, had no opportunity to meet to discuss problems and progress.

Unlike an educational establishment, the length of time an individual stays in a penal institution is determined, not by the length of the course, but by the length of the sentence. In borstal this is indeterminate, ranging from six months to two years.[1] Apart from this, the only period of time in the institution which is predetermined is a six-month vocational training course. Boys know that enrolment on a course means that they are committed to another six months in the institution.

Uncertainty about the length of time a boy will be in the institution, plus the fact that uppermost in all his decisions is his desire to leave the institution at the earliest opportunity, obviously militates against any long commitment on his part in terms of vocational or educational courses. Thus in one borstal the effect of a shortening of the over-all training period was that 'there became a tendency on the part of the rather better

[1] Thus, unlike an educational establishment, the structural situation in a borstal is one which gives early discharge to those who respond successfully (by its own standards) and retains those who fail to respond. A logical consequence of this situation is that a boy may be released because he is responding, but before he has achieved a great deal in educational terms.

potential training material to visualize the simple mathematics of their own case and realize that vocational training, if not available quite early after their arrival . . . would automatically preclude the possibility of an early discharge' (Johnson, 1967). Trade Instructors confirmed that some boys were discouraged from signing up for a six months course because of the effect it might have on their discharge.

In addition, although the syllabuses of the trade training courses in borstals are based on the requirements of the City and Guilds examination, opportunities to take the examination are affected by whether completion of the course coincides with bi-annual examination dates; this, as instructors pointed out, was not always the case, and some boys would complete the course and be discharged before the examination date. The uncertainty was obviously a factor which affected all examination work. It was one of the main reasons why Tutor Organizers chose to enter boys for RSA examinations which are held four times a year, as opposed to GCE.

As educationists in a penal institution, Tutor Organizers also have to come to terms with the fact they are dealing with a population which is never static; at the institutions visited, boys are arriving and being discharged on average once a fortnight. If every boy is to have six hours education a week, recruitment to classes has to be a continuous process, and is not affected by termly or yearly divisions of time. When questioned about this Tutor Organizers pointed out that all classes, apart from vocational training, were run on an open-ended, somewhat *ad hoc*, basis, which obviously affected their content and approach.

Finally it could be argued that the present uniform structure of borstal training not only militates against the effectiveness of educational and vocational training *per se*, as will be argued in the following sections, but that this uniform structure also assumes a rigidly defined and narrowly interpreted role for education.

(D) ORGANIZATIONAL STRUCTURE

In their discussion of the central organization of the Prison Department, the Prison Governors

describe the development of the Prison Service as being one

of piecemeal additions to the original para-military structure . . . Each of these additions, usually concerned with
specialist needs and techniques, is equipped with its own
hierarchy, channels of departmental communication, and
Head Office pressure group. In the absence of agreement on
basic aims, which would facilitate integration and the
establishment of priorities, the department can be reasonably
described as an aggregation of secondary interests more or
less continually in conflict with each other (Cmnd. 599,
1966–7, p. 65).

An example of this divisiveness is the fact that, despite what
might be considered as a natural overlap, Education and
Vocational Training have emerged as two separate departments
at the Prison Department in the Home Office; in the case of
the latter, two of the trade courses, bricklaying and painting,
come under the jurisdiction of another department, the Works
Department. Thus, in this one area, policy decisions are made
by three departments.

1. VOCATIONAL TRAINING

When questioned about the relationship between Vocational
Training and their own department, most Tutor Organizers
pointed to the fact that it was their responsibility to provide an
allied evening class, which it is compulsory for every trainee to
attend one evening a week. But as one Tutor Organizer pointed
out: 'I could refuse to have these instructors and employ my
own teachers.' S. F. Johnson (1967) refers to the varying
reactions on the part of the Tutor Organizer, a professional
teacher, to vocational training:

Some profess to have 'nothing to do with it, it's the Dep's
job'; some rather condescend to provide a number of allied
evening classes, but even to some of these . . . the feeling
seems inbred that the 'V.T. evening class' provides a perk for
the C.I.O.[1] rather than anything much of an educational
nature: to others the C.I.O. has no standing as a teacher or
he would be employed as a teacher in a college of technology.

In three of the institutions visited, Education and Vocational

Trade Instructors are officially described as Civilian Instruction Officers.

Training had a considerable degree of integration; in one, the Tutor Organizer held regular meetings with all the Trade Instructors and as a result acted as their representative at institutional staff meetings. This situation was felt to be to everyone's advantage. In the remainder of the institutions visited, Education and Vocational training functioned as separate departments.

The Civilian Instruction Officer is a skilled craftsman. In six months, spending eight hours a day in class contact, he aims to cover both the theoretical and the practical aspects of a trade course based on the City and Guilds examination.[1] It is at the training borstal that the decision is made as to whether a boy takes a course in vocational training. The methods of selection vary, although in the majority of borstals visited, it was by means of a Trade Board, on which all interested parties were represented. The Trade Instructor, Tutor Organizer and someone of the rank of Assistant Governor or Deputy Governor. However, in two institutions, the selection was entirely the responsibility of the Trade Instructors. Furthermore, as a result of the situation already outlined, additional trade tests were carried out by Trade Instructors in four of the borstals visited.

After their appointment, instructors are sent by the Prison Department for a fortnight's course at an Industrial Centre, so that they can learn how to teach their craft. In view of the extreme shortness of the course, it was not surprising to find that in the majority of cases their methods on the theoretical side, as evidenced from the boys' books, relied mainly on instruction rather than discovery, and copying out of information.

The conditions of their work frequently confined them with groups of boys for long hours, often in buildings scattered around the borstal. This physical isolation, coupled with the fact that their individual specialist trades tended to isolate them one from another, resulted in a situation where most of them worked in a lonely, separated manner.

Many of them seemed to be sincere, dedicated men who were genuinely interested in passing their trade skills on to the boys, in the belief that this was in the boys' interests. Despite the

---

[1] In one borstal the full-time employment of a technical teacher, who taught the vocational trainees half a day a week, relieved the trade instructors of the theoretical work and gave them some free time.

difficulties which they work under,' their results, in terms of examination successes, seem to be encouraging. Of 432 boys entered for external examinations, a 67·1 percentage of passes was obtained. (Cmnd. 3408, 1966, p. 32.)

It would seem highly desirable that in all institutions these instructors should at all times be encouraged to have closer contact with each other, with the Tutor Organizers and teachers, and with the institution as a whole. More communal exploration of aims and methods would help the institution as a whole, and these men in particular, as was the case in the borstal where the Tutor Organizer held regular meetings with all Trade Instructors.

2. EDUCATION

The responsibility for education in borstal institutions, defined as that department administered by a Tutor Organizer, is shared by the Prison Department and the Local Education Authority. The former bears the financial responsibility; the latter provides the teachers, including the Tutor Organizer, to run the various courses. As a result of this arrangement, both the Prison Department and the Local Education Authority are in a position to influence educational policy in borstals.

The education provided in borstal institutions is regarded by the Local Education Authority as having the same status as an evening institute. As such, borstals come under the jurisdiction of the Local Inspector for Further Education. Some of the differences, however, between the population in borstals and evening institutes have already been indicated. There is the additional fact that attendance at classes in borstals is not a voluntary decision, but is part of a training process, which the boys are compelled to undergo; the age range is limited to between fifteen and twenty-one. Also a sizeable proportion (33 per cent) of the population comes under the definition of backward in terms of reading-age.

The Reading Test distribution of a group of 1,245 receptions in 1960, in comparison with the distribution in 1948–9 of eighteen-year-old adult males, is given in the following table.[1]

[1] This information was obtained as a result of a private communication with the Educational Psychologist at the Wormwood Scrubs Allocation Centre. The test used with the borstal receptions is the Schonell's oral reading test, whereas the

TABLE 52

Reading Test distributions of Borstal Boys
in comparison with 18-year Adult Males

	Superior	Good average	Low average	Backward	Semi-literate	Illiterate
Reading age	14½–15	13½–14	12–13	9–11½	7–8½	Up to 6½
Borstal receptions %	7·6	23·2	36·2	23·9	5·8	3·3
Adult Males* %	23·7	39·4	19·4	13·5	2·6	1·0

* *Reading Ability* (1950), p. 49.

There are no comparable figures for the population at evening institutes, but it is unlikely that people with reading deficiencies would enrol for courses demanding good reading ability. Consequently, the range of education provision demanded is likely to be different from that in borstal, especially in view of the fact that particular emphasis is given to remedial education.

Tutor Organizers' answers to questions on the extent of backwardness indicated that the size of the problem varied between institutions but all had to allow for it in their education programme. It is difficult, however, to give an accurate indication of the differences between institutions, as Tutor Organizers' definitions of backwardness varied.

So far as the Local Education Authority was concerned, it was apparent from the interviews with Tutor Organizers that although the Authorities were prepared to give the Tutor Organizer support, the initiative had to come from him. Some Tutor Organizers added that they could not expect their Local Inspectors to be aware of particular problems concerned with educational provision in borstals. Furthermore, the situation is obviously not helped by the fact that some Local Authorities

Watts-Vernon Silent Reading Test was used in the case of the Survey of Adult Males. The Educational Psychologist points out that a comparison of the Reading Test distributions of borstal receptions in 1955 with those in 1960 showed that they were almost identical. It is unlikely that this would be the case in a national sample; the differences between the two distributions shown in Table 52 are likely to have increased in the twenty years since the survey into adult literacy was carried out.

may only be responsible for one penal institution, thereby making comparison impossible between penal institutions within that same Authority. Thus, subject to the approval of his Governor, responsibility for the choice of subjects in his education programme falls entirely on the individual Tutor Organizer. He can also determine the allocation of hours between day and evening classes.

Tutor Organizers indicated that any influence which the Prison Department chose to exercise over their educational policies was through the Department's financial control. Each borstal receives an annual grant to spend on books and equipment. Applications to spend this money have to be made to Head Office via the Administration Officer in each institution. Consequently, all requests for educational equipment are considered by Civil Servants working in the Prison Department and most of the queries which arise are on economic or security grounds, as opposed to educational.

It would appear that both Local Education Authorities and the Prison Department give Tutor Organizers little positive advice and guidance on the particular educational problems they have to deal with.

3. THE INSTITUTIONAL STRUCTURE

(a) The Institutional Board

Although they work in penal institutions, Tutor Organizers never become members of the Prison Service. In order to take up an appointment in a borstal institution, they are temporarily seconded from their Local Education Authority for a period of three to five years. Tutor Organizers have no official rank in prison service terms, and are, consequently, outside the personnel hierarchy which exists in penal establishments. When asked about this, the majority of Tutor Organizers were not prepared to give themselves a ranking; they suggested that they were appointed as advisers to the Governor on educational matters, and as such were only answerable to him.

The original aim in transferring the responsibility for educational provision in penal institutions to the L.E.A. was to ensure that this service was in the hands of those professionally qualified to organize it. It would seem that the advantages of this arrangement have been neutralized by the relative isolation of the Tutor Organizer within the total bureaucratic structure, for the power and responsibility of individual groups within this structure 'are in large measure related to the complexity of their individual structure' (T. and P. Morris, 1963, p. 211). One result of a situation of this kind is that specialists, such as Tutor Organizers, religious officials and welfare officers 'belong to a kind of limbo in that while they enjoy a measure of ascribed status they exert virtually no power. Their offices are under-bureaucratized and they have no appreciable body of subordinates responsible to them.' It was apparent from the interviews with Tutor Organizers that, in the absence of this complex supporting structure, they had to depend largely on their personal contacts and powers of persuasion in order to establish, and maintain, their professional status, and gain recognition that they have a contribution to offer in the eyes of the rest of the borstal staff.

However, it was apparent that lack of official rank inside the hierarchical, demarcation of work-structure which exists in the prison service allowed for a certain amount of flexibility in the interpretation of the role of Tutor Organizer. One of the consequences of their lack of rank was, as all Tutor Organizers pointed out, that the attitude of the Governor was the fundamental determinant of their role within the institution.[1] Thus their role could be an important or minor one, and could change with a change in Governor, as was the case in one institution.

The indeterminate sentence, and the grade system, are central to training in all institutions, and as such influence every aspect of life in borstals. An individual progresses through an institution by means of Training Boards. Each boy is interviewed at various stages of his term in the institution, and in the light of reports made by various members of the Board, a decision is reached by the Governor as to whether the boy is promoted into a higher grade and therefore nearer to his final discharge. In an institution run along these lines, membership of a Board must affect the influence an individual has on the

[1] Some indication of the Governor's attitude to the education department, and its status within the institution, is shown in the allocation of Discipline Officers, on a full-time basis, to assist the Tutor Organizer. In three of the institutions visited, a member of the Discipline Staff is permanently available to assist the Tutor Organizer, and undertakes particular responsibilities, such as the organization of the reference library, or the cataloguing and ordering of film material. In other institutions the Tutor Organizer has to carry out his responsibilities single-handed.

institution as a whole, and on the staff and boys within it. For certain members of the institution, their rank automatically entitles them to membership of the Board; for the Tutor Organizer the position is less clear-cut. In five of the institutions visited the Tutor Organizer's opinion was sought at all grades of promotion. In two he only sat on the Trade Board and assisted in the selection of boys for vocational training; in one he was not available as his appointment was on a part-time basis. However, despite their presence on the Institutional Board, the role of the Tutor Organizer within the institution as a whole was very circumscribed. Only two of those interviewed were consulted on matters concerning the over-all training policy of the institution, and, consequently, took an active part in the formulation of all policy.

(b) The Discharge Programme

Borstal has been described as 'essentially a remedial and educational system' (Cmnd. 645, 1959, p. 9). The term educational is descriptive and refers to borstal training in its entirety. The existence of an educationally orientated training structure largely controlled by members of the Prison Service, may, therefore, limit the educational area for which the Tutor Organizer is responsible. In five of the institutions visited, promotion to the Discharge Grade is linked with a training programme designed to prepare boys for their impending release. The organization of these Discharge Programmes might reasonably have been the responsibility of the Tutor Organizer. In fact, in all five institutions they come under the Governor's direct responsibility and take various forms. Their main aim is to prepare boys for life outside the institution. Speakers are invited in to talk and answer questions; discussions are sometimes organized with members of the discipline staff; in some institutions, boys in the Discharge Grade are moved into another part of the institution and given a greater degree of freedom. As these activities take place in the evening, attendance at evening classes is discontinued or severely limited. Thus, when Tutor Organizers in these five institutions were questioned about specific ways in which they were helping to prepare boys for release through, for example, the discussion of employment and work, their answers indicated that this was catered for in the Discharge Programme. As a result of these arrangements, a whole area of important problems are placed outside the responsibility of the Tutor Organizer, and only dealt with in the last month of training.

(c) Group counselling

The introduction into borstal training of group counselling and case-work techniques indicates the Prison Department's acceptance of modern sociological and psychological theory as necessary components of a reformatory system. Group counselling was in practice at all of the institutions visited except one, where the case-work approach was used. The usual method was to have group discussions between staff and boys which were held one evening a week. In only one institution visited could the Tutor Organizer be said to be playing an active part in the group counselling programme. It is evident, however, that the Prison Department does not expect Tutor Organizers to have a professional interest in group counselling, for as they point out: 'Although the direction of group counselling is regarded as appropriate for the lay staff, the activity may obviously present special interest to some Medical Officers and Chaplains, and such interest will be welcomed.' (Prison Commission, 1962).

(d) The library

Library facilities within borstal institutions were available long before Tutor Organizers were first appointed, and were run by the available staff under the over-all supervision of the Chaplain. The appointment of Tutor Organizers has not necessarily resulted in the integration of the library within his area of responsibility. Consequently, in six of the institutions visited, there is little or no connection between the library and the education programme. Thus, a situation exists in these institutions where books on loan from the local library are shared out between the houses or kept in a central library controlled by a Discipline Officer who unlocks it for only limited periods of time. The use of library facilities as part of the work done in education is impossible. In such a situation, the library, and consequently reading, becomes associated with leisure as distinct from education. As one Discipline Officer in charge of a library commented, when questioned about integration between the library facilities and the Education Department: 'I don't think the boys would want to mix their leisure interests with the work they do in the Education block.' Unfortunately, as one Tutor Organizer pointed out, this attitude may well influence the choice of available books: 'They only get Wild Westerns as this is all there is a demand for.' In addition, the fact that leisure facilities within a penal institution are limited, because of the nature of the institution, may well become the rationale for placing limitations on the amount of reading material available.

In one closed institution, however, a close interrelationship has been developed between the library, the education department and the training programme as a whole. Here, as an integral part of their training, boys complete a project of their own choice. Its completion involves a considerable degree of freedom so far as access to books in the library and other materials is concerned; a Discipline Officer pays a weekly visit to the local library to draw out the necessary reference books, and there is close co-operation between all members of staff, which includes the House Staff, Tutor Organizer and the Governor.

(E) THE FUNCTION OF THE TUTOR ORGANIZER

In all institutions visited the Tutor Organizer's responsibilities covered the following areas:

(a) The organization of day classes;
(b) The organization of evening classes which fall into three main categories:
    1. Classes whose content is geared to examination requirements, which include those for vocational trainees;
    2. Classes which provide remedial work in basic subjects;
    3. Recreational classes, whose main aim is to extend an interest or encourage a new one.
(c) The allocation of boys to classes;
(d) The appointment of teachers;
(e) The drawing up, or approving, of syllabuses.

The responsibilities outlined above are considerable, and are made more so when allied with the additional difficulties of working within the framework of a penal institution, where the demands of security may often conflict with educational aims. Still further difficulties are caused by the problem of professional isolation, which most Tutor Organizers were conscious of. Salaries and conditions of work do not reflect the responsibilities and knowledge such an appointment could demand. Thus, as Tutor Organizers pointed out, the fact that they are employees of different Local Education Authorities, and not the Prison Department, means that there is no consistent policy related to conditions of work, such as the length of vacations, working hours, and even salaries. The absence of a career structure for Tutor Organizers within the Prison Service results in appointments being short term, which severely limits the possibility of ideas and methods being developed within penal education by individuals over several years. It is inevitable that such conditions would not only discourage applications for any appointment, but also militate against a general over-all policy with regard to educational provision and consistency in its application.

Educational provision within the borstal framework presents its own peculiar problems, which arise both from the structure of the institution and the particular population it contains. Under the present conditions of service, the body of experience which a Tutor Organizer will build up, as a result of, for example, a five-year appointment in a borstal, cannot be used for further developments within the system, but will be dispersed at the end of his secondment. One of the results of this situation is that only two of the Tutor Organizers interviewed had previously had teaching experience in a penal institution. Recently, the Prison Department has provided Tutor Organizers some slight opportunity to learn something about their new job before actually taking up an appointment; prospective full-time Tutor Organizers do spend a week, and part-time Tutor Organizers three days, in a borstal before starting work. Most of the Tutor Organizers interviewed had not had this opportunity and had come from primary and secondary modern schools, consequently some having had no previous experience of teaching this particular age group, as well as colleges of further education, into an institution whose organizational structure and population needs were quite different from those encountered in their previous experience.

K   133

As part of any induction course to borstal training where the emphasis is on allocation, and differences between institutions, a visit to an Allocation Centre and an explanation of testing techniques would seem an essential prerequisite for any Tutor Organizer taking up an appointment. This, however, is not official policy, although Tutor Organizers can, of their own volition, arrange to make a visit. Thus, although there is a battery of educational tests administered at the Allocation Centre, five of the Tutor Organizers interviewed administered further tests to all new arrivals at their institutions. When questioned about the reasons for further testing, it appeared that Tutor Organizers needed the confirmation and reassurance that resulted from tests which they had administered themselves. As these tests merely reinforced information on 'developed' ability already available, as a result of the allocation procedure, in the boys' records, it does suggest a breakdown in communication between the Allocation Centre and the individual institutions. Another reason for Tutor Organizers administering further tests may well be that this reinforces their professional status within an organization where they feel their position threatened. However, some tests administered by Tutor Organizers were somewhat crude (see Appendix D).

The fact that there are failures by the Prison Department in appreciating the problems which a professional teacher has to face on his appointment as a Tutor Organizer, is not surprising in view of the absence of any career structure within the Service. One of the results of the absence of a career structure is that no Tutor Organizer ever ascends the promotion ladder into the hierarchy of the Prison Department at the Home Office. Consequently, policy decisions in the field of education are made by an Administrator who has not had experience of education within a penal institution.[1]

Faced with this difficult professional situation, with the

[1] In October 1967, a new appointment was created when an administrator with educational qualifications became responsible for education in Prison Service establishments. The original post of Director of Education and Welfare had been abolished in 1950 (see Cmnd, 8356, 1950, p. 6). The advertisement for this new post, together with the further information sent in answer to an enquiry about the post, made it clear that someone with experience in the field of L.E.A. administration would be appointed. There was no reference to educational experience in the penal field. The fact that this particular emphasis was given to the new appointment suggests an underestimation by the Prison Department of the differences between educational provision in a Technical College and a penal institution.

further difficulty of being a very small group widely scattered in borstals and prisons throughout the country, Tutor Organizers have attempted to establish a professional body of knowledge on teaching in penal institutions, through their annual conference and by publishing information. Most Tutor Organizers interviewed seemed to be dedicated and sincere teachers, believing strongly in what they were doing, despite the fact that, as has been demonstrated, they were often confronted with difficult and isolated conditions in which to work.

(F) EDUCATIONAL PROVISION

As has already been indicated, the borstal population covers a wide range of intelligence. In some borstals this range is confined within particular limits; in others no limits are imposed as a result of the allocation procedure.

1. BACKWARDNESS IN THE BASIC SUBJECTS

All of the Tutor Organizers interviewed had to make some provision for a proportion of their population who required remedial work in the basic subjects; although the size and degree of backwardness varied between institutions. In two of the institutions visited, a teacher was employed full-time to take day classes for boys who came into this category. In other institutions teachers were employed part-time, and boys requiring help were directed to evening classes.

This awareness of, and emphasis upon, the problem of backwardness amongst the borstal population has already been indicated. Both teachers and Tutor Organizers commented on the paucity of reading material whose content was suitable for young adults in this particular age group. They pointed out that their students were, on the whole, acutely conscious of, and embarrassed by, their own inabilities, and obviously did not respond to books whose approach was too juvenile for them, and which they may have been familiar with in the past.

This would seem to suggest that new techniques and texts have a vital part to play in teaching young adults to read, especially when it is realized that they have behind them experience of years of failure.[1] At present each institution is left to find its own solution to the problem, and, in the main, the methods used were a mixture of those found in both junior and secondary schools. Thus, material such as flash cards, simple sentence completion, comprehension exercises, and games such as Scrabble and Lexicon, were used. Boys were encouraged to write after visual stimuli, such as photographs, had been discussed, and letter-writing was encouraged; reading material was, in the main, a selection of secondary school readers for backward pupils, some of which made attempts at controlling vocabulary. One institution had been experimenting with Stenorettes, whereby students can listen to recording of texts whilst, at the same time, attempting to read them. So far as backwardness in numeration is concerned, the content of classes was geared to what was felt to be the everyday needs of the boys, such as budgeting, income tax and rates, simple measurements. The teaching methods seemed, on the whole, to be along traditional lines (see Appendix E).

The problem of backwardness amongst adults would seem to be one where the role of an advisory service, perhaps organized by the Local Education Authority, would be invaluable to Tutor Organizers. Local Advisers could disseminate information on successful methods, and also give support to Tutor Organizers in their requests to Governors and the Prison Department for opportunities to experiment. The function of an advisory service might also include the production, and evaluation of, new methods and materials.

2. OPPORTUNITIES FOR BOYS WHO ARE INTELLECTUALLY
ABLE TO EXTEND THEMSELVES

Information as to the proportion of boys amongst the borstal population who seem to be above average intelligence has already been given. Visits included one to an institution, whose population as a result of the allocation procedure, contained 'boys of superior intelligence and a reasonable level of matur-

[1] An organization which has had considerable experience of dealing with the same problem is the Army; Michael Pollard (1967), describes the work of the Army School of Preliminary Education at Corsham. The methods outlined in this article are an advance on any seen at institutions visited. The Army's experience and knowledge could be invaluable to the Prison Department in planning future developments.

ity'.[1] Here the Tutor Organizer, who was part-time, had been responsible for organizing a nationally recognized twenty-week course for boys at the borstal, which, as he explained, had been accepted as the equivalent of the first year of the Ordinary National Certificate in Business Studies. The twelve boys who enrolled on the first course were being taught two days a week and spending another three mornings on directed reading, in addition to attending evening classes. The Tutor Organizer explained that, as a result of being recognized whilst at borstal as mature students, boys who might not have had the requisite number of 'O' levels before training, could be accepted, on release from borstal, into a Technical College at second-year level. In two other institutions visited there were some facilities for a few boys to pursue more advanced study during the day; in one this was by means of an individual correspondence course; in the other, boys were taught one or possibly two mornings a week. In a fourth institution one boy had been enrolled full-time at the local Technical College. The main opportunities for examination work were provided in evening classes, which were, in the majority of institutions visited, limited to GCE and RSA in English and Mathematics, the majority of boys attending each class once per week. One institution offered a choice of five subjects.[2]

When questioned about the opportunities for the more intelligent boys, Tutor Organizers, whilst admitting that they were not adequate, gave as reasons for this the indeterminate length of time boys were in the institution, the difficulties of

[1] Information obtained as a result of a private communication with the Borstal Allocation Centre at Wormwood Scrubs.

[2] Unlike the examination successes resulting from Vocational Training, there are no longer central records of examination success resulting from the work of the Tutor Organizers and their staff, although figures are available in individual borstals. In one borstal visited, the figures for the three years, 1965–7, are as follows:

| Year | GCE 'O' Level | | | RSA |
	English Language	Woodwork	Arithmetic	English Language
1965	2	5	10	7
1966	—	2	6	3
1967*	1	4	2	3

* The figures for 1967 are incomplete, as candidates had been entered for the examinations in December.

examination dates, and the fact that small numbers in individual institutions meant that it was uneconomic to offer a wide variety of courses.[1] It is this situation which forces the teaching emphasis on to consolidation of what has been learnt in the past, rather than to developing latent potential, with obvious detrimental consequences, so far as obtaining qualifications is concerned. As an illustration of this situation, both Tutor Organizers and Trade Instructors, when questioned about their criteria for trade selection, emphasized the importance of a certain level of mathematical knowledge and literacy. In the existing conditions, it would seem difficult to bring a boy up to this level in the time available, prior to starting the course.

The main educational opportunity for boys of above average ability were the opportunities provided for trade training. That this is officially accepted as the main opportunity can be seen in the fact that, at one institution visited, an increase in the allocation of boys of above average ability had been accompanied by an expansion in the opportunities for trade training. Another institution catering for more intelligent boys offered the only trade course in Instrument-Making.

The opportunity to learn a trade during training is an important component of a sentence to borstal, but it was felt that this should not be a substitute for more academic outlets for boys who have the ability to benefit from them. Lack of other opportunities within the institution may result in a boy having the ability to complete a trade course, but not the interest or inclination to take it up as a job on release.

3. ALLOCATION TO EDUCATIONAL CLASSES

Allocation to classes is in the case of those in basic subjects, examination work, or in those related to vocational training, as a result of guidance from the Tutor Organizer. It is compulsory for all boys on a trade course to spend one evening a week in an allied class. In four borstals, attendance at certain classes is compulsory for all boys, either throughout or at a particular

[1] Although the average length of borstal training, which includes the time spent in allocation, is fourteen months (Cmnd. 3408, 1966, p. 15), the fact that boys went through an Induction, and/or a Discharge Programme, in all the institutions visited, meant that the time boys were available for attendance at classes was reduced by an average of three months. The length of time boys attended classes varied between institutions, ranging from a maximum of thirteen months to a minimum of six months.

138

stage in their training (see Appendix E). In the case of the remaining classes in the education programme, which can be broadly defined as recreational, boys are allowed a free choice, which is of course dependent on vacancies.

The content of courses and teaching methods, in all the institutions visited, are obviously affected by the fact that all classes (except those for vocational trainees) have a constantly changing membership, and that teachers are part-time. When questioned about how they dealt with the problem of continuous turnover in their population, Tutor Organizers said that some subjects are taught entirely on an individual basis. Thus, English and Maths seem, in the main, to be taught in this manner. Boys, on arrival, are fed into small classes at the appropriate level, and are able to progress at their own pace within the group, and, where necessary, are moved into another class, working at a higher level. The fact that the teachers are part-time, however, must militate against the effectiveness of this method, which is dependent on accurate diagnosis, communication of information on individual boys, as well as continuity of approach. It was not surprising to find a recently appointed teacher unaware of the fact that he had been sent a group of receptions for diagnostic reasons.

In those subjects which do not lend themselves so easily to the individual approach, the syllabus is arranged so that each session is self-contained, or divided into topics which can be dealt with within a short period of time (see Appendix E). This method is used in all subjects which appear on education programmes, apart from practical classes and those in English and Mathematics. The result is that it is impossible to teach any subject sequentially, thus presenting considerable difficulties so far as subjects such as Science, French, and some aspects of History are concerned. It is very difficult for the group as a whole to consolidate what has been learnt and consequently experience a sense of achievement. In the majority of cases the actual syllabus is drawn up by the individual teachers, and there seems no consensus between teachers as to the areas which might be covered. The exception to this is those classes at which attendance is compulsory, where the syllabus may be drawn up by the Tutor Organizer.

It could be argued that this *ad hoc* situation, where class membership changes frequently, where individual teachers are seen once a week, and where there is often a lack of educational goals, or even a consistent pattern of work, is particularly unsuited to the needs of delinquents. In some respects, it would seem an all too familiar pattern of educational experience for these boys. Quite a number of the teachers observed made few concessions to the particular needs of the population, or attempted to present a subject in any way which was either imaginative or different. Other teachers, working under the same difficult conditions, did manage to create an atmosphere of involvement, and, as a result, there seemed to be some measure of individual or group achievement.

4. SECURITY

It is obvious that the need for security, and the emphasis given to it by individual Governors, will have implications for the education programme in borstal institutions. Security is primarily the concern of the Discipline Staff, who will obviously be very conscious of it, knowing that they will carry the main responsibility should any breakdown occur;[1] security was naturally more of a problem in closed than open institutions.

The need for security in a closed institution severely limits freedom of movement. Teachers will have difficulty in gaining access to classrooms, and are dependent on Discipline Staff when they wish to move from one part of the building to another. The library may only be unlocked for certain limited periods of time, which inhibits freedom of access during evening-class hours. Movement of individuals and groups from one particular room to which they have been assigned is also restricted. At one borstal visited, the notes for the guidance of teachers pointed out that: 'Whilst falling out to visit the lavatory is not forbidden, it should be strongly discouraged. If it is considered essential that a lad should leave the room, then he must be told to report direct to the Education Office. After class, please inform the Education Office of any lad who has been given this permission to leave the room.' If a teacher wishes to take a group outside the main security block, perhaps to do some practical work in a workshop, this has to be carefully supervised and may be discontinued altogether in the winter because of the risk involved in moving boys around after dark.

[1] The system of half sheet reports, which are a permanent record of an individual officer's failure to carry out his duty, must increase this concern for security.

In all institutions a careful check has to be kept on class numbers, and an officer is on duty in the corridor outside class-rooms. Requests for equipment to run a particular class are checked for security reasons by an Administration Officer in individual borstals before being forwarded to the Prison Department. All tools and equipment which can be used are carefully checked. The opportunity to go outside the institutions is, in general, limited to boys who have reached their Senior Training Grade, which, as one Tutor Organizer pointed out, may not necessarily correspond to their educational requirements. In only one institution visited, however, did the Tutor Organizer feel that the implementation of the Mountbatten Report, resulting in a tightening of security, had affected work in the Education Department.

In these ways it can be seen that conditions of work in borstals are very different from those which exist in a purely educational institution, such as a College of Further Education.

5. FACILITIES AND EQUIPMENT

It is rare that borstal institutions are purpose-built, and this has its effect on the facilities for education. In four of the institutions visited classes are scattered around the institution, sometimes in rooms which have to be used for other purposes during the day. This creates organizational problems and adds to the individual teacher's isolation. In the two most recently built institutions of those visited, rooms are uniform in size and all contain desks and chairs. As one Tutor Organizer pointed out, this assumes a uniformity in educational requirements, which is just not the case. There is obviously a need for a more informal setting at times.

So far as audio and visual aids were concerned, standard equipment in every institution visited is a cine and film strip projector, record player and tape-recorder. In two institutions, the only person who can operate the projector is a Discipline Officer, a state of affairs obviously making its use less flexible. Some institutions have obtained extra equipment, such as overhead and loop projectors, and Stenorettes. Television sets, are, however, regarded by the Prison Department as recreational items and therefore it is not possible for Tutor Organizers to purchase one for educational purposes. Although borstals have television sets, these are attached to individual houses, which makes their use for educational purposes difficult.

141

V

An Alternative Role for Education

It would seem appropriate in a study such as this to conclude with recommendations for an alternative role for education as part of borstal training. The chapter, therefore, begins with a summary of the important factors relating to education to have emerged from the study, and continues by outlining an alternative role for education as part of borstal training. There follows a discussion on the organizational and structural changes which would be necessary to implement an alternative educational role, and the chapter ends with a discussion on research and development work which, it is argued, should be an essential part of experiment and change in education in borstal. The chapter is divided into the following sections:

(A) SUMMARY OF THE IMPORTANT FACTORS OF A BORSTAL POPULATION WHICH HAVE RELEVANCE TO EDUCATION

(B) EDUCATION—ITS DEVELOPMENT AND PRESENT ROLE IN BORSTAL TRAINING

(C) EDUCATION—AN ALTERNATIVE ROLE
1. *Basic skills*
2. *The acquisition of new skills and knowledge*
3. *The creation of new value systems and behaviour norms*
4. *The provision of recreational, cultural, and artistic opportunities*

(D) STRUCTURAL AND ORGANIZATIONAL CHANGES
1. *The role of the professional educationist in borstal training*
2. *The need for a career structure*

(E) THE NEED FOR RESEARCH

(A) SUMMARY OF THE IMPORTANT FACTORS
OF A BORSTAL POPULATION WHICH
HAVE RELEVANCE TO EDUCATION

As has already been indicated, it was thought relevant, as part of an examination of education in borstal training, to try to isolate those characteristics in the previous educational experience of a sample of borstal boys, which would seem to be important when considering, along with other factors to have emerged from this study, a new role for education within borstal training. This section proposes then to summarize those characteristics in the previous educational experience of the boys considered important for later discussion.

The aetiology of delinquency points to a great many factors which might be thought to be the cause of, and subsequently associated with, this kind of behaviour. Some of the factors known to be associated with delinquent behaviour have also been shown to affect adversely educational experience, for example social factors. Thus, as was expected, the proportion of boys from the present sample who had attended schools, which were selective on ability, was far fewer than for the population as a whole.[1] One of the consequences of this is that only 10 of the boys interviewed had obtained any formal examination qualifications before leaving their state school, although a further 6 had passed examinations whilst at Approved School.

If it could be maintained that low intelligence is associated with delinquency, this might be an explanation of why so few boys, in a sample drawn from a borstal population, had attended selective schools, and even fewer obtained formal qualifications. However, a survey of research into the relationship between delinquency and low intelligence suggested that the association was slight, if it existed at all. It pointed to the considerable evidence which suggested that social factors associated with delinquency, such as membership of a low socio-economic class, are likely to have had an adverse effect on

[1] The boys' answers to the *questionnaire* showed that 22 boys (6 per cent of the sample) had attended either a grammar or technical school, a much smaller proportion than the national average of 19 per cent. It is also less than the 10 per cent from semi- and un-skilled backgrounds, who are selected for grammar or technical education. (Report of the Central Advisory Council for Education (England) 1960, Vol. i, p. 12.)

intellectual development, and to affect performance in tests of intelligence, especially those relying heavily, or solely, on verbal ability.

The score distribution of the present sample in a non-verbal test of general intelligence (Raven's Progressive Matrices, 1938, 20-minute version (Revised Order, 1956)) showed that 68 per cent of the sample obtained a score which was above average, compared to a population norm of 50 per cent. However, when the non-verbal scores were amalgamated with the scores on the verbal test of intelligence (Abstractions CP Test 1), it was found that 45 per cent of the sample had an IQ score of 100+. These facts tend to support the argument that social factors have an influence on intellectual development and may have implications for the present educability, in narrow academic terms, of the sample. It suggests that in any borstal population, there is a considerable number of boys lacking in the resources of language needed to pursue an academic education. It would seem important, then, to investigate ways of developing these resources.

A further factor which must be taken into account was the considerable disruption which the sample experienced during its school career. One hundred members of the sample had been sent to an Approved School or Detention Centre before they had reached school-leaving age. In addition, a quarter of the sample said they had been absent weekly whilst attending secondary school. Furthermore, 126 boys had experienced the kind of disruption which results from a family removal, or a removal into a home, or a long illness.

So far as the sample's attitude towards education was concerned, some ambivalence emerged. As had been expected, the majority of those boys who had been free to do so left school at the earliest opportunity; only 17 boys (4·7 per cent) stayed on at school into the fifth year. Of the boys attending state schools, only 30 (11·5 per cent)[1] said that they would have liked to have stayed on longer, whereas 122 (46·6 per cent) said that they had

[1] Although this figure does not include any of the 100 boys who had been removed to an Approved School or a Detention Centre by the age of fifteen, it is a considerably smaller proportion of the population at risk than was found in a national sample. It was found that 16 per cent of boys who had attended secondary modern and all-age schools, and 22 per cent of all boys who had attended grammar and technical schools had wanted to stay on longer than they did. (Report of the Central Advisory Council for Education (England), 1960, Vol. ii, pp. 22–4.)

wanted to leave school earlier than they did. Further evidence of a dislike of school was to be found in the extent of truancy which the sample admitted to. Of 82 boys who admitted to weekly absence at junior school, 41 gave dislike of school as the sole reason, and of 91 boys who admitted to weekly absence at secondary school, 59 gave dislike of school as the sole reason. In addition, 189 (52·1 per cent) of the sample admitted to staying away at some time from their secondary school because they did not like it. However, replies to subsequent questions suggest that this dislike was not a total dislike of school. Thus, only 24 boys (6·6 per cent) replied that they had found nothing interesting at school, whereas 150 (41·3 per cent) said that they had found at least two subjects interesting. The two most frequent reasons given for interest was that they had enjoyed the subject; and that they could see some point, or achieve something tangible, in pursuing the subject. Such an involvement would seem to be fundamental to the learning situation, and the converse may be one of the major reasons why certain aspects of school were disliked.

So far as their teachers were concerned, a minority, 71 boys, felt they were not interested in them, and 212 boys said that their teachers were able to control them, and were fair and reasonable. This last comment, however, must be set against the fact that only 8 boys said that there was no corporal punishment in their schools, and that 170 (46·8 per cent) remembered being caned once a week. This may well have resulted in the boys considering that one of the normal, and perhaps best, methods of control was corporal punishment.

The sample's experience of further education, in addition to those who had experienced this as a result of a period of time at an Approved School or Detention Centre, was greater than had been expected. Ninety-five boys (26 per cent) of the sample had attended further education classes, but amongst this group there was a high degree of wastage, a trend also found at national level.[1] At the time of completing the *questionnaire*, 276

[1] The proportion of boys who had had no full or part-time further education at all (omitting those who had experienced this at Approved Schools or Detention Centre) was 74 per cent and is a very much larger proportion than that found in a national sample, where it was found that 46 per cent of boys who had attended secondary modern schools, and 19 per cent of boys who had attended grammar or technical schools had not experienced further education. (Report of the Central Advisory Council for Education (England) 1960, Vol. ii, p. 56.)

(76 per cent) said that they were interested in further study. The question was, however, deliberately general, and did not limit the suggestion of further study to borstal institutions.

During the visits to borstal institutions, Tutor Organizers were asked to assess the boys' degree of interest in education. These varied considerably. Of the 8 interviewed, 4 replied that once the idea had been carefully introduced, the majority of boys were really interested. Two said that the majority of the boys in their institutions regarded education simply as another aspect of borstal training to be accepted, in the same way as everything else. The remaining Tutor Organizers replied that the great majority of boys had not the slightest interest in continuing their education during borstal training. These answers illustrate that any real assessment of the situation, as deduced from the Tutor Organizers' general impressions, so far as the total borstal population is concerned, is difficult. The individual Tutor Organizers' general assessment of the situation is likely to be affected by the role his department plays in the individual institution, and as has been shown earlier, this varies considerably between institutions. However, so far as the boys are concerned, a sentence to a borstal institution is likely to be equated with punishment, rather than training, and this attitude could spill over into all aspects of borstal life, of which education is a compulsory part.[1] Any hostile attitude to education must be looked at in the context of this particular situation, and where the kinds of restrictions enforced during the day are carried over into the educational programme, this will obviously reinforce any tendency to equate education with punishment. However, a greater enthusiasm and interest for education might be engendered if certain changes in the total environment in borstal were brought about.

So far as their work experience was concerned, 89 boys (25 per cent of the sample) said that they had found nothing they had learnt at school had been of use to them since they had left; only 63 (17 per cent) had found more than one subject useful. In addition, only a small minority could recollect receiving through the school what might be described as com-

[1] Thus D. M. Lowson (1967, pp. 95–6) found that 77 boys of a sample of 100 discharged from borstal institutions perceived the intention of the authorities in sending them to borstal as punitive, or to deprive them of their freedom. A further 21 referred to the inconsistency, in their opinion, between what was said and actual practice.

prehensive advice on work prospects, and this was shown, from the findings of other research, to be a not untypical experience. An examination of the sample's work record showed that this was characterized by a high job turnover. Only 117 boys (32 per cent) had been in the same job for at least a year. A breakdown of the figures relating to the longest period in any one job indicated that, when compared with earlier borstal populations, there was a remarkable consistency in this particular aspect of experience. The longest period in any one job has been found to be highly indicative of later behaviour; the shorter the period, the worse the future prognosis (Mannheim and Wilkins, 1955, p. 145). It is, therefore, an important aspect of pre-institutional experience which is very relevant indeed to borstal training. And it would appear to be the rationale behind the policy which advocates that: 'The need to train a Borstal boy to stick at a hard day's work and do it well remains one of the major elements of training' (Cmnd. 7777, 1948, p. 52).

High job turnover has also been shown to be inversely related to the degree of skill involved in a particular job (Baldamus 1951; Willmott, 1966, pp. 115–16). An analysis of the last job held showed that 256 boys (70·5 per cent of the sample) had been employed in unskilled or semi-skilled work. Yet, 146 boys (40·2 per cent), when asked about their future plans and ambitions, said that they wanted to get a new job involving some degree of skill and/or responsibility. It might be argued that these aspirations are provided for in borstal, for there are opportunities to learn a trade during training, which equips boys with skills enabling them to obtain greater satisfaction from their work, and consequently greater stability. However, it has been shown that the opportunities are limited; the issue being further complicated by the fact that official figures relating to work taken up by boys released from borstal show that 'slightly under 30 per cent entered the trades for which they had been trained' (*Report of the Advisory Council on the Employment of Prisoners*, 1962, p. 12). The fact that the majority of boys who are taught a skill during training are not taking it up on release might have important implications for any proposal to widen vocational opportunities during training.

A comparison of the number of previous convictions and institutional experience of the present sample with the borstal population as a whole showed that the experience of the two populations was not significantly different. Comparison with the figures produced by Alan Little (1965) from a 10 per cent sample of all borstal receptions 1950–56, confirmed that longer criminal records and previous institutional experience were increasing trends, which were partly responsible for changes in the borstal population.

An analysis of the sample's leisure activities showed that these were limited. It was shown that an important determinant of leisure activities was membership of a social class, with its consequent cultural and social environment.

(B) EDUCATION—ITS DEVELOPMENT AND
PRESENT ROLE IN BORSTAL TRAINING

Before considering a new role for education within borstal training, it would seem important to summarize the development and present role of education as part of training, in order to highlight those areas where the need for change is apparent. This section will, therefore, concern itself with such a summary.

An examination of the development of education within penal institutions has shown that its introduction in the nineteenth century was concomitant with the acceptance of reformation, as opposed to deterrence, as the purpose of being sentenced to an institution. Education was synonymous with reform and thought to be an insulation against further delinquent behaviour. This factor, in combination with the educational and social climate of the time, determined its content, which in the early reformatory schools consisted, in the main, of religious teaching and industrial training; the latter being 'of especial value, as affording the best means of enabling children to provide for themselves the means of independent support' (Select Committee, 1853, p. iv).

The more widespread acceptance of the need for reformation and its application to an older age group resulted in the establishment, at the beginning of the twentieth century, of borstal institutions. The initial concept of training in these separate institutions, for young people between the ages of sixteen to twenty-one, was based on the belief that young delinquents needed to learn a respect for authority and accept their position in a stratified society amongst 'the ranks of honest and industrious labour' (Ruggles-Brise, 1921, p. 99). The function of education within this total concept was, on the one hand, to train the inmate for work, and on the other through 'exhortation and moral persuasion' . . . 'to elevate and instruct'. Thus, as in the early reformatory schools, education was conceived as having two separate and distinct functions.

It has been shown, however, that the advent of Sir Alexander Paterson, resulted in the rejection of the idea that borstal training could achieve its objectives as a result of the application of external moral exhortation. Under his leadership the concept of training was that of the totally educative environment, modelled on the kind of environment already in existence in the public school. Under the new regime the personal example, and emulation, of members of staff was believed to be of paramount importance in the process of reform, and there was a minimum of specialist functioning by the staff. The continuing belief in the importance of work as a component of training, however, resulted in an expansion of the opportunities for vocational training linked in some cases with the introduction of instruction by qualified teachers. Any other educational provision was the responsibility of the borstal staff, and as a consequence was mainly concerned with teaching constructive leisure pursuits. Although the content of education, other than vocational, was by this time much more broadly based, the over-all supervision of these educational activities was the responsibility of the institution chaplain, illustrating that the relationship between religion and education still existed at this time. The fact that an authoritative account published in 1952 places education as a subdivision of a chapter on the Chaplain's Department indicates that it is only quite recently that education has officially received an independent status (Fox, 1952, pp. 201–8). Furthermore, Annual Reports of the Prison Commissioners indicate that until 1950, the report on education in prisons and borstals was always provided by the Chaplain Inspector.

The main post-war developments in borstal training, in the opinion of the Home Office, have been in 'the extension of vocational training in skilled trades and of education in its widest sense' (Cmnd. 645, 1959, p. 9). This has been reflected in the recognition of the need to introduce educational specialists into borstal training and the appointment of Tutor Organizers with over-all responsibility for educational provision in particular institutions.

It has been argued, however, that the fact that educational specialists were grafted on to a well-established training pattern, complete with a supporting bureaucratic structure and its own 'educational' goals and value system, had certain implications for the role of the professional educator. This situation meant that those controlling the dominant organization within borstal were able to impose their own narrow definition of the role of the professional educator within borstal training. In addition, as a consequence of the existence of a common training pattern, the role of education became global and undifferentiated in its application to different institutions. Furthermore, the limitations imposed by the existing organizational structure have meant that education has been constricted and prevented from playing its full role in any innovations which have been introduced during the past fifteen years or so into borstal training as a whole. This has resulted in the increasing isolation, rather than integration of the Tutor Organizer and his staff; one example has been shown in the omission of the education staff from contributing to the recently introduced group counselling sessions.

Further limitations on the role of education within borstal training are the result of the particular function which has been assigned to vocational training within the total structure. As has been argued, trade training has always remained quite separate from the remainder of the educational programme. The traditional emphasis on the importance of work as a vital component of borstal training, and the fact that opportunities for trade training are seen as a logical development of this emphasis, has meant that vocational training has been identified with work rather than education; consequently, this training is the daily occupation of that proportion of the population who are enrolled on courses. Thus, a division has emerged between vocational training and the remainder of the educational programme, a state of affairs quite alien to other educational institutions where the role of the professional technical teacher is seen as complementary to the practical work of the craftsman.

It has been consequently argued that the present situation in borstal institutions places severe limitations on the achievement of purely educational (and likewise vocational) objectives.

It might be argued, however, that the present proportion of time, and emphasis, given to educational (and vocational) goals, as part of a total training pattern orientated to the needs of a delinquent population, is adequate for the needs of that population. An examination of the development, and current practice of borstal training, suggests, however, that the fundamental elements of this training, as inherited from the Paterson ideal, are largely based on a middle-class conception of the needs of the working-class delinquent, having been developed within the context of a hierarchical society which saw the purpose of training as enabling delinquents constructively to take their place within that society. Educational provision in borstal today would seem to be a logical development from such a total conception; the main educational opportunity to have emerged for the more able boy is a chance to enrol on a trade training course, which might be said to reflect the ceiling of working-class expectations; and for the backward, the main educational opportunity would appear to be the attainment of minimum literacy to enable him to play more efficiently his limited role in society. As Roger Hood (1965, p. 142) comments: 'Sir Lionel Fox's authoritative statement of borstal training principles made in 1952 reads very much like the pre-war writings of Paterson. Since 1952 there have been no revolutionary changes in the system.'

It has been argued, furthermore, that all educational activities (including vocational), whether taught in day or evening classes, are marginal in comparison with other aspects of training, such as work, and that the evening classes in particular could be interpreted as a convenient way of occupying the boys' evening leisure time, resulting in some cases perhaps in providing an interest which will continue on release.

Thus, the educational (and vocational) policy in borstals, as conceived by the Home Office, is determined not with reference to the human potential or other positive goals, but on a preconceived idea of the future life-style of the boys after release. Furthermore, the total training pattern seems to have taken little cognizance of changes in the structure of modern society. The outdated terms borstal 'boy' and 'lad', still in current use, are overt examples of an outmoded attitude, towards young people between the ages of fifteen to twenty-one. For example, the modern borstal boy cannot be considered in isolation from the context of the post-war teenage culture, and it is likely, moreover, that the early school-leaver, which applies to the majority of borstal boys, is most susceptible to such a culture, the life-style of which is very different to that of the 1930s (Downes, 1966, pp. 129–34). D. M. Lowson (1967, p. 8) argues that the present day borstal boy, unlike the borstal boy of the 1930s, has

> a very different view of his place in society these days when so much attention is paid to this impressionable, free-spending section of the community, and when the teens are looked on as a consummation, with later a decline from this halcyon period. The working-class teenager of today sees the years to the early twenties as the time of greatest intensity of living and grudges any time not spent in pursuit of personal satisfactions. His committal to borstal represents a snatching from the feast, a transition from the autonomous, assertive, favoured group to becoming a unit in a dependent, manipulated mass. At a time when the traditional paternalistic class system carries little weight with the majority of citizens, there are few less likely to defer to those more favourably placed on the social scale than the working-class teenager.

While one might not want to agree with all of D. M. Lowson's emphases and generalizations, the implications of his argument would seem important for borstal training.

The Prison Department is obviously aware of the changes and new demands of our society, a point continually made in annual reports (Cmnd. 496, 1957, p. 177; Cmnd. 2030, 1962, p. 27; Cmnd. 3088, 1965, p. 19). There is little evidence, however, of any attempt on its part to initiate radical change into the basic training structure in order to meet these changes and new demands.[1] The Prison Department's insistence on retaining

[1] See Hood (1965, pp. 142–61) for a survey of post-war training ideas. The annual report for 1962 (Cmnd. 2030, p. 28) contains a reaffirmation of the Prison Department's belief in traditional methods. 'The traditional method of borstal training, based on the house system with its competitive features, a good day's work, education and recreation in the evening, the grade system which allows increased responsibility and trust to those in the later stages, and, running through all, the interest and attention of the staff, is still followed by many borstals particularly those dealing with a large roll and difficult training material. It is a good training structure . . . and still produces results.'

the Paterson ideal must be a source of frustration to the people who are in daily contact with a changed situation, and who have to work out solutions to new problems resulting from the pressures of a changed society, within this outmoded frame of reference. As the Deputy Governor of one institution visited pointed out, an indeterminate sentence and the underlying concept that an inmate 'earned' his release had an adverse effect on the goals of the case-work approach which was being practised at his institution. The length of time a boy would spend at this institution was determined by his individual needs, which after allocation to this particular institution were diagnosed at the beginning of his stay, and not by a constant reviewing of his behaviour to discover whether he was earning his release. The fact that there was a discrepancy between the future trainee's perception of his sentence as being indeterminate and the norms of this particular institution inevitably caused conflict and undermined trust. For example, boys with personality disorders (and this particular institution received many such boys) tended to withhold information which they thought might prejudice their release, believing that 'earning' one's release meant not stepping out of line. However, the case-work approach requires an opening up on the part of the individual, admittance of having problems and need for help, and for the individual to be himself rather than play a role. Open relationships between staff and inmates is fundamental in this approach and is not helped by this conflict of values.

It would seem then that, looked at in relation to the kind of society to which the modern borstal boy will return on release, there are several aspects of the present training pattern which are inappropriate to his needs.

It is inevitable that a sentence to an institution involves loss of individual freedom and responsibility for one's own life, and this experience may be particularly painful to the teenage delinquent.[1] The present method of training in borstal could be said to reinforce this state of affairs rather than mitigate it through allowing some involvement by the boys in decisions which affect life in the institution. Inmate self-government has

[1] D. Matza (1964, pp. 155–60, 165–9 and 188–91) argues that the young delinquent is particularly concerned with the precept of manliness and with maintaining the symbols and behaviour that exemplify this status. As such he will strongly resent any action which deprives him of this status such as that which denies him freedom of action.

been introduced on a limited scale in some borstals (Kenyon, 1951; Bishop, 1960) but the principle of self-government has not spread to borstals in general. The process of training is, in the main, a highly structured situation in which boys are directed in a round of ceaseless activity;[1] the fact that inmates should be kept occupied often seems the most important consideration, rather than an evaluation of the tasks that they are set to do; the need for time to think, listen, discuss, talk or set out problems, and in other ways to experience direct personal communication with peer groups or adult friends does not seem to be as well catered for as these other activities. Governors who might attempt to cater for this need must be frustrated by an official policy which lays down that forty hours per week must be spent in work, and a further six in education. A highly structured environment of this kind, rather than engender a feeling of individual responsibility could in fact reinforce a delinquent's image of his own irresponsibility and inadequacy, and is certainly no preparation for being released to a loosely structured, poorly supportive social environment. Within such a highly controlled environment, the concept of the indeterminate sentence and the grade system implies an imposition of acceptable norms of behaviour by those in authority as opposed to a working through of personal difficulties on the part of the individual, guided and supported by the staff, leading to self-discovery, and a consequent real internalization of values on his part.

In addition, as has already been indicated, it is still assumed that the basic elements of training in operation at the moment are essential to the needs of all boys sentenced to borstal. Unfortunately, so long as this assumption exists, the goals and values of any treatment and experimental approach will continue to be subordinated to the total training pattern. This has been shown to apply to the role of education in borstal training, but the point is equally valid so far as the application of modern theories and techniques in psychology, psychiatry and sociology are concerned.

The implications of the arguments so far advanced suggest that a more diversified structure, based on individual needs,

---

[1] A working day in borstal starts at 8 a.m. and continues with breaks for meals, until 8 p.m. four evenings a week. The boys go to bed at 9 p.m. (Cmnd. 599, 1966–67, p. 260).

would seem to be required in the training and rehabilitation of young delinquents (see Hood, 1965, pp. 217–20; Rose, 1960; Miller, 1964, for a discussion of possible alternatives). Unfortunately, however, the emergence of the teenage culture, one aspect of which seems to be a strong sense of generational loyalty and a questioning of authority and tradition, has not unnaturally been paralleled by a demand for greater 'discipline' in dealing with adolescent deviance. This demand appears to have been reflected in the Criminal Justice Acts, 1948 and 1961, the former resulting in the setting up of Detention Centres; the latter resulting in the combining of borstals and young prisoners' centres into one system, emphasizing security and discipline as opposed to experimentation. It also made explicit the view that some social deviance was too severe to benefit from a wholly reformatory regime and introduced long-term prison sentences as an alternative to borstal. The present climate of opinion seems to be not conducive to experiment, and tends to reinforce the disciplinary, as opposed to treatment,[1] role of borstal institutions.

It is suggested, however, that the validity of this emphasis, and in fact borstal training as a whole, is called into question by the results of this method of training as indicated by the present re-conviction rate, for which the latest figures available at the present time show that of those boys released from borstal a minimum of three years, 67·7 per cent have been re-convicted (Cmnd. 3304, 1965, p. 47). This would seem to provide a powerful argument for more experimentation, and it is now proposed to outline theoretically a new role for education, within a more diverse structure of reformatory training.

(C) EDUCATION—AN ALTERNATIVE ROLE

It has been argued that the rationale for introducing education (including vocational training) into borstal training was reformative. However, it has also been argued that the main principles behind the kind of reformative training currently in operation are based on an outmoded conception of the needs of borstal trainees. This has led to a situation in which any new

[1] The term treatment refers to the application of certain professional skills such as psychiatry and sociology, to the problems of deviant behaviour.

thinking and new ideas, instead of radically affecting the content of the training, have been either gradually absorbed into and consequently transformed by the main training programme, or have remained peripheral to it. Group counselling, as currently practised, might be considered as a recent example of the former condition, education an example of the latter. Consequently, the introduction of professional teachers into borstals, and the recognition of the need to expand education, has not had the kind of impact on borstal training that it might have had.

It would seem then that if education is to have a greater impact on the total training programme (and it is the main purpose of this chapter to argue it should) there is a need to re-think the principles underlying the present pattern of reformative training. It is suggested that if this re-thinking were done, and made a greater attempt, than seems to happen at present, to provide for the actual needs of the modern borstal boy, some of which have been highlighted in this particular study, the role of education might then well become more central to any future training programme.

Before continuing by outlining some of the ways whereby education could take on a new role, it is proposed to touch on some of the important concepts which should underpin a programme of reformatory training, in which education could make a more central contribution.

If borstal training is to be truly reformative, there would seem to be a paramount need for boys to realize that, so far as behaviour is concerned, there are several possibilities from which to choose. The domination in the Prison Service of a para-military regime, which because of the interchangeability of staff between borstal and prison also carries over into borstal training, affects the life-style pervading borstal training. It is suggested that this life-style is restrictive and offers only a limited set of possibilities about behavioural patterns to the trainees. For example, one of its most serious consequences is that it removes from an individual almost total responsibility for his actions. It has been shown earlier in this study that the horizons of many boys sentenced to borstal training are severely circumscribed, and it could, therefore, be argued that the present pattern of training reinforces, rather than ameliorates, a restricted outlook, and consequently behavioural patterns.

156

If training is to offer borstal boys new insights regarding behaviour, and relationships, it could be argued that an imaginative educational programme has an important role to play, for this kind of programme would have within it a profoundly humane attitude which, it is hoped, would have its effect upon an individual, by opening new awareness and revealing new horizons. Furthermore, if new attitudes and values are to be internalized within the individual, there must be a climate in which this can flourish. It would seem fundamental that there is the right kind of atmosphere and opportunities within which delinquents try to come to terms, within themselves, with new awareness and values, rather than have these imposed upon them. An imaginative educational programme could open up new possibilities for boys, which could lead to individual revaluing of a life-style.

It is also important to realize that there would appear to be a considerable intellectual potential among borstal boys, and in order to satisfy this potential, it would seem essential to offer them more challenges, especially educational, than seem to be at present offered. The kind of dull routine that many boys undergo for most of their time during training might well be reinforcing any existing intellectual frustrations, which can only reinforce negative attitudes. Boys who can be intellectually pushed, and who are not, may soon turn their abilities to working the system, rather than being worked on, in the right way, by it.

It is now proposed to offer, in some detail, a theoretical model for education, based on the concepts outlined above, and within a more diverse structure of reformatory training. In the discussion which follows it is proposed to use the term education in a broader sense. Consequently, when the term is used it will include vocational training.

Educational provision, at present, could well be perceived as a minor part of a total training pattern, whose objectives are often in conflict with the goals of other aspects of this training. This must cause confusion in the mind of the individual, and it is obvious that he will be motivated towards what seems the most attractive goal in the total situation, namely release. Consequently, if education is to play a really valid role in the rehabilitation of delinquents, the imbalance between it and other aspects of training must be corrected.

An essential prerequisite to achieving this is the removal of the present artificial distinction between 'work', as opposed to 'education', and its replacement by a recognition that the emphasis given to particular aspects of training is determined by the needs of the individual. This would imply a recognition of the fact that it may be more important to his future rehabilitation into society for a boy to spend the greater part of his time during training in 'educational' activities, as opposed to 'work', a state of affairs which does not exist at the moment. Whatever is decided in the case of a particular boy, the relationship of the total training programme, including education, to long and short-term goals must be absolutely clear to him. This would seem vital, if involvement and motivation are to be achieved.

The method of approach in the initial stages would also seem fundamental to future individual motivation and co-operation. Decisions should be arrived at on the basis of discussion, so that the boy feels that every attempt is being made to cater for his particular educational needs. Education should be presented as an on-going process, not necessarily finishing at fifteen, and the development of individual ability should be shown to be as equally important to the needs of society as it is to the individual. One hopes that this emphasis will not only satisfy a boy's individual needs, but will also indicate that he has a link with, and a contribution to make to, society as a whole. It was pointed out by some Tutor Organizers at the institutions visited that a not untypical comment to information on educational matters was: 'What use are classes to me now? I've got by very well on what I have learnt so far,' or: 'It's done me no good in the past. It's not likely to make any difference now.' In the light of their previous experience, this kind of argument from boys is to be expected. It is suggested that if an individual's sights are raised, a boy will no longer feel it necessary to justify his self-image. As another Tutor Organizer discovered, from his experience of interviewing borstal boys: 'Many of these boys seem unaware of their own ability and the ways in which it might be extended and developed.'[1] The fact that many boys

---

[1] Experimental projects in the U.S.A. to increase the educational achievement of institutionalized offenders have found similar underestimations (McKee, 1967, p. 18). (Venables (1967, p. 161) in discussing the effect of anticipatory socialization on students at Technical College, also suggests a low self-image, as a result of the influences of home and school.

will have no identifiable aspirations, or be aware of possible outlets, suggests there is a need for real imagination in order to generate enthusiasm for educational objectives. It would seem essential that the education staff have time to show each boy that they have a sympathetic awareness of his particular interests. In addition, they must have time to acquire a knowledge of suitable job and training possibilities, so that they can best advise each individual. In this way educational objectives may begin to have some real validity for boys sentenced to borstal.

An important consideration in the provision of education is a recognition of the status of the students involved. This would seem to have particular application to the provision of education in borstal institutions (Matza, 1964, pp. 155–60, 165–9, 188–91). Young delinquents, the majority of whom finished their full-time education at the earliest opportunity, will obviously resent education if it in any way implies a return to the juvenile status they experienced whilst at school. Crucial in any recognition of changed status is the relationship between teacher and taught; it would seem desirable that this should be on a more adult basis than in the past. The learning situation should try to lend itself to a new approach; boys need not always be under the direct supervision of a teacher. Where possible more individual programming might be devised and the teacher could be available for consultation and evaluation of progress; this change in emphasis implies a more adult status than had been experienced at school and at the same time aims for participation and responsibility from the individual in decisions which affect his future life. An additional factor which may increase motivation is that the emphasis in the individual approach can be on success rather than failure, which may have been the emphasis in the past when direct comparisons between individuals were being made.

The kind of approach outlined above would obviously involve the employment of teachers on a full-time basis. Only in this way would it be possible to achieve the essential liaison between a Tutor Organizer and his staff if education is to play a more important role in borstal training, and education programmes are to be tailored to individual needs. The employment of more full-time teachers would ensure that those boys who might benefit from spending at least part of each day in educational activities would be able to do so. Education could, therefore, become a positive aspect of training and not merely an erosion of leisure time.

It is now proposed to outline some areas where education might be developed and expanded within borstal training.

1. BASIC SKILLS

It has already been suggested in the examination of previous school experience, and performance on the intelligence tests, that many boys sentenced to borstal training are likely to be deficient in the basic skills of language communication, both oral and written, and numeration. Deficiency in basic skills must be thought of in relative terms and will consequently apply equally to the boy who simply requires a refresher course before embarking on a vocational training course, as it does to the boy who is very backward and perhaps nearly illiterate. That these deficiencies should be diagnosed and attempts made to remedy them would seem an essential to all other aspects of training. For example, P. H. Shapland (1967) suggests that the non-verbal/verbal discrepancy which is known to exist among delinquents has implications for the benefits to be gained from group counselling. This is particularly important so far as the ability to use one's mother tongue, both orally and in written form, is concerned, not only for purely educational reasons, but also for social and personal reasons. If a part of the rehabilitation of delinquents is to try to get them to understand themselves and others, to develop them emotionally, and help them towards better personal relationships, then the ability to use language, both flexibly and fluently, is of paramount importance, for it is by means of language that all of us begin to come to terms with the experiences we encounter (see Flower, 1966 for a discussion of this point of view). The less articulate and developed a delinquent's use of language is, the more likely it will be that he does not begin to fully understand and consequently come to terms with, many experiences he encounters daily. The same argument is, of course, true for those in charge of delinquents.

In order to discover deficiencies in the basic skills, a standardized battery of achievement tests will need to be given to every boy and this might well be carried out on arrival at the training borstal.[1] This information would provide the basis on which the Tutor Organizer, or a member of his department, could then discuss with the individual concerned a number of possible short-term goals, for example the need to remedy a particular deficiency in numeration or literacy, so that he might then begin to work towards certain long-term educational goals. This would have application, for example, to boys who may have potential for vocational training, but are prevented from starting a course because of certain deficiencies in Mathematics. A full-time teaching programme might quickly remedy this situation.

The results of the achievement tests are likely not only to reveal differences in individual achievement in the constituent sub-tests, but also a wide range of achievement within a particular borstal population. The practical implications of this situation would seem to be that educational programming must be on a more individualized basis, designed to enable a boy to move at his own pace. In the case of boys who are very backward, some programme learning techniques and teaching machines may well need to be used, and because of their novelty might have better success in teaching basic skills than more traditional methods, which have failed for these boys in the past. Individual programming where possible also attempts to provide a solution to the problem of educational provision for a population that is never static but which is continually recruiting and discharging its members.

It has been suggested that a deficiency in basic skills may well prevent boys from obtaining the maximum benefit from all other aspects of training, for example further education opportunities, group counselling, and the day-to-day need to communicate effectively with people who are trying to offer help and guidance. If this is accepted, it would seem essential that boys who have a deficiency are able to spend frequent and concentrated periods of time during the day remedying this situation. This is vital, not only if future training in the institu-

---

[1] It has been shown in Chapter II, Section F, and Chapter IV, Section B, that the allocation procedure is often not affected by the information obtained from intelligence and vocational tests. It would seem more practical, therefore, and avoid the present duplication, if the main responsibility for educational testing was shifted from the Allocation Centre to the individual training borstals. Thus Tutor Organizers, who will have to programme for individual needs, would also be responsible for ascertaining them.

tion is to benefit, but also if individual interest is to be maintained.

2. THE ACQUISITION OF NEW SKILLS AND KNOWLEDGE

If one assumes that an individual's total score in the Standard Progressive Raven Matrices non-verbal test 'provides an index of his intellectual capacity, whatever his nationality or education' (Raven, 1956, p. 1), it would seem that the intellectual capacity of a large number of boys in borstal is above average, and that approximately one-fifth obtain a score which places them among the top 10 per cent of the population on this particular test. Whilst one does not want to over-estimate the results of this one test, they do seem to suggest, bearing in mind the total argument on intelligence put forward earlier, that a large number of boys in borstal may well be more intellectually able than certain criteria would appear to indicate. For example, the small number of boys who attended a grammar school; and the small number who have obtained a qualification in nationally recognized examinations.

The only extensive provision in borstal training today, which offers a sustained intellectual challenge, is the vocational training courses. Whilst not wishing in any way to denigrate the challenge these courses offer, and the satisfaction they may give to an individual, it does seem that there might be other intellectual challenges which could be more rewarding and demanding to many of these boys, and that the educational programme in borstal ought to be trying to tap the potential which seems to be there. This is given further emphasis from the fact that three-quarters of the sample, in answering the *questionnaire*, said that they were interested in further study, and 40 per cent were anxious to obtain, on release, a job involving some skill and/or responsibility.

In addition, these boys are members of a society in which education has become one of the main means of social mobility, and where consequently the need for qualifications has ever-increasing emphasis (Little and Westergaard, 1964). This study has indicated some of the factors which militate against certain members of our society (which includes many boys sentenced to borstal training) from taking full advantage of the existing educational provision, and it is suggested that this situation provides a powerful argument for providing another opportunity for boys to develop their intellectual potential during training. Many of these boys at their present educational level are unlikely to move outside the ranks of the unskilled worker, and the trend towards mechanization is likely to restrict further their opportunity for upward mobility. If one accepts the arguments of the delinquent sub-culture theorists, it is this failure to realize aspirations and expectations through legitimate channels that results in the kind of behaviour which seeks these satisfactions in illegitimate channels (Cohen, 1955; Cloward and Ohlin, 1960; Downes, 1966).

On the basis of the argument advanced so far it would seem common sense to try to provide a creative outlet for intellectual potential rather than let it become even further distorted. Full-time education along the lines of that offered in further education could provide the challenge which many of these boys need.

However, any suggestion for the extension of opportunities to acquire new skills and knowledge during borstal training is likely to be countered by the argument that those already provided are not used to full advantage. Thus the Governor of Feltham in answer to a question about the advisability of extending trade training facilities replied that: 'We are having great difficulty in persuading boys to take up the existing facilities' and finds this 'a little strange . . . [as] they are quite attractive and useful courses' (Cmnd. 599, 1966–67, p. 259). Further support for this argument is provided by the small number of boys who take up a job in the trade for which they have been trained on release. One explanation of this may be the lack of alternative opportunities, which may result in a boy enrolling on a trade course, rather than face the boredom of a dull routine, although he may not have the interest and inclination to take the trade up as a job on release. However, an explanation for this cannot be found by looking at the problem in isolation from the total organization of borstal training, which it has been argued is a factor motivating strongly against an individual's perception of the value of further education during training (see Venables, 1967, pp. 151–4 for a discussion of motivating factors in trade courses). It is suggested that changes in organization along the lines outlined in this study are essential, if there is to be an extension of the educational opportunities in borstal.

163

There are obviously a number of difficulties which will create problems for those trying to extend educational opportunity, especially for more able boys. One major problem is the small number of boys in each borstal, which means that it will be difficult to provide a range of viable courses. Another problem is the indeterminate sentence which may mean that some boys start a course but are released before finishing it.

In order to ensure that boys would be able to spend a reasonable amount of time in pursuing more challenging educational objectives, it is envisaged that the arrangements and methods of working would be along the lines already outlined; teachers involved would be employed on a full-time basis and boys would spend part of each day on educational activities. Where possible it would seem essential that a close link with a local College of Further Education is made, so that boys could attend some courses daily which could not be provided by the existing educational staff in borstal. One additional beneficial result of a link of this kind would be to enable the delinquent to come into contact with a more stable peer group in society, and to identify with the outside world rather than feel rejected by it.

Although each institution will probably only be able to offer a limited number of intellectually challenging courses, there could be a reasonable variety if they are imaginatively conceived in conjunction with those offered wherever possible by local Colleges of Further Education. And if imaginative and individual programming is devised, using, where suitable, programme learning techniques, the number of alternatives offered could be sufficient to challenge many of the boys.

This kind of approach would also have some carry-over into the arrangements for vocational training courses which would now be seen as an integral part of the whole education programme. Recruitment to all courses might, therefore, become an on-going process and not limited as at present to six-monthly periods; the employment of full-time technical teachers working in close liaison with the trade instructors would give the latter the extra time needed for the approach to be on an individual level. Where suitable, the use of programme learning techniques, which are already being discussed for use in vocational training, would lend support to this new approach, and enable boys to progress at their own speed and to their own level (Cmnd. 3408, 1966, p. 32).

It would also be profitable if attempts were made to introduce greater flexibility into examination dates. The report (Cmnd., 3408) also states that there has already been considerable co-operation on behalf of external examining bodies, who 'have agreed to hold hold two examinations yearly instead of one' largely to cater for the particular needs of penal establishments. Recent changes in the approach to industrial training, and the consequent setting up of Industrial Training Boards from 1964 onwards, suggests that any attempt to improve training facilities would receive a sympathetic hearing. It might be fruitful if representations were made about examination dates for borstal.

It would seem crucial for an individual's motivation to work at this level, and to ensure a carry-over on release, that the boys concerned are aware of the available opportunities to use their new qualifications once they leave the institution, and that this is taken into consideration in the arrangements for after-care. The opportunity to learn new skills or knowledge is in itself obviously not sufficient to enable a delinquent to obtain a more satisfying and constructive place in society on release. This provision needs to be fully supported by a policy which attempts to alleviate the factors which may prevent an ex-borstal boy from using his new skill or knowledge.[1] It suggests the need at the beginning of training to explore job and educational opportunities as they appertain in the area to which an individual is planning to return, and to relate this to educational goals. Only one of the institutions visited made a systematic attempt through the probation service, at the beginning of training, to ascertain employment opportunities in the area to which the boy would return on release, and then related this information to the kind of employment (vocational training in particular), he pursued during training. The fact that in most institutions enrolment on a trade course is not preceded by a careful investigation into the possibilities of a boy getting a job in that trade on release, may be one reason why some boys, having completed a course, do not continue in that trade on being discharged from the institution. In addition, there seems

---

[1] The need to take cognizance of the situation on release, and some methods of dealing with it, are described in the reports of experimental projects in vocational training carried out in the U.S.A. (*The MacLaren Vocational Center*, 1967, pp. 25–6; *16th Progress Report*, Draper Correctional Center, 1967, Appendix E.)

to be a place for a public relations policy which attempts not only to enlist the support of future employers, trade officials and educational institutions by keeping them informed of what is going on in borstal institutions but which also invites their co-operation in any re-appraisal of particular educational provision.

3. THE CREATION OF NEW VALUE SYSTEMS AND
   BEHAVIOUR NORMS

It cannot be expected that the provision of educational facilities so far outlined would be sufficient in themselves to ensure the successful rehabilitation of the borstal boy into society. One essential element must be the provision of some direct re-socialization experience aimed at modifying the negative and delinquent attitudes of borstal trainees, and substituting more positive and humane attitudes. It is not sufficient, for example, to provide a boy with the opportunity to learn a skilled trade if, at the same time, no attempt is made to modify his perception of the value of work; employment records, prior to present committal, suggest that many boys sentenced to borstal training may well have acquired an attitude which devalues the importance of conventional work careers (Downes, 1966, pp. 236–9).

It could be argued that the need to try to modify delinquent attitudes and values is already recognized in borstal training. Group counselling, for example, is practised at all the institutions visited. The main aim in introducing this technique into penal establishments was, as the Prison Commissioners (1962) point out, 'to help correct, in some degree, the distorted view which many inmates have of themselves and of society, and which is often responsible for the behaviour which has brought them into conflict with the law'. Groups are led by lay members of staff who 'retain complete discretion to use information as they think fit either in the interest of security and good order of the institution or in the interests of a particular individual'. It is, however, likely that boys are aware of this fact, and this situation within the context of a penal institution, in which detention is indeterminate and release is earned, may inhibit completely open and frank discussion because of the fear that certain things said may delay one's discharge from the institution. In addition, it was apparent at the time of the visits to borstals, that not all the institutions had adequate facilities for training those lay staff involved in counselling, nor were they receiving adequate advice from the Prison Service psychologists. A lack of proper training can only aggravate a situation in which there will be in any case role conflict, for in counselling situations borstal staff are expected to be confidants and guides, whereas in other situations, outside the group, they must revert to the role of the more traditional authority figure (Morrison, 1960, p. 287).

It is suggested that if the organization of group counselling were to become the responsibility of the education department in borstal institutions, some of the existing problems and conflicts might be overcome, or at least alleviated. If group counselling were part of an educational programme which was not perceived by the boys as simply another aspect of the kind of total structure existing at present, it might be possible to create more favourable conditions for the engendering of new attitudes and values. (Morrison, 1960, pp. 283–93 discusses group counselling within a penal setting.)

The introduction of this proposal would imply that the Tutor Organizers in borstals, and if possible some of the members of their department, should have a knowledge of group dynamics. It would suggest that this knowledge should be a condition of appointment, or that Tutor Organizers should be seconded by the Prison Department, in order to attend a suitable course. Tutor Organizers with this qualification would be able to provide continuous in-service training for members of the lay staff who were involved in counselling. 'The training system of choice here would appear to involve regular counselling groups for counsellors, these being run on a mixed-experience-teaching basis' (Morrison, 1960, p. 293; Jones, 1966, discusses training method). Provision of this kind would seem essential if it is accepted that intensive forms of treatment do not only have to be carried out by the psychiatrists or highly trained case-workers, but that Prison Officers 'could be as effective, or more effective, than so-called professional workers in treatment efforts, given that they were provided with a modest degree of behavioural knowledge through in-service training' (Gibbons, 1965, pp. 161–3).

It is further suggested that in the kind of education programme which has so far been outlined, and within a total environment orientated to training, such as that which exists in borstal institutions, it ought to be possible to move towards milieu management treatment (McCorkle *et al.*, 1958; Pilnick *et al.*, 1967). This is a total therapeutic environment in which group therapy is one aspect 'in which the situation in all its details represents an experiment in social living, so that by learning how to adjust to the institution, the inmate also learns how to manage himself in a law-abiding fashion in the free community' (Gibbons, 1965, pp. 163–74).

It would seem important to point out that the techniques of group therapy at present practised in borstal institutions, and which it is suggested might be the responsibility of the education department, are not necessarily suited to the needs of all boys sentenced to borstal training. To assume this would be to ignore the fact 'that offenders are characterized by various patterns of definitions rather than by a single set of beliefs, attitudes, and the like which set them off from . . . non-delinquents'.

Obviously individual interpretations of events and understandings of a given situation will vary from boy to boy, as will the experiences which produce them. Consequently, 'no single kind of therapy activity can be expected to accomplish treatment'. It is to be expected then that some boys will require very specialized individual treatment, such as psycho-therapy, and other boys, who show no obvious anti-social or adjustment problems, may require no treatment at all. Thus, Gibbons (1965), after identifying nine delinquent types (pp. 74–97) and six patterns of treatment (pp. 129–88) puts forward recommendations for the way in which the two could be matched (pp. 228–52).

4. THE PROVISION OF RECREATIONAL, CULTURAL
AND ARTISTIC OPPORTUNITIES

The fact that the habitual leisure activities of many boys sentenced to borstal are very limited and that consequently there is a need to try to widen the individual's horizons and experience during training have already been discussed. It has also been suggested that one of the most important considerations in the present educational provision in borstal institutions is to widen leisure interests (Home Office, 1960, p. 58).

It is felt, however, that one of the fundamental needs of delinquents 'is to engage in and be rewarded adequately by the society in which they live' (Downes, 1966, p. 264); this need applies to the whole life experience and should not be seen as only applying to particular aspects, such as work or non-work. It would seem fundamental in any attempt to satisfy this need that a guiding principle should be that of involvement and active participation on the part of individuals in decisions which affect their lives. The proposals for education outlined so far have attempted to introduce this approach; it might be possible to extend this concept even further while at the same time attempting to widen an individual's horizons; and recreational, cultural and artistic facilities could provide such an opportunity.

In addition, it is suggested that provision should be made to compensate for the negative aspects of institutional life; consignment to an institution can be a painful process resulting not only in a loss of freedom but also autonomy, as well as the absence of physical comforts and normal heterosexual contacts. All of these experiences could be said to undermine an inmate's self-image resulting from his way of life outside the institution (Sykes, 1958, pp. 63–83). It points to the need to provide legitimate opportunities for borstal boys to re-establish their self-image in relation to the society of which they are now a member. In some respects recognition of this need is already acknowledged in the variety of sporting, outdoor pursuits and voluntary social service activities in various institutions (Cmnd. 3408, 1966, pp. 17–20).

In order to realize the aims which have been outlined above, it is felt that educational activities in the evening should not have the total compulsion that exists at the moment. There should be more element of choice in the way an individual spends the time after 'work'. It is further suggested that if the boys were in some measure responsible for determining the evening activities, this would increase their inclination to participate.

In any choice of the kind of provision which might be made in the evenings it would seem important to emphasize the active involvement of everybody concerned in decision-making and in the choice of activities; ideally one wants to have a situation of flexibility which makes it possible for groups to be created to meet a particular demand. These groups could be assisted,

169

as at present, by a variety of people drawn from both inside and outside the institution; furthermore, boys might run their own groups within the over-all supervision of the education department. It would not seem essential that groups should be organized by teachers; the important criteria is that whoever assists the groups should have the ability to communicate a particular interest imaginatively, and a willingness to try to understand the members of the group as people rather than simply as delinquents. If one agrees with D. Matza's assumption (1964, pp. 1–30) that a substantial majority of juvenile delinquents are not 'radically differentiated from the rest of conventional youth' then a willingness to understand them would seem essential as a counter-balance to the delinquent self-image which may result from a sentence to a penal institution.

Although it is envisaged that certain groups would be open-ended, as is the case at present, it would seem essential that provision should also be made for closed groups; this would enable the growth of group loyalties and group achievement, perhaps resulting in the production of some concrete evidence of the combined effort. It would also seem essential that facilities should be available for those boys who want to sit quietly and read in comfortable surroundings, the library being one obvious room for this. There should be other opportunities, in addition to those already mentioned, for the boys to meet people from outside the institution. This would seem to present another way of establishing contacts with other institutions such as Colleges of Education and Universities catering for young people. The opportunity of working on joint projects or making informal social contact with students, through, for example, discussion groups, would help to reinforce stable peer group norms, as opposed to delinquent norms and values. Contact of this kind might also help in the realization, so far as borstal education is concerned, that this education is also further education.

There would also seem to be a place for arranging meetings along the lines of those which are organized by student unions. Boys could invite speakers to address them, and could be responsible for entertaining them. This might, in part, take the place of some of the present Discharge Programmes. It would seem essential that an opportunity for discussion and mutual exchange of views with a wide range of people, rather than the formal lecture and question procedure, should be available throughout an individual's stay in the institution, and would be part of the on-going process of preparation for the return to society. Programmes of this kind would seem essential if prejudices and misconceptions about each other on the part of both the delinquent and the general public are to be eroded.

There would obviously be a need for sensitive guidance and supervision if this kind of contact is to be mutually beneficial, and the education department would seem to have an obvious role to play in this.

Finally, it would seem beneficial to the general life of the institution, and obviously to the programme of education, if boys could be encouraged to participate in some decisions related to the general day-to-day running of the borstal. In this way one would hope to establish a feeling of commitment and involvement to the training programme, while at the same time preparing individuals for a responsible involvement in the society to which they will return.

In conclusion, it would seem important to emphasize, however, that the proposals which have been outlined are not conceived to apply in their entirety to all borstal institutions. Rather they are an outline of the particular contribution education might make as part of a programme of reformatory training; the extent to which an educational contribution is required will depend ultimately on the needs of the particular individual concerned.

(D) STRUCTURAL AND ORGANIZATIONAL CHANGES

It has been argued that the introduction of professional specialists, such as Tutor Organizers, into borstal institutions did not result in a re-examination and re-definition of the existing value system, but that the new specialists and their departments were grafted on to an existing 'training' structure. This has resulted in a lack of integration seen clearly in the individual borstal, where, for example, vocational and educational departments are separate. This same divisiveness exists in the Head Office of the Prison Department, where the responsibility for education and vocational training is shared between three departments. The divisiveness could be said to be reinforced by a system of communication, which tends to be one way and authoritarian rather than one of interaction and dialogue (Garrity, 1964). The organizational framework could therefore be said to encourage each individual department of the Prison Service to pursue its own goals and values, which may conflict with those of other departments, rather than encourage integration and common aims. It has been suggested that in such a situation the interests of the Tutor Organizer's department have often been circumscribed and subordinated, and this has been accentuated because unlike other departments education is not supported by its own bureaucratic structure.

It would appear, therefore, that the proposals outlined in the previous section could not be implemented in the existing structure and are consequently dependent on structural and organizational changes both in the Head Office of the Prison Department and in individual borstals. It is proposed in the following section to discuss some of the changes which seem fundamental if educational goals are to be attained within a training structure.

1. THE ROLE OF THE PROFESSIONAL EDUCATIONIST IN BORSTAL TRAINING

An examination of the present role of Tutor Organizer has indicated that any attempt to redress the present imbalance between training and educational goals must involve a redefinition and extension of the role of the professional educator within borstal training. The theoretical model for an educational contribution to borstal training envisages the expansion of the present opportunities for obtaining new skills and knowledge. Consequently, the Tutor Organizer will need more full-time teachers on his staff. The model also presupposes the integration of vocational training into the educational programme, and it is envisaged that the Tutor Organizer would have over-all responsibility for all education within the institution which would now include vocational training.

In addition, it is suggested that the education department could become more integrated into the total training structure if it were realized that the professional knowledge of the Tutor Organizer and his staff had relevance to all members of the institution, both staff and boys. This implies a further extension of the role of Tutor Organizer and could include the official recognition of his contribution to Discipline Staff training, through, for example, guidance on counselling techniques, or in relation to Discipline Staff promotion examinations. At present all Discipline Officers have the same basic training, which ensures that they are interchangeable between prison and borstal institutions. This suggests there is a need to provide continuous in-service training in borstal institutions for Discipline Staff, if they are to adjust to the particular role expected of them in a borstal training regime. The Tutor Organizer's department could make an important contribution to this process. Such recognition would establish the professional status of the Tutor Organizer. It would also seem important for inmate, staff relationships that the Tutor Organizer should try to provide in the education department facilities which could be shared by both staff and boys. In one institution visited the Tutor Organizer felt that the fact that a French course had also been attended by staff wives had greatly contributed to its success and to better relationships in the institution. One of the results of this kind of contribution to the total life of the institution could be that members of staff have first-hand evidence of the relevance of education to the over-all training programme. It is obviously important that staff have a positive conception of the educational provision, if their co-operation is to be gained in the achievement of educational goals.

It is obvious, however, that real recognition and acceptance of educational goals by the institution as a whole will not be achieved so long as the position of Tutor Organizer carries status but no real power within the hierarchy of authority. This applies at both institutional level and within the governing structure of the Head Office of the Prison Department.

Yet, it is interesting to note that some Tutor Organizers, when interviewed, defended the present situation on the grounds that, as outsiders, they have more freedom of action than if they were members of the Prison Service. They argued that in their present position they were not circumscribed in their actions through being part of a hierarchical structure within the Prison Department. Furthermore, they maintained that a system of short-term appointments to the post of Tutor Organizer ensured that there was a constant influx of new educational ideas into the penal service, and prevented individual Tutor Organizers from atrophying by being too long in one particular borstal.

Although the arguments regarding the Tutor Organizer's comparative freedom appear to be attractive and to have some validity, when one comes to examine closely what actually happens in borstal, one finds, as has already been argued, that the Tutor Organizer's actions are circumscribed because of the minor role that education plays in borstal training, and that they may be even further circumscribed, as his role is subject to the individual Governor's interpretation, which may not necessarily be a favourable one. In addition, a short-term appointment will inhibit long-term planning and commitment, which in turn circumscribes the Tutor Organizer's actions, and contribution to the establishment. Were he to have an official status within the Prison Service hierarchy, his role would be more clearly defined, and if, as has been argued, education were to play a greater role in borstal training, he would be less circumscribed than at present.

As for the argument regarding the influx of new educational ideas into the Prison Service, this can be brought about in a variety of ways. Perhaps the most obvious are the individual Tutor Organizer's own desire to keep himself abreast of new educational ideas, coupled with attempts to break down the isolation of penal education from education in other institutions.

It would seem then that if Tutor Organizers are to gain equal recognition for educational objectives and values within the total training programme, the education department, like other departments, must be fully internalized within the penal structure. (The present situation in the Forces, so far as education is concerned, might be considered a good parallel.) The structural changes which this would necessitate must, however, allow for the fact that the development of education within the Prison Service is as dependent on links outside the service as on integration within it. Consequently, some special arrangements might have to be made with local authorities, for example, so that these links might be forged and maintained.

At the institutional level, the internalization of the education department implies that the position of the Tutor Organizer becomes a full-time appointment to the Prison Service, and not one in which the appointee is, as at present, seconded from his Local Education Authority for a period of time. The appointment, with over-all responsibility for all educational activities in a particular institution, would carry equivalent status as other departmental heads, such as the Chief or Administration Officer. As such, the Tutor Organizer would be automatically represented at meetings of departmental heads, and would be involved in discussions of total training policy, neither of which necessarily happens at present.

It would also seem important to the attainment of power and authority within the institution that Tutor Organizers have the support of their own bureaucratic structure, in the same way as other departments. The employment of more teachers on a full-time basis would go some way to achieving this, but it is also important that a number of Discipline Staff should be attached to the Tutor Organizer's staff to assist in the work of the education department. This would help to break down the isolation of the specialist department which frequently occurs within such a stratified structure as the Prison Service, and would lead to the expansion, rather than contraction of, the role of the Discipline Officer, as a result of closer contact with professional teachers. The existence of a bureaucratic structure within the education department would also release the Tutor Organizer from some aspects of the daily administrative running of his department and enable him to devote more time to experimenting and planning educational policy and to discussion of the over-all training programme both with his own department and within the institution as a whole.

It has been necessary to outline in some detail proposals for more recognition of another interest group within the administrative structure of an institution. It must be emphasized that the purpose of these proposals is not to subordinate the goals of other departments to those of education, but to achieve equal recognition and status for educational goals. To achieve this, however, would also seem to require a redefinition of the administrative structure at all levels. It will be necessary to encourage each department to regard its contribution towards a common aim as being more important than the imposition of its own particular norms on the other departments, and consequently on the life of the institution and the future life-style of the inmates.

Finally, it would seem highly desirable that if there is to be integration of education and vocational training within institutions, integration should also take place within the Home Office itself. The creation of a department which has over-all responsibility for all aspects of education, and subsumes the existing, fragmented departments into itself, would seem to be essential if a new role for education is to be developed.

2. THE NEED FOR A CAREER STRUCTURE

The redefinitions and extensions of the role of education within borstal training necessarily imply a reassessment of the qualifications needed for the post of Tutor Organizer. All Tutor Organizers should be trained teachers, but it would also seem important that their experience and training should have prepared them to deal with young delinquents who have many personal and social problems. Consequently, it would seem desirable that Tutor Organizers had taught in secondary or further education and in addition had some kind of experience or training in the application of the social sciences. This might take one of several forms, such as a training in counselling techniques, or a diploma in one of the social sciences, or training in, or experience of, work in some aspect of the Youth Service. Alternatively, this might be a degree qualification in one of the social sciences, followed by further training and experience as a teacher.

As has already been indicated, the continuity and conservation of educational provision and the employment of highly trained teachers is almost impossible so long as the present conditions of employment for teachers in borstal institutions exist.

The need to build up a career structure within the Prison Service would seem essential if well-qualified teachers are to be attracted to the post of Tutor Organizer, and if a body of experience is to be built up and conserved. A proper career structure would seem equally important to the recruitment of the right kind of full-time teachers, from whom future Tutor Organizers could be appointed. The internalization of the education department within the Prison Service must not mean, however, that the only real opportunities for teachers are within the Service. (If this were to be the case, there would be a strong argument for retaining the present situation.) There must be easy transfer in, and out of, penal education, which can only be achieved if a career in penal education parallels that in other educational institutions, so far as posts of responsibility are concerned, for example, and if increments and pension rights are transferable. Unless this were guaranteed, there would be difficulty in recruiting imaginative and experienced teachers, who while prepared to serve several years in the Prison Service might wish eventually to transfer to another kind of educational institution.

A career structure in penal education would also need to be closely integrated with the total secondary/further educational provision, and not be in isolation as at present. One way of ensuring this is to develop and maintain links with other educational institutions and consequently involve their staff and students in the life of a borstal institution. By involving other educational institutions one would not only counteract the problem of the professional isolation of the teacher in penal institutions but would also provide other teachers and their students with the opportunity to experience the environment of such an institution. This would lead to a greater knowledge and understanding of the problems involved, and also to a greater awareness of the opportunities that are available in this particular area of education.

A career structure for Tutor Organizers, however, must not be confined to work within the institutions. The most important policy decisions concerning borstal institutions are made in the Head Office of the Prison Department, which would seem to indicate that there is a need for educational goals to be represented in the hierarchy of authority which exists outside individual institutions. One way of achieving this representation would be to create certain posts in which the appointees would have over-all guidance for the educational provision within a number of penal institutions, in a manner similar to Local Authority advisers and inspectors. It is envisaged that the creation of such posts would provide the essential link between the policy-making body at Head Office and the Tutor Organizers in the field; it might also enable more positive use to be made of the advisory services of the various Local Education Authorities. Creation of these posts would provide the career structure already in existence in other departments of the Prison Service, from which the administrative appointments to Head Office could be made. This would not only ensure that educational goals were represented in policy decisions at this level but also the administrator responsible had had experience of education in penal institutions.

(E) THE NEED FOR RESEARCH

The proposals for an educational contribution to borstal training have been put forward in the form of a theoretical model; their validation, which could be broadly defined as their relevance to the future needs of borstal trainees, has yet to be assessed. In order that assessment can be carried out in a scientific manner, it would seem important that an in-built research programme should be conceived of as an integral part of borstal training; this implies that research workers should play a role in planning the actual form of training, as well as be responsible for a continuous evaluation of the methods which are being used (Hood, 1965, p. 217).

Experimentation with the educational aspect of training suggests the need for the establishment of research projects in borstal institutions in collaboration with University Schools of Education or Colleges of Education. In this way controlled and scientific experimentation into both the content, approach and success of learning in borstal institutions could be carried out in collaboration with educational specialists. For example, the role of programmed learning or the problems of adult illiteracy could be systematically investigated by experts in these particular fields, and their findings disseminated to other borstals.

The introduction of research workers should help achieve a greater degree of integration between penal and educational institutions, and would provide a source of support and constant feedback and dialogue for the full-time teaching staff in the institution.

One method of approach might be to set up in one or possibly two institutions a research project into educational aspects of training with a view to establishing their validity for more widespread application to borstal training.

It has already been pointed out that the proposals for an educational contribution to borstal training have relevance in some degree to the needs of all boys. Consequently experiment and research should be concerned with a wide spectrum of boys and not a particular narrow group. It would seem desirable then that research should be carried out in an institution where an important consideration in the allocation decision has been the need for secure conditions, as well as in an open borstal. In addition to research work, there would also be experiments in development work. Once again University Schools of Education and Colleges of Education could be involved. For example, groups of students training to be teachers could, as part of their training, work regularly in a borstal institution, helping the full-time staff in introducing and teaching new materials. The introduction of students would facilitate the individual approach suggested in an earlier section; would establish a contact between the boys and other people of their own age, and might encourage prospective teachers to consider working in penal education. Material for this work might come from current Nuffield projects, such as the Resources for Learning Project or the Humanities Project. Alternatively, it could be devised by a University School of Education, or College of Education in collaboration with the staff at the borstal.

CODA

The purpose of this study has been to examine the development and present practice of education in borstal institutions, and its relevance to the needs of boys who have been sentenced to borstal training.

It has been shown that the realization that education has a role to play in any programme of borstal training has long been accepted. It has been suggested, however, that its present role is limited and circumscribed by its relationship to the total training structure, and that the latter is based on a set of concepts and principles which are no longer entirely relevant to the needs of the modern borstal boy.

This study has attempted a re-thinking of the role of education, one aspect of borstal training, and in so doing has inevitably questioned the validity of other aspects of this training. Proposals have been suggested for a different, and it is hoped a more successful approach, in which education plays a greater role. The validity of these proposals will need to be assessed if further re-thinking is to flourish.

One thing seems certain. The re-conviction rate of boys dis-

179

charged from borstal indicates that the present method of training is failing with a considerable proportion of boys, and that this number has been increasing steadily since 1955.[1] This evidence suggests that there is a need for a radical re-thinking of the principles on which borstal training has been developed over the last fifty years.

[1] Records, over a three-year period, of boys discharged from borstal in 1955, show that 47·7 per cent had not been re-convicted within that time; for 1962 (the latest year for which figures are available) the proportion is 33·3 per cent. (See *Report on the Work of the Prison Department*, Statistical Tables, 1965.)

Appendices

APPENDIX A

Abstractions C.P. Test 1

Wherever you see a dot, there is ONE letter or figure missed out.
Write letters or figures just above the dots.

1. A B C D .
2. 9 8 7 6 5 .
3. bad B sad S lad L had .
4. 2 4 6 8 10 . .
5. hot cold wet dry fast slow down . .
6. 212 323 434 545 . . .
7. grass green sky blue soot . . . . .
8. than an throughout out think . . .
9. Sunday 1 Monday 2 Saturday .
10. peat pea note not bowl . . .
11. 1d. inch 1s. foot 3s. . . . .
12. shark hark ark spill pill . . .
13. no on ten net deer . . . .
14. C 18 D 16 E 14 F 12 . . .
15. head hat foot shoe hand . . . .
16. she he still ill slow . . .
17. A Z B Y C X D W . .
18. January March May . . . .
19. finger hand arm toe foot . . .
20. we our she her he . . .
21. bag beg big . . . bug
22. he ha end and rein . . . .
23. 864 753 642 531 . . .
24. Wednesday Tuesday Friday Thursday Saturday
    . . . . . .
25. great get tarry try blind bid chain . . .
26. RZKT TRZK KTRZ . . . .
27. beneath bath swallow slow torrent . . . .
28. sheathe heath eat .
29. sloops pool unity tin zone . .
30. bread dread ham jam nail . . . .
31. umpire rum pie search she car estate tea . . .

Turn over and go straight to question 32

NUMBER.............................. .... NAME...

32. dough cough bough teal seal . . . .
33. B C E H L .
34. rain into tone . . . . atom
35. ALZ DMX GNV JOT . . .
36. sleet hail greet recline lie falsehood bag . . . .
    dismiss
37. DeF HiJ LmN . . .
38. 100 baa 201 cab 106 bag 543 . . .
39. dare ease fate h . . .
40. TOWN VQYP CITY . . . .

Literacy C.P. Test 102

Number............................... Name..

EXAMPLE 1: Cats like....................................*milk*, mittens, maize, mulch.
EXAMPLE 2: Snow is.. ....black, red, *white*, blue.

1. In winter it is...........................hot, cold, warm, sultry.
2. One writes with a............ ....ruler, rubber, pin, pen.
3. If a room is vacant it is...................................empty, damp, miser-
   able, hopeless.
4. Many ships make up a...... ....flock, fleet, flight, fleece.
5. One eats with a knife and.............................frock, force, fork,
   forceps.
6. A man who makes suits is a............................salesman, fitter,
   tailor, suitor.
7. The camel has a......................................bump, lump, hump, hemp.
8. A person who writes music is a...........................composer,
   compositor, composition, component.
9. In the morning you tidy your hair with a...........................come,
   cone, comb, corn.
10. To scare means to................ ....hurt, frighten, help, avoid.
11. Books may be borrowed from a...........................shop, church,
    garage, library.

12. A period of a hundred years is sometimes called a.............................
    decade, annual, century, centurion.
13. A man who runs away from danger is a.............................caviller,
    courier, cavalier, coward.
14. A girl dresses well to look.............................elevated, electric,
    elected, elegant.
15. To avoid upsetting people you should be.............................tacit,
    tactful, tawdry, taciturn.
16. To damage means to.............................pay, kill, beat, injure.
17. In December in England most trees have.............................many
    leaves, fruit, nuts, bare branches.
18. The snake went.............................running, jumping, swimming,
    gliding . . . away.
19. Electric light comes from the.............................switch, bulb, flex,
    fuse.
20. When the weather is stormy it is.............................windy,
    drizzly, sunny, foggy.
21. To acquit means to.............................agree, punish, depart,
    let off.
22. A person who is difficult to please is.............................flagrant,
    fastidious, fascinating, fabulous.
23. Selfish people are.............................egocentric, endogenous,
    esoteric, ectomorphic.
24. Most eccentric people are very.............................individualistic,
    indiscreet, industrious, indistinct.
25. Very hard menial work is just.............................durable,
    dredging, drudgery, dreaded.
26. To have catholic tastes means to like things that are.............................
    divine, religious, serious, diverse.

APPENDIX B

Questionnaire completed by a sample of 363 boys sentenced to borstal training

Below are some questions regarding the kind of education you have had. Everything you write will be treated as confidential and will in no way affect what happens to you in the future. Please answer these questions as carefully and as fully as possible. Where several alternatives are given always tick more than one if appropriate.

1. At what age did you leave school?   Years   Months

2. Why did you leave then?

3. Did you want to leave school at an earlier age than you did?

    YES
    NO

    If YES why did you want to leave earlier?

4. Did you want to leave school at a later age?

    YES
    NO

    If YES why did you want to stay on longer than you did?

5. Did you pass any exams before you left school?

    YES
    NO

    If YES what exams were they?

    G.C.E. 'A' Level
    G.C.E. 'O' Level
    R.S.A.
    Your own School Leaving Certificate
    Name any other

    Tick any exam that you sat, and list alongside the subjects in which you passed.

185

6. During your time in junior school were you absent on average:

> once or twice a term
> once or twice a month
> once or twice a week

7. Were you absent

> (1) because of illness
> (2) because you did not like school
> (3) for both reasons

8. During your time in secondary school were you absent on average:

> once or twice a term
> once or twice a month
> once or twice a week

9. Were you absent

> (1) because of illness
> (2) because you did not like school
> (3) for both reasons

10. Was your education ever interrupted for any length of time for any of the following reasons:

> (1) You moved house
> (2) You had a serious illness
> (3) You were sent to a residential institution other than a school

If answers to 1 or 2 is YES try and give time you were away from school.

11. Did you sit an exam at the age of 11?

> YES
> NO

If YES, did you pass it?

> YES
> NO

Question 12 onwards refers only to your SECONDARY SCHOOL career.

12. What kind of school did you go to after 11?

  Comprehensive
  Grammar
  Secondary Modern
  Technical
  Approved School
  Any other

  Tick all types of secondary school you attended. If you attended more than one school write down your age when you went there and how long you attended.

  (For the following questions if you attended more than one secondary school, choose the one you attended longest and answer all the questions on this.)

13. Was the school mixed
  single sex

14. What subjects did you study at secondary school?

English	Physical Education	Others:
History	French	
Geography	German	
Arithmetic	Latin	
Geometry	Woodwork	
Algebra	Metalwork	
Pottery	Art	
Music	Games	
Social Studies	Engineering	
Scripture	Gardening	
Biology	Technical Drawing	
Physics	Current Affairs	
Chemistry	Drama	
General Science		

15. Write as much as you like in answer to the following question:

  Which of the subjects you learnt at school have you found most useful in life and in what way?

16. How did the school prepare you for when you left?

  Did it tell you: Answer YES or NO

  (a) All the different kinds of work available to you in your area.
  (b) How to apply for any job you might want.

187

17. If the answer to any of 16 a, b, is YES, how were you given this information? Please give as full an answer as possible.

18. Did you discuss and learn about the following things at your school? Answer YES or NO.

    (a) How you claim benefits if you were unemployed or sick.
    (b) What happened to the money that was taken away from you in tax and insurance.
    (c) To have a hobby or interest outside your job.
    (d) To have an interest in foreign countries and their people and want to travel abroad.
    (e) To understand the news and follow what was going on in the world.
    (f) To be interested in local politics.
    (g) How to cast your vote.

19. What subjects did you enjoy most at school and why? Please give as full an answer as possible.

20. What do you remember about your teachers at SECONDARY SCHOOL? Were at least three quarters of the staff:

    (a) Able to control you and fair and reasonable.
    (b) Able to control you but unfair so you never knew how they might behave towards you.
    (c) Interested in you and your future.
    (d) Unable to control you.
    (e) Not interested in you.

21. Was the cane or other form of corporal punishment used in your school?

    YES

    NO

    If YES was it

    (a) *Often* used by *most* of the staff.
    (b) *Often* used by *some* of the staff.
    (c) *Often* used by *only* the head and deputy head.
    (d) *Rarely* used by *only* the head and deputy head.
    (e) Were you personally caned:
        Daily/twice a week/once a week/once a fortnight/ three times a term/once a term/never?
    (f) Why were you caned?

Appendices

22. Do you feel most of your teachers really knew what you were like or tried to find out?

> YES
> NO

23. What did your teachers think about you?

24. In view of the way you behaved at school, do you feel the picture most of them had of you was a fair one?

> YES
> NO

25. Did you attend any Further Education classes after you left school?

> YES
> NO

If YES

> (a) Evening
> (b) Day release
> (c) What subjects did you study?
> (d) How long did you attend.
> (e) Did you gain any qualifications through these classes?
>
> > YES
> > NO
>
> If YES—what were they?

26. With the wider experience of life you now have what subjects would you like to know more about? You need not limit yourself to normal school subjects.

27. Are you ever bored during your leisure time?

> Frequently   Hardly ever
> Moderately

28. How do you like to spend your leisure time? If you have any hobbies list these. Answer as fully as you can.

189

29. When you leave here what would you really like to do and become? Answer as fully as possible.

Your name:

Age: Years: Months:

Additional oral questions, arising from the questionnaire, which were answered by a sub-sample of 39 boys

2. Why did you leave then?

   Would you go into more detail on the answer you have written to this question?

5. Did you pass any exams before you left school?

   If answered no

   Did any of the pupils at the school you were attending take external exams?

   What exams did they take?

   Did you want to take them?

   If answered yes

   Why did you not take them?

   If answered no

   Why did you not want to take them?

   If answered yes to question 5

   In what ways do you think your exam passes have helped you since you left school?

6, 7, 8, 9. If the respondent has indicated that he absented himself at least once a month from school because he did not like it:

   What was it that you did not like about school?

   What action did the school take when you were away?

   What did your family say and do?

190

14. What subjects did you study at secondary school?

    Respondents were asked if they could describe how they were taught a selection of six of the subjects they had ticked in answer to this question. The subjects were selected in rotation.

15, 16, 17, 18. Do you feel that what you did at school prepared you for life and work after you left?

    Why do you say this?

20. What do you remember about your teachers at secondary school?

    Why have you ticked this particular alternative in answer to this question? Can you go into more detail as to how your teachers behaved?

21. Was the cane or other form of corporal punishment used in your school?

    If the respondent had indicated that he was caned three times a term or more frequently he was asked:

    Did the cane stop you doing the thing for which you were caned?

    Why do you say this?

22. Do you feel most of your teachers really knew what you were like or tried to find out?

    All the interviewees were asked: Did your teachers talk to you about matters other than those concerned with your school work, for example what you might have done at the weekend?

    Were you in trouble with the police whilst you were still at school?

    Did the school know about this?

    What did they do?

25. Did you attend any Further Education classes after you left school?

    If their answers indicated that they had had no experience of Further Education respondents were asked: Were there facilities for you to attend evening or day release classes after you left school?

191

Why did you not enrol?

If their answers indicated they had started a course but had not completed it the respondents were asked:

Why did you not complete the course for which you enrolled?

27. Are you ever bored during your leisure time?

    If answered frequently or moderately:

    Why do you think it is that you are bored in your leisure time?

29. When you leave here what would you really like to do and become?

    Would you go into more detail as to why you wrote what you did in answer to this question?

Schedule of questions used in the oral interview with Tutor Organizers

1. How well would you say these boys have been educated prior to their committal to training?

   To what extent do you feel the schools they have attended are responsible for what you describe?

   Would you say that inadequate education is a contributory factor in delinquent behaviour?

   How far?

   In what ways?

2. How interested are the boys in the idea of continuing their education during training?

   Why do you say this?

   Do you find that there is any change in attitude towards education as training progresses?

3. In theory what contribution do you think education has to make to the total training programme in this institution?

4. Are you able to offer a variety of courses which are adequate for the particular needs of the population here?

5. Do you think it is a good arrangement for the majority of boys to work during the day and come to classes in the evening?

6. How do you deal with the continuous turnover in population which takes place in borstal?

   What effect does this have on teaching method?

   Does this situation have any effect on the opportunities for examination work?

   What is the approximate length of time boys are available to attend classes?

7. Are the Vocational Training and Education Departments run as two separate departments in this institution?

   Would you say that the opportunities to learn a trade here are adequate?

   Is the attainment of a particular level in English and Mathematics an important consideration in the selection of boys for trade training?

   Do you find there is a discrepancy between the recommendations made by a Vocational Guidance Officer at the Allocation Centre and the actual practice in this institution?

8. Does the Education Department take any part in helping boys to find work on release?

   Are you responsible for organizing discussions concerned with the conditions and problems of the work situation?

9. As a result of their work in the Education Department, how much contact are the boys able to have with life outside the institution?

10. Are you responsible for making follow-up arrangements for boys to continue with a particular course of study after their release?

11. In what particular ways would you say your education programme was trying to widen an individual's horizons, and extend his range of interests?

12. What information is available to you on an individual's previous education experience?

    Are you able to have any contact with schools which boys have attended in the past?

13. What is the range of intellectual ability for which you have to cater here?

    On what information are you basing your answer?

14. What proportion of your population is completely illiterate?

    Apart from the previous group, what proportion of your population requires remedial work in English and/or Mathematics?

How are you defining backwardness in your answer?

On what criteria do you base the selection of boys who need to attend remedial classes during the day?

15. How are boys allocated to particular classes?

16. What opportunities are there for boys of above average intelligence to extend themselves?

> What proportion of your population are able to take advantage of these opportunities?

> How do you select those boys who have the opportunity to do educational work during the day?

17. Is it compulsory for boys to attend a certain number of evening classes a week?

Are certain classes compulsory?

> Tutor Organizers were then questioned about particular classes which appeared on their programmes; facilities which were available and approach used.

18. Do you have any difficulty in recruiting teachers to work here?

Are you able to have regular discussions with your teachers as to over-all educational policy?

How often does this take place?

Do the teachers have much influence on the training programme as a whole here?

19. What audio visual aid equipment do you have here?

20. Do you feel isolated in any way as a teacher working in a penal institution?

Do you have an opportunity to express your opinion on the institution boards?

In the allocation of grades do you feel that work done in education carries the same weight as other considerations?

Are you consulted in the formulation of over-all training policy?

What would you say your rank was within the institutional hierarchy?

How sympathetic are the borstal staff to what you are trying to do in education?

Does what you have said apply to all of the staff here?

21. In what way does your Local Education Authority contribute to the education programme carried out here?

    What is the contribution of the Head Office of the Prison Department?

    To what extent and in what way is the Governor able to influence the work of the Education Department?

    How much co-operation is there between your Local Authority and the Prison Department over educational policy in this institution?

22. To what extent do the demands of security affect what you can do?

    Have there been any changes which have affected the Education Department, as a result of the Mountbatten Report?

Schedule of questions which were put to the Vocational Training Instructors

1. By what method are boys selected to train in your particular trade?

   (If the reply indicated that additional testing was carried out in the training borstal the instructor was asked why this was necessary, in view of the trade testing which took place at the Allocation Centre.)

2. How many boys on your courses have been recommended to do this particular trade by the Allocation Centre?

   Do you have boys on your courses who have not been recommended as suitable for trade training by the Allocation Centre?

   What proportion of the total number on the course?

   Why is there this discrepancy between the decisions of the Vocational Guidance Officer and the actual practice in this institution?

3. Do you assist in the selection of boys for your trade?

 On average how many boys will apply to do a course?

 How many are selected?

 On what criteria do you base your selection of boys for the course?

 Is a certain attainment level in Mathematics and English an important consideration?

 What is this attainment level?

4. Do you find that the fact that boys are sent here for an indeterminate length of time affects trade training in any way?

5. Is it possible for you to give an adequate training in your trade within a borstal institution?

APPENDIX D

Examples of educational tests administered at the training borstals

No............................ Surname..

Christian Name(s)..

What kind of books do you like?
Have you any hobbies? If so, what?
Have you any special interests in sport?

Every lad *must* go to classes once he achieves Training Grade and is promoted to a Training Wing. Have you any special preference? e.g. Art, Music, Gardening and Farming, First Aid, Carpentry, Handyman Classes, M/Vehicles, Refereeing/Sport, French, T/ Drawing. CIRCLE YOUR INTERESTS.

You may also, if your standard is low, require extra classes in English and Arithmetic—and you will be notified of these.

MAKE A NOTE IN YOUR DIARY OF YOUR ANSWERS ABOVE!

Attempt the following:

(a) Fill in the missing words:

1. In winter the nights are l............................
2. A whale is a m............................
3. It is never too late to l............................n
4. We waited in a q............................e
5. Telstar is a man-made sat............................
6. Duke of Ed............................'s Award
7. A s............................ in time saves nine
8. The lamp hangs from the c............................g
9. The Houses of P............................t
10. The Ch............................take the Church Parade

198

(b) Do the following sums—(do working overleaf)
1. $16+9 =$
2. $41+26 =$
3. 1s. 6d. $+9$d. $=$
4. 4s. 3d. $+6$s. 6d. $=$
5. $16-6 =$
6. $161-40 =$
7. $14\div2 =$
8. $29\times2 =$
9. $64\div4 =$
10. $31\times5 =$
11. $\frac{2}{5}$th of £1 $=$
12. 6s. 8d. $\times6 =$
13. $\frac{1}{2}\times\frac{1}{2} =$
14. $\frac{1}{2}\div\frac{1}{2} =$
15. A car does 30 m.p.g. How many gallons needed for 75 miles?
16. A car does 30 m.p.g. How many gallons needed for 210 miles?
17. A car does 30 m.p.g. How many miles would it travel on 1 pint?
18. What is the square root of 64?
19. What is the Formula for the area of a square?
20. What is the Formula for the area of a circle?

1	2	3	4			5
	6			■		
7					8	
9		■		■		■
10		11	■	12		
13						■
	■		■	14		

(c) Complete the following crossword:

Clues

Across

1. There are primary and secondary ones
6. You must obey it
7. Soldier with much service
9. Abbreviation of 'Avenue'
10. Jelly has to . . .
12. There . . . 20 in a score
13. A knight . . . . . . wandered in search of adventure
14. You pay to Government

Down

2. Skilful
3. Worn on head
4. Bill . . . John money
5. 92,000,000 miles away
7. Flowers arranged in
8. Main artery from heart
11. Score at Rugby
12. Small busy insect

ADD $+$	MULTIPLY $\times$	FRACTIONS

ADD $+$

1.
$$14$$
$$37+$$
___
$$=$$

2.
$$285$$
$$739+$$
___
$$=$$

3. $5+6+4$
ANS. $=$

4. $13+17+9$
ANS. $+$

SUBTRACT $-$

5.
$$38$$
$$23-$$
___
$$=$$

6.
$$743$$
$$347-$$
___
$$=$$

7. $81-39$
ANS. $=$

8. $243-29$
ANS. $=$

ADD and SUBTRACT

9. $28+17-9$
ANS. $=$

MULTIPLY $\times$

10.
$$43$$
$$3\times$$
___
$$=$$

11.
$$46$$
$$7\times$$
___
$$=$$

12.
$$438$$
$$47\times$$
___

DIVIDE $\div$

13. $4)96$

14. $8)264$

15. $29)1073($

16. $\dfrac{396}{9}$
ANS. $=$

17. $7\times6\div3$
ANS. $=$

18. $(5\times4)+(12\div16) =$

FRACTIONS

19. $\frac{3}{4}+\frac{1}{8} =$

20. $1\frac{7}{8}+2\frac{3}{4} =$

21. $\frac{5}{8}-\frac{1}{2} =$

22. $1\frac{2}{3}-\frac{1}{8} =$

23. $\frac{5}{6}$ of 1 ft. $=$
ins.

24. $\frac{3}{5}$ of £1 $=$
sh.

25. $\frac{1}{4}\times\frac{2}{3} =$

26. $3\frac{3}{5}\times1\frac{2}{3}$
ANS. $=$

27. $\frac{1}{4}\div\frac{1}{2} =$

28. $2\frac{4}{5}\div1\frac{2}{5}$
ANS. $=$

201

DECIMALS

29. $0·24+0·6+33·0 =$

30. $33·5-9·03 =$

31. $1·3 \times 1·3 =$

32. $13·2 \times 0·22 =$

AREAS

33.

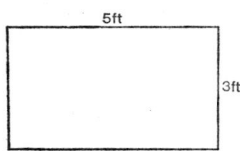

5ft

3ft

AREA =

34.

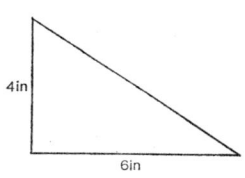

4in

6in

AREA =

35.

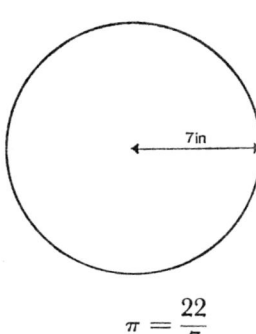

7in

$$\pi = \frac{22}{7}$$

AREA =

36.

```
|←————— 16ft —————→|
```

8ft 5ft 5ft 3ft 6ft 6in 5ft

This is a drawing of one wall of a room leaving the door and window out, what area remains to be painted?

ANS. =

37. Plumbers' solder is 67% lead and 33% tin. What weight of tin will be needed to make 100 lbs. of solder?

ANS. =

38. What is 20% of 75?

ANS. =

39. What is the cost of 3,500 bricks at £7 10s. per thousand?

ANS. =

40. What is the square root of 64?

ANS. =

41. If L = 120t−12, what is the value of t if L = 228?

ANS. =

42. $(a+b)(a-b) =$

43. Solve the equation
$3x-4 = 5$
$x =$

202

One institution used two differential aptitude tests, Numerical Ability Form A and Verbal Reasoning Form A which were produced by the Psychological Corporation, New York, U.S.A. The norms cf these tests had, however, only been standardized on an American High School population.

APPENDIX E

Syllabuses of basic subjects in institutions visited

Revision and Remedial Mathematics

As the attainment and ability of the lads concerned varies considerably any scheme of work designed for them must be very flexible and cover a wide range. It must be sufficiently comprehensive and practical to interest and extend each student whatever his level in the initial stages. Methods employed will be varied to suit individual requirements.

It is hoped that enough ground will be covered by the following outline syllabus to keep all students profitably occupied even if they should remain in the class for the full period of their borstal training.

Lesson time—1½ hours per week

Diagnostic tests

Individual work according to test results commencing at the most suitable point in the scheme of work

Simple rules—number—money—weights and measures

Areas

Simple problems involving the above

Shortened methods—aliquot parts

Compound quantities—L.C.M. and H.C.F.

Fractions—multiplication—division—simplification—brackets

Percentages—profit and loss—simple and compound interest

Practical problems of mensuration—areas. Costing and quantity surveying specifically related to available Vocation Training Courses which the student may be studying

Decimals—four simple rules

The Metric System

Ratio and proportion

Simple algebra, geometry and trigonometry if appropriate

Logarithms

The following text-books are available for use:

An Arithmetic of Everyday Affairs
Your Work and Wages
Kingway Mathematics for Seniors (Amber and Blue Series)
Mathematical Topics for Modern Schools

204

The predominating factor which will be always borne in mind is that abstract and theoretical themes are of little or no real value in this context, the emphasis must be firmly placed on real-life situations which are meaningful and can be readily understood.

Basic subjects of English and Arithmetic will appear, as far as possible, within a framework of Social Studies.

It may be that a teacher will *in fact* be teaching both English and Maths, but most classes will be so divided that the teacher will specialize on one (thus taking 2×1-hour classes in one evening but with two groups). Generally the books *Counting the Cost* and *Social English* provide the basis for study—and for most lads a minimum of 16 weeks will be needed. Of course, many will remain in the group for (much) longer. Remedial classes (particularly in English) may precede or parallel the Social Studies groups. A cyclical approach should be used, as lads may enter or leave the group at any point during the term—equally, this approach lends itself to the difficult conditions prevailing where lads may attend regularly, or may from time to time be working, on home leave, etc.

Rather than attempt to break up the syllabus in great detail I put forward the following main headings (and leave it to individual teachers to expand, vary, etc. in the light of their own individual experience).

ENGLISH

Communicating with people
  (a) for pleasure
  (b) for gain
  (c) to obtain information
  (d) to get/learn of a job

Using one's leisure
Knowing about people
  (a) general knowledge
  (b) specialized knowledge
  (c) newspapers and magazines
  (d) criticism

ARITHMETIC

  (a) budgets
  (b) incomings and outgoings
  (c) rates and taxes
  (d) 'other' deductions

Syllabus of a course which it was compulsory for all boys to attend throughout training
E.F.S. (Education for Society)

There will be three main topics:
  You and others
  You and the community
  You and the world

205

Books etc. so far available:
  Liberal Studies—L.S.
  Progressive Literacy—P.L.
  Take Home Booklets—T.H.B.
  Talking About Money—T.A.M.
  Useful Literacy—U.L.
  Educational Production Wallcharts—W.C.
  National Savings Booklets—N.S.B.

You and others   AUTUMN TERM

Topic	*Material Available*	
Keeping in Touch		
Communicating with others	Use of English	U.L.
Clear instructions, some	Accent on Accent	U.L.
letter writing, etc	Comprehension	P.L.
	Clear Instruction	P.L.
	The Essay	U.L.
	Dear Me and You Sir	T.H.B.
After Work		
Reading for pleasure, TV	Television	P.L.
Films, Music, Radio,	The Reading Habit	U.L.
Sport, etc	Music Hath Chorus	U.L.
	Invitation to a Dance	U.L.
	Adventure	U.L.
	Sport	U.L.
	Further Education	P.L.
	Leisure for Pleasure	T.H.B.
	Holidays	P.L.
Money Troubles		
Use of Ready Reckoner	Ready Reckoners	
Shopping, Personal Budget,	Choice, Luck and Skill	P.L.
H.P., Mortgage, Credit	Facts and Figures	P.L.
terms, etc	Money	P.L.
	Personal Economies	T.A.M.
	Talking About Money	T.A.M.
	Building Society and You	T.H.B.
	Shopping	T.A.M.
	Family Housekeeping	T.A.M.
	Thinking about Money	N.S.B.

206

It's a Paper World

Payment of bills, filling in forms, simple graphs, etc	Various forms will be available, e.g. Tax, labour, etc
	Several Arithmetic textbooks are also available for graphs

Pressures on You

Effects of Mass Media	Telling the Teenagers	U.L.
Pressures of Advertising.	Advertising	U.L.
Neighbourhood, Parents,	The Glass of Fashion	U.L.
Gangs, etc	Good Manners	P.L.
	The Commercials	P.L.
	Class or Status	P.L.

What's in the News?

Matters of great importance that are in the news	Wall Maps
	World, Europe, Africa, Asia, America, Australia, etc

You and Your Community   SUMMER TERM

You and Your Town

Local Government	You and Your Town	W.C.
Functions and activities,	Rate Demand	T.H.B.
Employers, Finance, etc	Running the Town	L.S.
	Town Planning	L.S.
	Spending for the neighbourhood	N.S.B.

Running the Country

Central Government	The British Constitution	W.C.
The Monarchy, Houses of	Elections and Parliament	W.C.
Parliament, Electoral	The Monarchy	W.C.
system, Party system,	Civil Service	W.C.
Civil Service, etc	Community or Chaos	T.H.B.

Do We Need Laws?

Why we have laws, how	Law and Order	P.L.
they are administered,	Watch and Ward	T.H.B.
Police, Jury, Courts, etc	Motoring	P.L.
	The Law	W.C.

We have Never Had it so Good

Welfare State	T.A.M.
Work	T.H.B.
Standards of Living	L.S.
Education	U.L.
Through Three Generations	L.S.
The Good Old Days	T.A.M.
The Cost of Living	T.A.M.

Getting on with the Boss

Labour relations in Britain, Trade Unions and Their Changing Role, Automation, Redundancy, the Structure of Industry, etc	From Dick Whittington to Act of Parliament	T.H.B.
	Change the Unions	T.H.B.
	Problems of Redundancy	T.H.B.
	Joining a Trade Union	T.A.M.
	The Structure of Industry	W.C.
	The T.U.C.	W.C.

You and the World　　SPRING TERM

Paying our Way

Britain's Trade, Wholesale and Retail, Private Enterprise versus Nationalization, National Housekeeping, Exports and Balance of Payments, etc	Commonwealth Trade	W.C.
	Spending for the Nation	N.S.B.
	National Housekeeping (Budget, Nationalization, Pound note, Paying our way, etc.)	T.A.M.
Common Market	The raw facts (Imports and Exports)	T.H.B.

Before and After the War

Political and economic events leading to the two great wars. The position in 1938. Territorial changes since 1942, and present difficulties, of European countries.	Europe—History,	
	1870–1939	W.C.
	1939–1948	W.C.
	War	P.L.
	Africa	W.C.
	India, Pakistan	W.C.
	Far East	W.C.
	South East Asia	W.C.

Appendices

Syllabus of a course at which attendance was compulsory for all boys in their Senior Training Grade

LIBERAL STUDIES SYLLABUS

SUBJECT CURRENT EVENTS	SKILL ENGLISH	SKILL MATHS
Main political parties Government/Commons/Lords History and Development	English and general knowledge	General maths.
World's trouble spots	Reading	Time/Distance
Space Travel	Comprehension	Time/Distance Cost and revenue
U.K.—Emigration/Immigration Questions and problems of inter-racial communities		Money rules Ratio and proportion
Emergence states Status old and new	Reading	Cost/Time/Distance
Struggle for power U.S. and U.S.S.R. Britain's part Alignments and neutralities	Reading and Comprehension	

SUBJECT CURRENT EVENTS	SKILL ENGLISH	SKILL MATHS.
Topical subjects—news headlines The 24 hour clock—why and wherefore	Reading and Comprehension	Time tables G.M.T. and B.S.T.
Commonwealth replacing Empire Modern education development and ideas Comprehensive selection at 11		
Christian Unity Ecumenical Council	Reading Comprehension General knowledge	
The Atomic age Present and future significance The Computer age The Binary system (basic)		

SUBJECT CIVICS	SKILL ENGLISH	SKILL MATHS	FORMS
National Insurance Unemployment benefits	English Job-getting letter-writing, Comprehension, Reading, Spelling	Maths Four rules of money	Claim forms etc.

SUBJECT CIVICS	SKILL ENGLISH	SKILL MATHS	FORMS
Public health Sickness benefits	Comprehension Reading	Four rules of money Time	Appropriate forms
Income tax	Reading Comprehension	Rules of money Rebate	Tax
Reasons for tax	National expenditure—Chancellor—budget Parliament (Commons and Lords)—Monarchy		
Set-up of Parliament	Electoral systems (constituencies) The Ministries and their work		
Rent/Rates Reason for rates—sub-division	Housing Highway Health Education Public utilities	Four rules of money Valuation and assessment	Rates forms
House purchase	Reading Comprehension	Simple interest Percentages	Building Society pamphlets

SUBJECT CIVICS	SKILL ENGLISH	SKILL MATHS	FORMS
Set-up of Council	Electoral system of Councils (Wards) County Borough Rural Districts Urban Districts		
Immigration Assisted Passages	Letters of application Geography Reading	Four rules of money Time/Distance Decimal coinage	
Local Government	The Why and Wherefore The Rule of the 'Town Hall' The case for a 'Town Director'		
Political 'Isms'	Monarchies Presidencies Dictatorships Democracies Socialism Communism		

SUBJECT HOME ECONOMICS	SKILL ENGLISH	SKILL MATHS	FORMS
Budgeting	The meaning of money	Simple accounts and book-keeping	
Saving/Insurance	Comprehension Reading Spelling	Money Simple interest Fractions	Premium bonds Savings certificates Insurance policies
Hire Purchase	Reading Comprehension Spelling	Mortgages Interest Money Time Fractions Proportions	H.P. Rentaset The new act
Marriage Attitude to opposite sex Behaviour Courtship	Reading Comprehension Letters		Marriage Guidance pamphlets Youth Council booklets
Education	What's new in education today Further education/Evening Institutes/W.I./W.E.A. Technical Colleges Day release		

SUBJECT HOME ECONOMICS	SKILL ENGLISH	SKILL MATHS	FORMS
Education	What is a University?		
Cars/Motor cycles	Reading Comprehension Spelling	Money Time/Distance	Licence Insurance Highway Code
Holidays	Descriptive writing Route planning Letters of application	Money/Time/Distance	Travel catalogues
Entertainment/Leisure TV/Sports/Education	Discernment Comprehension Reading	Money Weights/Measures Time	
Salaries Wages	Reading, etc.	Standard deductions Money/Time Distance	Time sheets Logs
The Home To Rent or Buy	Reading Comprehension	The maths of house purchase, Upkeep, Purchase	
Rates and Taxes The reasons (revision of Civics)			

SUBJECT LEISURE	SKILL ENGLISH	SKILL MATHS	FORMS
Sport	Letter writing (Tickets) Descriptive writing	Averages Percentages Money Number	Pools
Entertainment	Discussion (Trends, fashions, Fan fickleness, Censorship)	Costing of tickets Budgeting for night out	
Cars/Bikes	Highway Code Questions Reading Comprehension Discussion	Money Time/Distance Fractions Metric capacity	Highway Code Licence forms H.P. forms
Radio/TV Records	Essays Favourite programmes Dictation Song writing Letter-requests	Money	Wireless licence
Clothes	Reading History of fashion Reasons for fashion	Length Area Four rules of money	

SUBJECT LEISURE	SKILL ENGLISH	SKILL MATHS	FORMS
Clothes	Natural and man-made fibres Clothes/Climate Geography		
Holidays	Reading Letters—information Geography	Money/Time/Distance Insurance	Railway time-tables Flight plans
Reading for information	(a) Newspapers, purpose Press Council—standards—analysis of content, advert, News agencies (b) Biographical literature —Fact, opinion, entertainment (c) Works of reference (d) Advertisement—purpose morality integrity		

SUBJECT LEISURE	SKILL ENGLISH	SKILL MATHS	FORMS
Reading for pleasure	Comprehension Short story writing Reading		
The art of discrimination in every day life	(a) Entertainment (b) Employment		

218

Bibliography

ANDRY, R. G. (1960), *Delinquency and Parental Pathology*, London: Methuen.

BANKS, F. (1958), *Teach Them to Live*, London: Max Parrish.

BALDAMUS, W. (1951), 'Types of Work and Motivation', *Brit. J. Sociology*, ii, 44.

BERNSTEIN, B. (1958), 'Some Sociological Determinants of Perception—An Enquiry into Sub-cultural Differences', *Brit. J. Sociology*, ix, 159.

BERNSTEIN, B. (1959), 'A Public Language: Some Sociological Implications of a Linguistic Form', *Brit. J. Sociology*, x, 311.

BERNSTEIN, B. (1960), 'Language and Social Class', *Brit. J. Sociology*, xi, 271.

BERNSTEIN, B. (1961), 'Social Structure, Language and Learning', *Educational Research*, iii, 163.

BISHOP, N. (1960), 'Group Work in Pollington Borstal', *Howard J.*, x, No. 3, 185.

BLANK, L. (1958), 'The Intellectual Functioning of Delinquents', *J. Social Psychology*, xlvii, 9.

BURT, C. (1925), *The Young Delinquent*, London: University of London Press.

CAPLAN, N. S. (1965), 'Intellectual Functioning', Quay, H. C. (Ed.): *Juvenile Delinquency Research and Theory*, Princeton, New Jersey: D. Van Nostrand Company Inc.

CARLEBACH, J. (1969), *Caring for Children in Trouble*, London: Routledge & Kegan Paul.

CARPENTER, M. (1851), *Reformatory Schools for the Children of the Perishing and Dangerous Classes and for Juvenile Offenders*, London: Gilpin.

CARTER, M. P. (1962), *Home, School and Work*, London: Pergamon Press.

CLOWARD, R. K. and OHLIN, L. E. (1960), *Delinquency and Opportunity*, New York: The Free Press.

COCKETT, R. (1967), *Psychological Testing in Remand Centres and Borstal*, Private Circulation for the benefit of the members of the Prison Service.

COHEN, A. (1955), *Delinquent Boys The Culture of the Gang*, New York: The Free Press.

COTSGROVE, S. and PARKER, S. (1963), 'Work and Non-Work', *New Society*, xli, 8.

Bibliography

DIXON, H. (1850), *The London Prisons*, London: Jackson and Walford.

DOUGLAS, J. W. B. (1964), *The Home and the School*, London: MacGibbon and Kee.

DOUGLAS, J. W. B., ROSS, J. M., HAMMOND, W. A. and MULLIGAN, D. G. (1966), 'Delinquency and Social Class', *Brit. J. Criminology*, vi, 294.

DOWNES, D. (1966), *The Delinquent Solution*, London: Routledge and Kegan Paul.

FLOUD, J. E. (ed.), HALSEY, A. H. and MARTIN, F. M. (1956), *Social Class and Educational Opportunity*, London: William Heinemann Ltd.

FLOWER, F. D. (1966), *Language and Education*, London: Longmans Green and Co.

FOSTER, A. L. (1959), 'A note concerning the intelligence of delinquents', *J. Clinical Psychology*, xv, 78.

FOX, L. W. (1952), *The English Prison and Borstal Systems*, London: Routledge and Kegan Paul.

GARRITY, D. L. (1964), 'Some Implications of Prison Organization for Penal Objectives', *Howard J.*, xi, No. 3, 166.

GIBBONS, D. C. (1965), *Changing the Lawbreaker*, Englewood Cliffs, New Jersey: Prentice-Hall Inc.

GLUECK, S. and E. (1950), *Unraveling Juvenile Delinquency*, New York: The Commonwealth Fund.

GUILFORD, J. P. (1959), 'Three Faces of Intellect', Wiseman, S. (ed.). *Intelligence and Ability*, Middlesex: Penguin Books.

HOLLOWAY, V. P. (1966), *Inadequacy from the Point of View of Allocation*, Private Circulation of a paper given at the Borstal Assistant Governors' Conference.

HOME OFFICE (1945, 1950, 1957, 1960), *Prisons and Borstals*, H.M.S.O.

HOOD, R. (1965), *Borstal Re-Assessed*, London: Heinemann.

HOOD, R. (1966), *Homeless Borstal Boys*, Occasional Papers on Social Administration No. 18, London: G. Bell and Sons Ltd.

HOWARD, D. (1960), *The English Prisons*, London: Methuen and Co. Ltd.

JAHODA, G. (1964), 'Social Class Differentials in Vocabulary Expansion', *Brit. J. Educational Psychology*, xxxix, 321.

JOHNSON, S. F. (1967), 'A Teacher's View of Vocational Training within a Penal Establishment', *Prison Service J.*, vii, No. 25, 26.

JONES, H. (1966), 'Prison Officers as Therapists', *Howard J.*, xii, No. 1, 34.

KENYON, H. (1951), 'The Concept of Shared Responsibility in Borstal Training', *Howard J*, viii, No. 2, 189.

220

Bibliography

LITTLE, A. N. and WESTERGAARD, J. (1964), 'The Trend of Class Differentials in Educational Opportunity in England and Wales', *Brit. J. Sociology*, xv, 301.

LITTLE, A. N. (1965), 'The "Quality" of Borstal Receptions', *Brit. J. Criminology*, v, 190.

LOGAN, R. F. L. and GOLDBERG, E. M. (1953), 'Rising Eighteen in a London Suburb', *Brit. J. Sociology*, iv, 323.

LOWSON, D. M. (1967), Borstal Training and After-Care, Unpublished M.A. thesis: University of Liverpool.

MADDOCK, J. (1967), 'Station in Life', *Brit. J. Sociology*, xviii, 435.

MANNHEIM, H. and WILKINS, L. T. (1955), *Prediction Methods in Relation to Borstal Training*, London: H.M.S.O.

MATZA, D. (1964), *Delinquency and Drift*, New York: John Wiley and Sons, Inc.

MAYS, J. B. (1954), *Growing up in the City*, Liverpool: The University Press of Liverpool.

McCORKLE, L. W., ELIAS, A. and BIXBY, F. L. (1958), *The Highfields Story*, New York: Holt, Rinehart and Winston, Inc.

McKEE, J. M. and CLEMENTS, C. B (1967), *Progress Report 1962–67*, Publication issued by the Rehabilitation Research Foundation, Elmore, Alabama.

MILLER, D. (1964), *Growth to Freedom*, London: Tavistock.

MORRIS, T. (1957), *The Criminal Area*, London: Routledge and Kegan Paul.

MORRIS, T. and MORRIS, P. (1963), *Pentonville—a Sociological Study of an English Prison*, London: Routledge and Kegan Paul.

MORRISON, R. L. (1957), 'Borstal Allocation', *Brit. J. Delinquency*, viii, 95.

MORRISON, R. L. (1960), 'Group Counselling in Penal Institutions', *Howard J.*, x, No. 3, 279.

PEEL, E. A. (1956), *The Psychological Basis of Education*, Edinburgh: Oliver and Boyd.

PILNICK, S. M., ALLEN, R. F., DUBIN, H. N. and YOUTZ, A. C. (1967), *Collegefields from Delinquency to Freedom*, Publication issued by the Collegefields Group Educational Center, Newark State College.

POLLARD, M. (1967), 'From the classroom, I.T.A. in the Army', *New Education*, iii, No. 11, 24.

PRISON COMMISSION (1962), 'Group counselling: an instruction by the Prison Commissioners', *Howard J.*, xi, No. 1, 37.

RAVEN, J. C. (1956), *Guide to using Progressive Matrices* (1938), Sets A, B, C, D and E, London: H. K. Lewis.

RAYNOR, J. M. (1967), 'The School Counsellor', Craft M., Raynor, J. and Cohen, L. (ed.): *Linking Home and School*, London: Longmans Green.

Bibliography

RELIGIOUS TRACT SOCIETY (1872), *Sarah Martin Prison Visitor of Great Yarmouth: the Story of a Useful Life*, London: The Religious Tract Society.

ROSE, A. G. (1954), *Five Hundred Borstal Boys*, Oxford: Basil Blackwell.

ROSE, A. G. (1960), 'Training for Young Offenders', *Penal Practice in a Changing Society*, London: I.S.T.D.

RUCK, S. K. (ed.) (1951), *Paterson on Prisons*, London: Muller.

RUGGLES-BRISE, E. (1921), *The English Prison System*, London: MacMillan.

SHAPLAND, P. H. (1967), 'Groups and the Ability to Communicate', *Brit. J. Criminology*, vii, 404.

SMITH, M. (1967), 'Fathers in Borstal', *Marriage Guidance*, x, 264.

STONES, E. (1966), *An Introduction to Educational Psychology*, London: Methuen and Co. Ltd.

STOTT, D. H. (1952), *Saving Children from Delinquency*, London: University of London Press.

SYKES, G. M. (1958), *The Society of Captives*, Princeton, New Jersey: Princeton University Press.

TRENAMAN, J. (1952), *Out of Step*, London: Methuen.

VENABLES, E. (1967), *The Young Worker at College—A Study of a Local Tech.*, London: Faber and Faber.

VERNON, P. E. (1956), *The Measurement of Abilities*, London: University of London Press.

VERNON, P. E. (1958), 'A New Look at Intelligence Testing', *Educational Research*, i, 3.

WEBB, B. and S. (1922), *English Prisons under Local Government*, English Local Government Vol. vi, London: Longmans Green and Co.

WILLMOTT, P. (1966), *Adolescent Boys of East London*, London: Routledge and Kegan Paul.

WISEMAN, S. (1964), *Education and Environment*, Manchester: Manchester University Press.

WOLFF, M. (1967), *Prison: the penal institutions of Britain*, London: Eyre and Spottiswoode.

WOODWARD, M. (1963), *Low Intelligence and Delinquency* (Revised edition), London: I.S.T.D.

Official Reports

Report from the Select Committee on Criminal and Destitute Children, 1853. Vol. xxiii, Parliamentary Papers 1852–53.

Report from the Departmental Committee on Prisons, 1895, (Cmnd. 7702).

Bibliography

Report of the Commissioners of Prisons, Pt. II, 1913–14, (Cmnd. 7601), H.M.S.O.
Report of the Commissioners of Prisons, 1930, (Cmnd. 4151), H.M.S.O.
Report of the Commissioners of Prisons, 1931, (Cmnd. 4295), H.M.S.O.
Report of the Commissioners of Prisons, 1936, (Cmnd. 5675), H.M.S.O.
Report of the Commissioners of Prisons, 1948, (Cmnd. 7777), H.M.S.O.
Reading Ability, 1950, Pamphlet No. 18, Ministry of Education, H.M.S.O.
Report of the Commissioners of Prisons, 1950, (Cmnd. 8356), H.M.S.O.
Report of the Commissioners of Prisons, 1955, (Cmnd. 10), H.M.S.O.
Report of the Commissioners of Prisons, 1957, (Cmnd. 496), H.M.S.O.
Penal Practice in a Changing Society—Aspects of Future Development (England and Wales), 1959 (Cmnd. 645), H.M.S.O.
Report of the Commissioners of Prisons, 1959, (Cmnd. 1117), H.M.S.O.
Report of the Commissioners of Prisons, 1960, (Cmnd. 1467), H.M.S.O.
15 to 18, Report of the Central Advisory Council for Education (England), Vol. i, ii, 1960. Ministry of Education, H.M.S.O.
Census 1961 England and Wales Preliminary Report, 1961, H.M.S.O.
Report of the Commissioners of Prisons, 1962, (Cmnd. 2030), H.M.S.O.
'Work and Vocational Training in Borstals' (England and Wales), *Report of the Advisory Council on the Employment of Prisoners*, 1962, Home Office, H.M.S.O.
Half our Future, A Report of the Central Advisory Council for Education (England), 1963, Ministry of Education, H.M.S.O.
Borstal Institutions England and Wales Draft Borstal Rules, 1964, H.M.S.O.
Report on the Work of the Prison Department, 1965, (Cmnd. 3088), H.M.S.O.
Report on the Work of the Prison Department, 1965, Statistical Tables, 1965, (Cmnd. 3304), H.M.S.O.
Classification of Occupations, 1966, Registrar General, H.M.S.O.
Criminal Statistics England and Wales, 1966, (Cmnd. 3332), H.M.S.O.
Report on the Work of the Prison Department, 1966, (Cmnd 3408), H.M.S.O.
Eleventh Report from the Estimates Committee Prisons, Borstals and Detention Centres, Session 1966–67, (Cmnd 599), H.M.S.O.
The MacLaren Vocational Center (1967). A report of a special demonstration conducted by the MacLaren School for Boys, Woodburn, Oregon, in conjunction with the Youth Opportunity Center, Portland, Oregon.
16th Progress Report (1967). Experimental and Demonstration Manpower Project for Training and Placement of Youthful Offenders. Rehabilitation Research Foundation, Draper Correctional Center, Elmore, Alabama.

223

Index

Index

teaching methods and materials, 9, 136, 141, 161
teenage culture, 24, 79, 152
Terman Merrill Scale, 48
tests, 18, 62, 134, 160–1 and Appendices A and D
  intelligence, 36–42
  'non-verbal' and 'verbal', 33
  psychological, 42–50
  reading, 126, 127
  trade, 117, 118
  see also Abstraction test CP1, Arithmetic test CP101A, Bennett Mechanical Comprehension test, Columbian tests, Literary test CP102, Raven Matrices test, Schonell's oral reading test, Watts-Vernon Silent Reading test, Wechsler-Bellevue intelligence test
trade
  training, 10, 17, 117, 118, 121, 124, 125, 138, 150, 151, 163, 165
  Instructors, 117, 118, 123–6, 138, 164
  see also tests, industrial training
Trenaman, J., 38, 54
truancy, 19, 50–4, 66, 145
Tutor Organizers, 53, 116–18, 121–8, 135, 139, 141, 146, 150, 158, 159, 161, 171 and Appendix C
  appointment and position of, 11–14, 128–135
  possible future role of, 172–8

United States of America, 36, 39, 158, 165
  reformatory at Elmira, 7, 8

Universities, contact with, 170, 178, 179

values, 157
  delinquent, 166
  middle-class, 9
  system(s), 142, 166, 171
Vernon, P. E., 41, 42, 44
vocational
  guidance, 50, 99, 117, 118
  training, 14–17, 42, 117, 118, 120–5, 137, 149, 150, 162, 164, 165
  training instructors, 121, 181

Watts-Vernon Silent Reading test, 127
Webb, B. and S., 6
Wechsler Adult Intelligence scale, 48
Wechsler-Bellevue intelligence test, 38, 40
Willmott, Peter, 20, 68, 147
Wiseman, S., 99
Wolff, M., 48
women in borstal institutions, 73, 173
Woodward, Mary, 36, 39
work
  in borstal training, 5, 7, 8, 12, 16, 17, 152, 158
  opportunities, 159, 165
  prospects, 146, 147
  see also attitudes of borstal boys, job(s)

Youth Employment Service, 98, 99

228

The International Library of

Sociology

and Social Reconstruction

Edited by W. J. H. SPROTT

Founded by KARL MANNHEIM

ROUTLEDGE & KEGAN PAUL
BROADWAY HOUSE, CARTER LANE, LONDON, E.C.4

CONTENTS

PRINTED IN GREAT BRITAIN BY HEADLEY BROTHERS LTD
109 KINGSWAY LONDON WC2 AND ASHFORD KENT

GENERAL SOCIOLOGY

Brown, Robert. Explanation in Social Science. *208 pp. 1963. (2nd Impression 1964.) 25s.*

Gibson, Quentin. The Logic of Social Enquiry. *240 pp. 1960. (3rd Impression 1968.) 24s.*

Homans, George C. Sentiments and Activities: Essays in Social Science. *336 pp. 1962. 32s.*

Isajiw, Wsevelod W. Causation and Functionalism in Sociology. *165 pp. 1968. 25s.*

Johnson, Harry M. Sociology: a Systematic Introduction. *Foreword by Robert K. Merton. 710 pp. 1961. (5th Impression 1968.) 42s.*

Mannheim, Karl. Essays on Sociology and Social Psychology. *Edited by Paul Keckskemeti. With Editorial Note by Adolph Lowe. 344 pp. 1953. (2nd Impression 1966.) 32s.*

Systematic Sociology: An Introduction to the Study of Society. *Edited by J. S. Erös and Professor W. A. C. Stewart. 220 pp. 1957. (3rd Impression 1967.) 24s.*

Martindale, Don. The Nature and Types of Sociological Theory. *292 pp. 1961. (3rd Impression 1967.) 35s.*

Maus, Heinz. A Short History of Sociology. *234 pp. 1962. (2nd Impression 1965.) 28s.*

Myrdal, Gunnar. Value in Social Theory: A Collection of Essays on Methodology. *Edited by Paul Streeten. 332 pp. 1958. (3rd Impression 1968.) 35s.*

Ogburn, William F., and Nimkoff, Meyer F. A Handbook of Sociology. *Preface by Karl Mannheim. 656 pp. 46 figures. 35 tables. 5th edition (revised) 1964. 45s.*

Parsons, Talcott, and Smelser, Neil J. Economy and Society: A Study in the Integration of Economic and Social Theory. *362 pp. 1956. (4th Impression 1967.) 35s.*

Rex, John. Key Problems of Sociological Theory. *220 pp. 1961. (4th Impression 1968.) 25s.*

Stark, Werner. The Fundamental Forms of Social Thought. *280 pp. 1962. 32s.*

FOREIGN CLASSICS OF SOCIOLOGY

Durkheim, Emile. Suicide. A Study in Sociology. *Edited and with an Introduction by George Simpson. 404 pp. 1952. (4th Impression 1968.) 35s.*

Professional Ethics and Civic Morals. *Translated by Cornelia Brookfield. 288 pp. 1957. 30s.*

Gerth, H. H., and Mills, C. Wright. From Max Weber: Essays in Sociology. *502 pp. 1948. (6th Impression 1967.) 35s.*

Tönnies, Ferdinand. Community and Association. *(Gemeinschaft und Gesellschaft.) Translated and Supplemented by Charles P. Loomis. Foreword by Pitirim A. Sorokin. 334 pp. 1955. 28s.*

SOCIAL STRUCTURE

Andreski, Stanislav. Military Organization and Society. *Foreword by Professor A. R. Radcliffe-Brown. 226 pp. 1 folder. 1954. Revised Edition 1968. 35s.*

Cole, G. D. H. Studies in Class Structure. *220 pp. 1955. (3rd Impression 1964.) 21s. Paper 10s. 6d.*

Coontz, Sydney H. Population Theories and the Economic Interpretation. *202 pp. 1957. (3rd Impression 1968.) 28s.*

Coser, Lewis. The Functions of Social Conflict. *204 pp. 1956. (3rd Impression 1968.) 25s.*

Dickie-Clark, H. F. Marginal Situation: A Sociological Study of a Coloured Group. *240 pp. 11 tables. 1966. 40s.*

Glass, D. V. (Ed.). Social Mobility in Britain. *Contributions by J. Berent, T. Bottomore, R. C. Chambers, J. Floud, D. V. Glass, J. R. Hall, H. T. Himmelweit, R. K. Kelsall, F. M. Martin, C. A. Moser, R. Mukherjee, and W. Ziegel. 420 pp. 1954. (4th Impression 1967.) 45s.*

Jones, Garth N. Planned Organizational Change: An Exploratory Study Using an Empirical Approach. *About 268 pp. 1969. 40s.*

Kelsall, R. K. Higher Civil Servants in Britain: From 1870 to the Present Day. *268 pp. 31 tables. 1955. (2nd Impression 1966.) 25s.*

König, René. The Community. *232 pp. Illustrated. 1968. 35s.*

Lawton, Denis. Social Class, Language and Education. *192 pp. 1968. (2nd Impression 1968.) 25s.*

McLeish, John. The Theory of Social Change: Four Views Considered. *About 128 pp. 1969. 21s.*

Marsh, David C. The Changing Social Structure in England and Wales, 1871-1961. *1958. 272 pp. 2nd edition (revised) 1966. (2nd Impression 1967.) 35s.*

Mouzelis, Nicos. Organization and Bureaucracy. An Analysis of Modern Theories. *240 pp. 1967. (2nd Impression 1968.) 28s.*

Ossowski, Stanislaw. Class Structure in the Social Consciousness. *210 pp. 1963. (2nd Impression 1967.) 25s.*

SOCIOLOGY AND POLITICS

Barbu, Zevedei. Democracy and Dictatorship: Their Psychology and Patterns of Life. *300 pp. 1956. 28s.*

Crick, Bernard. The American Science of Politics: Its Origins and Conditions. *284 pp. 1959. 32s.*

Hertz, Frederick. Nationality in History and Politics: A Psychology and Sociology of National Sentiment and Nationalism. *432 pp. 1944. (5th Impression 1966.) 42s.*

Kornhauser, William. The Politics of Mass Society. *272 pp. 20 tables. 1960. (3rd Impression 1968.) 28s.*

Laidler, Harry W. History of Socialism. Social-Economic Movements: An Historical and Comparative Survey of Socialism, Communism, Co-operation, Utopianism; and other Systems of Reform and Reconstruction. *New edition. 992 pp. 1968. 90s.*

Lasswell, Harold D. Analysis of Political Behaviour. An Empirical Approach. *324 pp. 1947. (4th Impression 1966.) 35s.*

Mannheim, Karl. Freedom, Power and Democratic Planning. *Edited by Hans Gerth and Ernest K. Bramstedt. 424 pp. 1951. (3rd Impression 1968.) 42s.*

Mansur, Fatma. Process of Independence. *Foreword by A. H. Hanson. 208 pp. 1962. 25s.*

Martin, David A. Pacificism: an Historical and Sociological Study. *262 pp. 1965. 30s.*

Myrdal, Gunnar. The Political Element in the Development of Economic Theory. *Translated from the German by Paul Streeten. 282 pp. 1953. (4th Impression 1965.) 25s.*

Polanyi, Michael. F.R.S. The Logic of Liberty: Reflections and Rejoinders. *228 pp. 1951. 18s.*

Verney, Douglas V. The Analysis of Political Systems. *264 pp. 1959. (3rd Impression 1966.) 28s.*

Wootton, Graham. The Politics of Influence: British Ex-Servicemen, Cabinet Decisions and Cultural Changes, 1917 to 1957. *316 pp. 1963. 30s.*
Workers, Unions and the State. *188 pp. 1966. (2nd Impression 1967.) 25s.*

FOREIGN AFFAIRS: THEIR SOCIAL, POLITICAL AND ECONOMIC FOUNDATIONS

Baer, Gabriel. Population and Society in the Arab East. *Translated by Hanna Szöke. 288 pp. 10 maps. 1964. 40s.*

Bonné, Alfred. State and Economics in the Middle East: A Society in Transition. *482 pp. 2nd (revised) edition 1955. (2nd Impression 1960.) 40s.*
Studies in Economic Development: with special reference to Conditions in the Under-developed Areas of Western Asia and India. *322 pp. 84 tables. 2nd edition 1960. 32s.*

Mayer, J. P. Political Thought in France from the Revolution to the Fifth Republic. *164 pp. 3rd edition (revised) 1961. 16s.*

CRIMINOLOGY

Ancel, Marc. Social Defence: A Modern Approach to Criminal Problems. *Foreword by Leon Radzinowicz. 240 pp. 1965. 32s.*

Cloward, Richard A., and **Ohlin, Lloyd E.** Delinquency and Opportunity: A Theory of Delinquent Gangs. *248 pp. 1961. 25s.*

Downes, David M. The Delinquent Solution. A Study in Subcultural Theory. *296 pp. 1966. 42s.*

Dunlop, A. B., and **McCabe, S.** Young Men in Detention Centres. *192 pp. 1965. 28s.*

Friedländer, Kate. The Psycho-Analytical Approach to Juvenile Delinquency: Theory, Case Studies, Treatment. *320 pp. 1947. (6th Impression 1967). 40s.*

Glueck, Sheldon and **Eleanor.** Family Environment and Delinquency. *With the statistical assistance of Rose W. Kneznek. 340 pp. 1962. (2nd Impression 1966.) 40s.*

Mannheim, Hermann. Comparative Criminology: a Text Book. *Two volumes. 442 pp. and 380 pp. 1965. (2nd Impression with corrections 1966.) 42s. a volume.*

Morris, Terence. The Criminal Area: A Study in Social Ecology. *Foreword by Hermann Mannheim. 232 pp. 25 tables. 4 maps. 1957. (2nd Impression 1966.) 28s.*

Morris, Terence and **Pauline,** assisted by **Barbara Barer.** Pentonville: A Sociological Study of an English Prison. *416 pp. 16 plates. 1963. 50s.*

Spencer, John C. Crime and the Services. *Foreword by Hermann Mannheim. 336 pp. 1954. 28s.*

Trasler, Gordon. The Explanation of Criminality. *144 pp. 1962. (2nd Impression 1967.) 20s.*

SOCIAL PSYCHOLOGY

Barbu, Zevedei. Problems of Historical Psychology. *248 pp. 1960. 25s.*

Blackburn, Julian. Psychology and the Social Pattern. *184 pp. 1945. (7th Impression 1964.) 16s.*

Fleming, C. M. Adolescence: Its Social Psychology: With an Introduction to recent findings from the fields of Anthropology, Physiology, Medicine, Psychometrics and Sociometry. *288 pp. 2nd edition (revised) 1963. (3rd Impression 1967.) 25s. Paper 12s. 6d.*

The Social Psychology of Education: An Introduction and Guide to Its Study. *136 pp. 2nd edition (revised) 1959. (4th Impression 1967.) 14s. Paper 7s. 6d.*

Homans, George C. The Human Group. *Foreword by Bernard DeVoto. Introduction by Robert K. Merton. 526 pp. 1951. (7th Impression 1968.) 35s.*

Social Behaviour: its Elementary Forms. *416 pp. 1961. (3rd Impression 1968.) 35s.*

Klein, Josephine. The Study of Groups. *226 pp. 31 figures. 5 tables. 1956. (5th Impression 1967.) 21s. Paper 9s. 6d.*

6

Linton, Ralph. The Cultural Background of Personality. *132 pp. 1947. (7th Impression 1968.) 18s.*

Mayo, Elton. The Social Problems of an Industrial Civilization. With an appendix on the Political Problem. *180 pp. 1949. (5th Impression 1966.) 25s.*

Ottaway, A. K. C. Learning Through Group Experience. *176 pp. 1966. (2nd Impression 1968.) 25s.*

Ridder, J. C. de. The Personality of the Urban African in South Africa. A Thematic Apperception Test Study. *196 pp. 12 plates. 1961. 25s.*

Rose, Arnold M. (Ed.). Human Behaviour and Social Processes: an Interactionist Approach. *Contributions by Arnold M. Rose, Ralph H. Turner, Anselm Strauss, Everett C. Hughes, E. Franklin Frazier, Howard S. Becker, et al. 696 pp. 1962. (2nd Impression 1968.) 70s.*

Smelser, Neil J. Theory of Collective Behaviour. *448 pp. 1962. (2nd Impression 1967.) 45s.*

Stephenson, Geoffrey M. The Development of Conscience. *128 pp. 1966. 25s.*

Young, Kimball. Handbook of Social Psychology. *658 pp. 16 figures. 10 tables. 2nd edition (revised) 1957. (3rd Impression 1963.) 40s.*

SOCIOLOGY OF THE FAMILY

Banks, J. A. Prosperity and Parenthood: A study of Family Planning among The Victorian Middle Classes. *262 pp. 1954. (3rd Impression 1968.) 28s.*

Bell, Colin R. Middle Class Families: Social and Geographical Mobility. *224 pp. 1969. 35s.*

Burton, Lindy. Vulnerable Children. *272 pp. 1968. 35s.*

Gavron, Hannah. The Captive Wife: Conflicts of Housebound Mothers. *190 pp. 1966. (2nd Impression 1966.) 25s.*

Klein, Josephine. Samples from English Cultures. *1965. (2nd Impression 1967.)*
1. Three Preliminary Studies and Aspects of Adult Life in England. *447 pp. 50s.*
2. Child-Rearing Practices and Index. *247 pp. 35s.*

Klein, Viola. Britain's Married Women Workers. *180 pp. 1965. (2nd Impression 1968.) 28s.*

McWhinnie, Alexina M. Adopted Children. How They Grow Up. *304 pp. 1967. (2nd Impression 1968.) 42s.*

Myrdal, Alva and **Klein, Viola.** Women's Two Roles: Home and Work. *238 pp. 27 tables. 1956. Revised Edition 1967. 30s. Paper 15s.*

Parsons, Talcott and **Bales, Robert F.** Family: Socialization and Interaction Process. *In collaboration with James Olds, Morris Zelditch and Philip E. Slater. 456 pp. 50 figures and tables. 1956. (3rd Impression 1968.) 45s.*

Schücking, L. L. The Puritan Family. *Translated from the German by Brian Battershaw. 212 pp. 1969. About 42s.*

7

THE SOCIAL SERVICES

Forder, R. A. (Ed.). Penelope Hall's Social Services of Modern England. *288 pp. 1969. 35s.*

George, Victor. Social Security: Beveridge and After. *258 pp. 1968. 35s.*

Goetschius, George W. Working with Community Groups. *256 pp. 1969. 35s.*

Goetschius, George W. and **Tash, Joan.** Working with Unattached Youth. *416 pp. 1967. (2nd Impression 1968.) 40s.*

Hall, M. P., and **Howes, I. V.** The Church in Social Work. A Study of Moral Welfare Work undertaken by the Church of England. *320 pp. 1965. 35s.*

Heywood, Jean S. Children in Care: the Development of the Service for the Deprived Child. *264 pp. 2nd edition (revised) 1965. (2nd Impression 1966.) 32s.*

An Introduction to Teaching Casework Skills. *190 pp. 1964. 28s.*

Jones, Kathleen. Lunacy, Law and Conscience, 1744-1845: the Social History of the Care of the Insane. *268 pp. 1955. 25s.*

Mental Health and Social Policy, 1845-1959. *264 pp. 1960. (2nd Impression 1967.) 32s.*

Jones, Kathleen and **Sidebotham, Roy.** Mental Hospitals at Work. *220 pp. 1962. 30s.*

Kastell, Jean. Casework in Child Care. *Foreword by M. Brooke Willis. 320 pp. 1962. 35s.*

Morris, Pauline. Put Away: A Sociological Study of Institutions for the Mentally Retarded. *Approx. 288 pp. 1969. About 50s.*

Nokes, P. L. The Professional Task in Welfare Practice. *152 pp. 1967. 28s.*

Rooff, Madeline. Voluntary Societies and Social Policy. *350 pp. 15 tables. 1957. 35s.*

Timms, Noel. Psychiatric Social Work in Great Britain (1939-1962). *280 pp. 1964. 32s.*

Social Casework: Principles and Practice. *256 pp. 1964. (2nd Impression 1966.) 25s. Paper 15s.*

Trasler, Gordon. In Place of Parents: A Study in Foster Care. *272 pp. 1960. (2nd Impression 1966.) 30s.*

Young, A. F., and **Ashton, E. T.** British Social Work in the Nineteenth Century. *288 pp. 1956. (2nd Impression 1963.) 28s.*

Young, A. F. Social Services in British Industry. *272 pp. 1968. 40s.*

SOCIOLOGY OF EDUCATION

Banks, Olive. Parity and Prestige in English Secondary Education: a Study in Educational Sociology. *272 pp. 1955. (2nd Impression 1963.) 32s.*

Bentwich, Joseph. Education in Israel. *224 pp. 8 pp. plates. 1965. 24s.*

Blyth, W. A. L. English Primary Education. A Sociological Description. *1965. Revised edition 1967.*

   1. Schools. *232 pp. 30s. Paper 12s. 6d.*

   2. Background. *168 pp. 25s. Paper 10s. 6d.*

Collier, K. G. The Social Purposes of Education: Personal and Social Values in Education. *268 pp. 1959. (3rd Impression 1965.) 21s.*

Dale, R. R., and **Griffith, S.** Down Stream: Failure in the Grammar School. *108 pp. 1965. 20s.*

Dore, R. P. Education in Tokugawa Japan. *356 pp. 9 pp. plates. 1965. 35s.*

Edmonds, E. L. The School Inspector. *Foreword by Sir William Alexander. 214 pp. 1962. 28s.*

Evans, K. M. Sociometry and Education. *158 pp. 1962. (2nd Impression 1966.) 18s.*

Foster, P. J. Education and Social Change in Ghana. *336 pp. 3 maps. 1965. (2nd Impression 1967.) 36s.*

Fraser, W. R. Education and Society in Modern France. *150 pp. 1963. (2nd Impression 1968.) 25s.*

Hans, Nicholas. New Trends in Education in the Eighteenth Century. *278 pp. 19 tables. 1951. (2nd Impression 1966.) 30s.*
Comparative Education: A Study of Educational Factors and Traditions. *360 pp. 3rd (revised) edition 1958. (4th Impression 1967.) 25s. Paper 12s. 6d.*

Hargreaves, David. Social Relations in a Secondary School. *240 pp. 1967. (2nd Impression 1968.) 32s.*

Holmes, Brian. Problems in Education. A Comparative Approach. *336 pp. 1965. (2nd Impression 1967.) 32s.*

Mannheim, Karl and **Stewart, W. A. C.** An Introduction to the Sociology of Education. *206 pp. 1962. (2nd Impression 1965.) 21s.*

Morris, Raymond N. The Sixth Form and College Entrance. *231 pp. 1969. 40s.*

Musgrove, F. Youth and the Social Order. *176 pp. 1964. (2nd Impression 1968.) 25s. Paper 12s.*

Ortega y Gasset, José. Mission of the University. *Translated with an Introduction by Howard Lee Nostrand. 86 pp. 1946. (3rd Impression 1963.) 15s.*

Ottaway, A. K. C. Education and Society: An Introduction to the Sociology of Education. *With an Introduction by W. O. Lester Smith. 212 pp. Second edition (revised). 1962. (5th Impression 1968.) 18s. Paper 10s. 6d.*

Peers, Robert. Adult Education: A Comparative Study. *398 pp. 2nd edition 1959. (2nd Impression 1966.) 42s.*

Pritchard, D. G. Education and the Handicapped: 1760 to 1960. *258 pp. 1963. (2nd Impression 1966.) 35s.*

Richardson, Helen. Adolescent Girls in Approved Schools. *Approx. 360 pp. 1969. About 42s.*

Simon, Brian and **Joan** (Eds.). Educational Psychology in the U.S.S.R. *Introduction by Brian and Joan Simon. Translation by Joan Simon. Papers by D. N. Bogoiavlenski and N. A. Menchinskaia, D. B. Elkonin, E. A. Fleshner, Z. I. Kalmykova, G. S. Kostiuk, V. A. Krutetski, A. N. Leontiev, A. R. Luria, E. A. Milerian, R. G. Natadze, B. M. Teplov, L. S. Vygotski, L. V. Zankov. 296 pp. 1963. 40s.*

9

SOCIOLOGY OF CULTURE

Eppel, E. M., and M. Adolescents and Morality: A Study of some Moral Values and Dilemmas of Working Adolescents in the Context of a changing Climate of Opinion. *Foreword by W. J. H. Sprott. 268 pp. 39 tables. 1966. 30s.*

Fromm, Erich. The Fear of Freedom. *286 pp. 1942. (8th Impression 1960.) 25s. Paper 10s.*
The Sane Society. *400 pp. 1956. (4th Impression 1968.) 28s. Paper 14s.*

Mannheim, Karl. Diagnosis of Our Time: Wartime Essays of a Sociologist. *208 pp. 1943. (8th Impression 1966.) 21s.*
Essays on the Sociology of Culture. *Edited by Ernst Mannheim in co-operation with Paul Kecskemeti. Editorial Note by Adolph Lowe. 280 pp. 1956. (3rd Impression 1967.) 28s.*

Weber, Alfred. Farewell to European History: or The Conquest of Nihilism. *Translated from the German by R. F. C. Hull. 224 pp. 1947. 18s.*

SOCIOLOGY OF RELIGION

Argyle, Michael. Religious Behaviour. *224 pp. 8 figures. 41 tables. 1958. (4th Impression 1968.) 25s.*

Nelson, G. K. Spiritualism and Society. *313 pp. 1969. 42s.*

Stark, Werner. The Sociology of Religion. A Study of Christendom.
Volume I. Established Religion. *248 pp. 1966. 35s.*
Volume II. Sectarian Religion. *368 pp. 1967. 40s.*
Volume III. The Universal Church. *464 pp. 1967. 45s.*

Watt, W. Montgomery. Islam and the Integration of Society. *320 pp. 1961. (3rd Impression 1966.) 35s.*

SOCIOLOGY OF ART AND LITERATURE

Beljame, Alexandre. Men of Letters and the English Public in the Eighteenth Century: 1660-1744, Dryden, Addison, Pope. *Edited with an Introduction and Notes by Bonamy Dobrée. Translated by E. O. Lorimer. 532 pp. 1948. 32s.*

Misch, Georg. A History of Autobiography in Antiquity. *Translated by E. W. Dickes. 2 Volumes. Vol. 1, 364 pp., Vol. 2, 372 pp. 1950. 45s. the set.*

Schücking, L. L. The Sociology of Literary Taste. *112 pp. 2nd (revised) edition 1966. 18s.*

Silbermann, Alphons. The Sociology of Music. *Translated from the German by Corbet Stewart. 222 pp. 1963. 32s.*

SOCIOLOGY OF KNOWLEDGE

Mannheim, Karl. Essays on the Sociology of Knowledge. *Edited by Paul Kecskemeti. Editorial note by Adolph Lowe. 352 pp. 1952. (4th Impression 1967.) 35s.*

Stark, W. America: Ideal and Reality. The United States of 1776 in Contemporary Philosophy. *136 pp. 1947. 12s.*
The Sociology of Knowledge: An Essay in Aid of a Deeper Understanding of the History of Ideas. *384 pp. 1958. (3rd Impression 1967.) 36s.*
Montesquieu: Pioneer of the Sociology of Knowledge. *244 pp. 1960. 25s.*

URBAN SOCIOLOGY

Anderson, Nels. The Urban Community: A World Perspective. *532 pp. 1960. 35s.*

Ashworth, William. The Genesis of Modern British Town Planning: A Study in Economic and Social History of the Nineteenth and Twentieth Centuries. *288 pp. 1954. (3rd Impression 1968.) 32s.*

Bracey, Howard. Neighbours: On New Estates and Subdivisions in England and U.S.A. *220 pp. 1964. 28s.*

Cullingworth, J. B. Housing Needs and Planning Policy: A Restatement of the Problems of Housing Need and "Overspill" in England and Wales. *232 pp. 44 tables. 8 maps. 1960. (2nd Impression 1966.) 28s.*

Dickinson, Robert E. City and Region: A Geographical Interpretation. *608 pp. 125 figures. 1964. (5th Impression 1967.) 60s.*
The West European City: A Geographical Interpretation. *600 pp. 129 maps. 29 plates. 2nd edition 1962. (3rd Impression 1968.) 55s.*
The City Region in Western Europe. *320 pp. Maps. 1967. 30s. Paper 14s.*

Jackson, Brian. Working Class Community: Some General Notions raised by a Series of Studies in Northern England. *192 pp. 1968. (2nd Impression 1968.) 25s.*

Jennings, Hilda. Societies in the Making: a Study of Development and Redevelopment within a County Borough. *Foreword by D. A. Clark. 286 pp. 1962. (2nd Impression 1967.) 32s.*

Kerr, Madeline. The People of Ship Street. *240 pp. 1958. 28s.*

Mann, P. H. An Approach to Urban Sociology. *240 pp. 1965. (2nd Impression 1968.) 30s.*

Morris, R. N., and **Mogey, J.** The Sociology of Housing. Studies at Berinsfield. *232 pp. 4 pp. plates. 1965. 42s.*

Rosser, C., and **Harris, C.** The Family and Social Change. A Study of Family and Kinship in a South Wales Town. *352 pp. 8 maps. 1965. (2nd Impression 1968.) 45s.*

RURAL SOCIOLOGY

Chambers, R. J. H. Settlement Schemes in Africa: A Selective Study. *Approx. 268 pp. 1969. About 50s.*

Haswell, M. R. The Economics of Development in Village India. *120 pp. 1967. 21s.*

11

Littlejohn, James. Westrigg: the Sociology of a Cheviot Parish. *172 pp. 5 figures. 1963. 25s.*

Williams, W. M. The Country Craftsman: A Study of Some Rural Crafts and the Rural Industries Organization in England. *248 pp. 9 figures. 1958. 25s. (Dartington Hall Studies in Rural Sociology.)*
The Sociology of an English Village: Gosforth. *272 pp. 12 figures. 13 tables. 1956. (3rd Impression 1964.) 25s.*

SOCIOLOGY OF MIGRATION

Humphreys, Alexander J. New Dubliners: Urbanization and the Irish Family. *Foreword by George C. Homans. 304 pp. 1966. 40s.*

SOCIOLOGY OF INDUSTRY AND DISTRIBUTION

Anderson, Nels. Work and Leisure. *280 pp. 1961. 28s.*

Blau, Peter M., and **Scott, W. Richard.** Formal Organizations: a Comparative approach. *Introduction and Additional Bibliography by J. H. Smith. 326 pp. 1963. (4th Impression 1969.) 35s. Paper 15s.*

Eldridge, J. E. T. Industrial Disputes. Essays in the Sociology of Industrial Relations. *288 pp. 1968. 40s.*

Hollowell, Peter G. The Lorry Driver. *272 pp. 1968. 42s.*

Jefferys, Margot, with the assistance of Winifred Moss. Mobility in the Labour Market: Employment Changes in Battersea and Dagenham. *Preface by Barbara Wootton. 186 pp. 51 tables. 1954. 15s.*

Levy, A. B. Private Corporations and Their Control. *Two Volumes. Vol. 1, 464 pp., Vol. 2, 432 pp. 1950. 80s. the set.*

Liepmann, Kate. Apprenticeship: An Enquiry into its Adequacy under Modern Conditions. *Foreword by H. D. Dickinson. 232 pp. 6 tables. 1960. (2nd Impression 1960.) 23s.*

Millerson, Geoffrey. The Qualifying Associations: a Study in Professionalization. *320 pp. 1964. 42s.*

Smelser, Neil J. Social Change in the Industrial Revolution: An Application of Theory to the Lancashire Cotton Industry, 1770-1840. *468 pp. 12 figures. 14 tables. 1959. (2nd Impression 1960.) 50s.*

Williams, Gertrude. Recruitment to Skilled Trades. *240 pp. 1957. 23s.*

Young, A. F. Industrial Injuries Insurance: an Examination of British Policy. *192 pp. 1964. 30s.*

ANTHROPOLOGY

Ammar, Hamed. Growing up in an Egyptian Village: Silwa, Province of Aswan. *336 pp. 1954. (2nd Impression 1966.) 35s.*

Crook, David and **Isabel.** Revolution in a Chinese Village: Ten Mile Inn. *230 pp. 8 plates. 1 map. 1959. (2nd Impression 1968.) 21s.*
The First Years of Yangyi Commune. *302 pp. 12 plates. 1966. 42s.*

Dickie-Clark, H. F. The Marginal Situation. A Sociological Study of a Coloured Group. *236 pp. 1966. 40s.*

Dube, S. C. Indian Village. *Foreword by Morris Edward Opler. 276 pp. 4 plates. 1955. (5th Impression 1965.) 25s.*
India's Changing Villages: Human Factors in Community Development. *260 pp. 8 plates. 1 map. 1958. (3rd Impression 1963.) 25s.*

Firth, Raymond. Malay Fishermen. Their Peasant Economy. *420 pp. 17 pp. plates. 2nd edition revised and enlarged 1966. (2nd Impression 1968.) 55s.*

Gulliver, P. H. The Family Herds. A Study of two Pastoral Tribes in East Africa, The Jie and Turkana. *304 pp. 4 plates. 19 figures. 1955. (2nd Impression with new preface and bibliography 1966.) 35s.*
Social Control in an African Society: a Study of the Arusha, Agricultural Masai of Northern Tanganyika. *320 pp. 8 plates. 10 figures. 1963. (2nd Impression 1968.) 42s.*

Ishwaran, K. Shivapur. A South Indian Village. *216 pp. 1968. 35s.*
Tradition and Economy in Village India: An Interactionist Approach. *Foreword by Conrad Arensburg. 176 pp. 1966. (2nd Impression 1968.) 25s.*

Jarvie, Ian C. The Revolution in Anthropology. *268 pp. 1964. (2nd Impression 1967.) 40s.*

Jarvie, Ian C. and Agassi, Joseph. Hong Kong. A Society in Transition. *396 pp. Illustrated with plates and maps. 1968. 56s.*

Little, Kenneth L. Mende of Sierra Leone. *308 pp. and folder. 1951. Revised edition 1967. 63s.*

Lowie, Professor Robert H. Social Organization. *494 pp. 1950. (4th Impression 1966.) 50s.*

Mayer, Adrian C. Caste and Kinship in Central India: A Village and its Region. *328 pp. 16 plates. 15 figures. 16 tables. 1960. (2nd Impression 1965.) 35s.*
Peasants in the Pacific: A Study of Fiji Indian Rural Society. *232 pp. 16 plates. 10 figures. 14 tables. 1961. 35s.*

Smith, Raymond T. The Negro Family in British Guiana: Family Structure and Social Status in the Villages. *With a Foreword by Meyer Fortes. 314 pp. 8 plates. 1 figure. 4 maps. 1956. (2nd Impression 1965.) 35s.*

DOCUMENTARY

Meek, Dorothea L. (Ed.). Soviet Youth: Some Achievements and Problems. *Excerpts from the Soviet Press, translated by the editor. 280 pp. 1957. 28s.*

Schlesinger, Rudolf (Ed.). Changing Attitudes in Soviet Russia.

2. The Nationalities Problem and Soviet Administration. Selected Readings on the Development of Soviet Nationalities Policies. *Introduced by the editor. Translated by W. W. Gottlieb. 324 pp. 1956. 30s.*

Reports of the Institute of Community Studies

Cartwright, Ann. Human Relations and Hospital Care. *272 pp. 1964. 30s.*
Patients and their Doctors. A Study of General Practice. *304 pp. 1967. 40s.*

Jackson, Brian. Streaming: an Education System in Miniature. *168 pp. 1964.* (*2nd Impression 1966.*) *21s. Paper 10s.*

Jackson, Brian and **Marsden, Dennis.** Education and the Working Class: Some General Themes raised by a Study of 88 Working-class Children in a Northern Industrial City. *268 pp. 2 folders. 1962.* (*4th Impression 1968.*) *32s.*

Marris, Peter. Widows and their Families. *Foreword by Dr. John Bowlby. 184 pp. 18 tables. Statistical Summary. 1958. 18s.*
Family and Social Change in an African City. A Study of Rehousing in Lagos. *196 pp. 1 map. 4 plates. 53 tables. 1961.* (*2nd Impression 1966.*) *30s.*
The Experience of Higher Education. *232 pp. 27 tables. 1964. 25s.*

Marris, Peter and **Rein, Martin.** Dilemmas of Social Reform. Poverty and Community Action in the United States. *256 pp. 1967. 35s.*

Mills, Enid. Living with Mental Illness: a Study in East London. *Foreword by Morris Carstairs. 196 pp. 1962. 28s.*

Runciman, W. G. Relative Deprivation and Social Justice. A Study of Attitudes to Social Inequality in Twentieth Century England. *352 pp. 1966.* (*2nd Impression 1967.*) *40s.*

Townsend, Peter. The Family Life of Old People: An Inquiry in East London. *Foreword by J. H. Sheldon. 300 pp. 3 figures. 63 tables. 1957.* (*3rd Impression 1967.*) *30s.*

Willmott, Peter. Adolescent Boys in East London. *230 pp. 1966. 30s.*
The Evolution of a Community: a study of Dagenham after forty years. *168 pp. 2 maps. 1963. 21s.*

Willmott, Peter and **Young, Michael.** Family and Class in a London Suburb. *202 pp. 47 tables. 1960.* (*4th Impression 1968.*) *25s.*

Young, Michael. Innovation and Research in Education. *192 pp. 1965. 25s. Paper 12s. 6d.*

Young, Michael and **McGeeney, Patrick.** Learning Begins at Home. A Study of a Junior School and its Parents. *About 128 pp. 1968. 21s. Paper 14s.*

Young, Michael and **Willmott, Peter.** Family and Kinship in East London. *Foreword by Richard M. Titmuss. 252 pp. 39 tables. 1957.* (*3rd Impression 1965.*) *28s.*

14

The British Journal of Sociology. *Edited by Terence P. Morris. Vol. 1, No. 1, March 1950 and Quarterly. Roy. 8vo., £3 annually, 15s. a number, post free. (Vols. 1-18, £8 each. Individual parts £2 10s.*

All prices are net and subject to alteration without notice

1268 H.B.